GOLF magazine's **handbook of golf strategy**

GOLF magazine's

HARPER & ROW, PUBLISHERS

handbook of
golf strategy

edited by Robert Scharff
and the editors of GOLF magazine

New York   Evanston   San Francisco   London

FIRST EDITION

STANDARD BOOK NUMBER: 06-011578-5

LIBRARY OF CONGRESS CATALOG CARD NUMBER: 73-138227

Contents

GOLF magazine's **handbook of golf strategy**

1. THINK Before You Play

It is an observable truism that day after day, week after week, and year after year, the average golfer labors along in the fairway vineyards without any noticeable improvement. It is equally true that you can only harvest what you plant. If you've sown good fundamentals into your golf swing, then you can only reap an excellent crop of good scores.

Golf's fundamentals are simple and, perhaps because of their simplicity, they are most often broken (or at least bent). In any case, we don't think it will hurt anyone to meditate on these precepts and to see just exactly where he may have strayed from the straight and narrow between tee and green. Personally, we think that anyone with a handicap of eight or more who gives this book an honest reading will help himself immeasurably.

In general, the game of golf can be summed up in the words *equipment, mechanics, thought,* and *strategy.* And somewhere among the causes and cures analyzed here should be the answer to your problem. In this book, while all four phases of the game will be discussed, the latter two will be covered in full detail. We will attempt to show that by employing thought and proper strategy, the average player can cut innumerable strokes from his game.

Developing Proper Attitude

If you're a poor golfer, chances are that anywhere from 40 to 70 percent of your trouble isn't in your swing. It's in your head!

Your trouble can be any one of a number of things: sheer idiocy in planning your shots, negative thinking that produces the exact disaster you talked yourself into, going for broke and winding up just that, or fear of a certain shot that makes an abject coward of your swing.

It happens to everybody. Consider the case of Gene Littler in the

U.S. Open at Olympic in 1966. He fired a 68 in the first round—and an 83 in the second round.

What happened? "If I knew what happened, it wouldn't have happened," he grunted in disgust.

Althea Gibson Darben blazed her way to a course record 68 in the first round of the Lady Carling Open—and chopped out an 88 in the second round.

What happened? "Everything."

In the Indianapolis Open, John Schlee shot a six-under-par 66 in the first round—and a 72 in the second round, scrambling.

What happened? "I couldn't seem to do anything right after a sleepless night," he groaned. "I went to bed and lay there all night. I just couldn't go to sleep."

You'd better believe him, says former PGA champion Wally Burkemo. "Getting the lead seems to bother some players worse than shooting a bad score," he observes. "They fret and worry all night about whether they can keep up the pace and whether they can continue to play that well. The result is that they worry themselves right off their game instead of enjoying their success and relaxing."

"I know one thing," Burkemo adds, "I sure hate to room with those leaders. A few years back I roomed with George Bayer when he had the first-round lead at Coral Gables. The next week I roomed with John Barnum when he had the first-round lead at Palm Beach, or maybe it was vice versa, but I was too sleepy to remember. Because every few minutes, all night long, the lights go on, and they sit up and smoke a cigarette right down to their fingernails. The lights go off and then, 15 minutes later, they're on again for another cigarette. All you get rooming with the leaders is bags under your eyes."

The moral of the story, he says, is that it's a common fault to think of yesterday instead of today. If you played well, you're afraid you won't be able to do it again. If you played poorly, you're fearful that things may get even worse. It is, in other words, more difficult to train your mind than it is to master your swing.

Gene Sarazen, one of the all-time greats who even today possesses enough of his boyish confidence to tee it up against anybody for one round, places the mental side of golf at 40 percent. "Too many players, amateur as well as professional, go out there and box shadows," he says. "They start playing well, and they don't believe in their own capabilities. It stands to reason that, if you are playing well, then you should have proved to yourself that you are capable of it. Some players get the feeling that they are playing over their heads and start getting cautious. When they do that, they're simply destroying themselves. That's what separates an Arnold Palmer from some other players with great talent. When he gets five under par, he wants to make it seven under. The others, when they get five under, just worry about holding on to it, and play themselves right into a bunch of killing bogeys, or worse."

Listening in, Johnny Johnston of Bear Park Golf Club in High Point, North Carolina, intervened that he would put the mental side of the game as high as 70 percent once a man has mastered the fundamentals. Playing well should give you a lift and confidence, he agreed, instead of causing you to draw back and start playing conservatively. Johnston carries a clipping in his wallet that sums up his feelings on the matter: "If you think you're good, you'll make it. If you don't think you're good, you won't."

Max Elbin of Burning Tree, the former president of the Professional Golfers' Association, places no percentage on the mental aspect of the game, and yet he is a firm believer in the theory that you have to "think your way to better golf."

"What separates winners from losers is the ability to think intelligently, and to avoid or minimize mistakes," he insists. "By this I mean mistakes in thinking as well as in making your shots. There's no question in my mind but that to play top golf you must balance both the mental and the physical sides." Two of his foremost precepts are: use good judgment and control your emotions.

Let's consider the first of these—use good judgment—and how the first shot he hit destroyed Bobby Nichols' chances of regaining his PGA championship at Firestone Country Club a few years ago. Nichols teed off with his driver, put the ball in the water, ended up with a bogey, and "things kept getting worse and worse because of that stupid start" as he shot a killing 81.

"I knew as soon as I hit the ball that I should have teed off with a three-wood," he muttered later. "The three-wood would have been straighter, there'd have been no chance of putting the ball in the water, and I'd still have been able to get home in two. Why didn't I hit the three-wood? Well, the truth of the matter is that I just wasn't thinking."

Along these lines, the late Tony Lema always contended that it was foolish to gamble on any shot. "Play the shot you know you can hit," he'd say, "and that removes it from the realm of the gamble. Always play the shot that, if it doesn't come off, will result in the least penalty. Hitting any shot is mechanical. It's thinking out the safest shot and the safest placement that is the real pay-off."

Former U.S. Open champion Ken Venturi substantiates this in another way. The slender Californian always is quick to credit Byron Nelson with taking him in hand as a young man and really teaching him how to play. "Naturally he started with my swing," Venturi explains. "He converted me from a flat, three-piece swinger into a one-piece upright swinger with greater control. But before he started working with me, Byron made me promise that I would listen to him unquestionably as far as strategy was concerned."

While in the process of changing his swing under Nelson's direction, Venturi lost his state amateur championship but never reverted to his former style. "But once we had the mechanical side satisfactory," he recalls, "I learned my greatest lessons riding in the car with Byron between exhibition appearances. At those times he'd explain why certain shots had failed to come off, why I shouldn't even have attempted certain other shots, always hammering at the necessity of thinking out a shot fully before playing it."

Temper and temperament also play a paramount part in the mental side of golf, and two prime examples are handsome Bob Goalby and thunderous Tommy Bolt.

Goalby, one of the most talented players on the tour, as attested by his eight consecutive birdies in winning the 1961 St. Petersburg Open, for years failed to live up to his promise. It wasn't until the last few years that he began to appear with regularity in the top echelon. "My trouble was that I stewed at myself," he admits. "I'd hit a bad shot, get mad at myself, and consequently hit more bad shots. Sam Snead opened my eyes not too long ago when we were paired together. He told me 'Why don't you take ahold of yourself and stop gettin' mad and beatin' yourself.' It sure made me think, and I knew he was right. I just had to learn to stop beating myself."

Bolt, whose four rounds in winning the 1958 U.S. Open at Tulsa are considered among the golfing classics, always was handicapped in the same manner. "A lot of people follow me just because they think I'll throw a club," Tommy analyzes. "Any time I miss a shot I cringe, just waiting for somebody to yell 'Throw it, Tommy.' It sure breaks up your concentration. You keep thinking they're hoping you'll blow a shot so they can see you go off like a skyrocket."

Learning to forget the last shot in favor of concentrating on the next one is one of the most difficult tasks a player faces when he joins the Tour, says young Chris Blocker, the husky blond from Jal, New Mexico. "I'd have to guess a lot of it is due to the fact that you want to get in the money so badly," he analyzes. "You know that every time you waste a shot you're just making it that much harder to survive the cut or move up in the field. When a shot here and a shot there can mean the difference between hamburger and caviar, it's mighty difficult to quit worrying."

Richard Crawford, another of the younger set, agrees with Blocker's reasoning. The kid from Arkansas points out that "there are two different games going on out there."

"The fellows who have it made can play one game, relaxed and unworried about the money," he points out. "The rest of us, all trying to get our foot in the door, feel that we have to strain and gamble to get there. I'd have to think that nothing succeeds like success, and once you've cracked the financial ice you can quit gambling with your desperation shots and settle down to playing it cool, calm, and collected."

This, in a way, can be translated into everyday play at your own club. How many times, just for a two-dollar Nassau, when everything is riding on the last hole, have you seen two opponents chop themselves out sixes or sevens when the most they should have had was a bogey? The answer is that they were more worried about the other man's shot than they were with their own, and their own concentration and effort was completely dissipated.

Al Geiberger summed it up in winning the PGA championship by four strokes, although he merely matched par. "I tried to forget the field and just play the golf course the best I could," he disclosed. "I didn't figure anybody was going to tear up that Firestone course. It's too tough. So I just went out and played against par and forgot what everybody else was doing."

It was a winning bit of psychology, a payoff for the mental side of golf. Certainly there were players in that star-studded field who hit it just as far and just as straight and could chip and putt as well as big Al. In the final analysis the answer had to be that he was geared better than anyone else in the thinking department.

Tom Weiskopf moaned during the Buick Open that he just "couldn't" play a soft, quick-stopping trap shot from those Warwick Hills bunkers. So he left it in the sand three times. Dave Ragan confessed that he had the "yips" on those three- and four-foot putts. The

result was that he missed three inside that distance—including one of
18 inches—in one round. As anyone on tour will tell you, he's too fine
a player to be doing that, but he had talked himself into it. It takes
twice as much talking in the self-lecture department to get out of such
miseries.

Frank Strafaci, seven-time New York Metropolitan Amateur champion and later director of golf at Miami's Doral Country Club, was
convinced for two years that at a critical point in a match he couldn't
help but get the shanks. In the first round of the 1965 British Amateur
he was two up with five holes to play and "subconsciously knew I was
going to shank." He did, to lose the fourteenth hole, and did it again
to lose the sixteenth and go all even. "On the eighteenth," he grimaces
at the memory, "I shanked my second shot, my third shot, and my
fourth shot and lost, one down."

Strafaci still had the shanks when he returned in 1966. En route to
the British he played in the Irish Amateur and, while in Ireland,
started working out the shanks by starting with his short pitches. "I
found out I had been moving my right shoulder over the shot," he
recalls. "It was that simple, and I knew I had licked the shanks. My
mental block was gone, and instead of freezing in front of the ball at
critical moments I convinced myself I could play the shot without
shanking."

Which brings to mind the time a player asked Ed Furgol, "Will you
take a look at my practice swing and tell me what's wrong?"

"What's the matter, are you nuts?" the forthright Furgol replied
acidly. "Everybody has a good practice swing. It's how you swing
when you have the ball teed up in front of you that tells the story." It
is Furgol's theory that, among amateurs principally, everybody has
two swings. There's the easy, fluid practice swing that is made without
pressure and tension. Then there's the other one at the ball, when you
tighten up all over and aim to smash it lopsided—meaning that your
mental processes have converted you from a sweet-swinging Dr. Jekyll
into a horrendously hacking Mr. Hyde.

A case in excellent point is a "customer's man" of our acquaintance
who set out to "throw" a match to an important buyer. Playing in an
uncaring fashion, without tension and pressure or the necessity of
winning, he shot the best round of his life. He simply couldn't lose for
winning.

Considering all the evidence at hand, it would seem without too
much question that the mental side of golf plays a tremendous part in

how you score no matter what your handicap. Probably the most important lesson a golfer can learn about the psychological side of this *most* psychological of all games is: It isn't enough to know that you *can* improve your game; you've got to *want* to improve it. When you have accepted both of these ideas—that you want to improve and that you can improve—you *will* improve. And, of course, the opposite is true. Without faith in yourself, you can't succeed. As trite as this may sound, it's surprising how many golfers are playing beneath their capabilities simply because they don't believe they can play any better.

If you're shooting in the 90's and never expect to shoot in the 80's, you never will. Once a golfer admits to himself that he can probably putt better than he's putting and drive better than he's driving, he's on his way to accomplishing these very improvements.

What Makes a Winner

Negative thinking has no place in golf. Uncertain in your club choice? Think you'll blow the shot? Think you'll miss that putt? Then, believe us, you will. Indecision, pessimism, negative thinking. These can do as much to ruin your round as someone yelling "Fire!" each time you start the club back. And every time you tee up an old ball on a water hole, you directly confess to your subconscious that you expect to knock it right into the drink, with the very favorable odds that you'll do just that.

In the "negative thinking" department go such things as not playing your game as you know it to be, steering the ball, and deliberately looking for trouble you can't possibly handle, instead of shooting for the open spaces and hitting for the fat part of the greens. Let's say you're a slicer, which most amateurs are. Well, then, don't stand heroically to the ball as if you were going to thread it straight through the narrow tree-lined tunnel. Aim it along the far left side, and give it plenty of room to go into its left-to-right dance without penalizing you too much. Postpone curing the slice for when you have the time to go to the practice tee. If you find your ball huddled hopelessly in the rough, take an iron, not a wood—forget the miracle shots. Why shoot blindly for the green on some vague hope that you "might" get home with a perfect shot and all the while knowing full well that, as sure as taxes, you'll hit those yawning traps. Play for the opening, even though you're short of the green. A good chip can still save your par. Think positively, and aim for safety.

Play percentage golf. If your game involves a good deal of slicing, on those narrow holes play your game and your slice by teeing on the right side and firing to the left.

With any obstacle, like trees, blocking a clean shot to the green, don't fight the odds. Play for the opening—save strokes, don't waste them.

With traps in front of and behind the green and the flag tucked in close, leaving little room for error, you should shoot for the fatter, safer area.

In fact, positive thinking can be spelled: *confidence*. Take a generous portion of that and stir it well with a hot putter, and you have the makings of a champion. Actually, the techniques and mechanics of playing the various shots vary but little among those who are able to make a good showing on the money-winning list. What you might refer to as the top echelon of the touring professionals is a group separated only by a few strokes here and there.

The winners keep the ball in play, fight off that costly bad round, have the putter working and, to our way of thinking, polish off the job because they are confident that they can come out on top. Golf pros such as Arnold Palmer, Jack Nicklaus, and Billy Casper hold that confidence is 90 percent of the game when you consider that, mechanically, there is so little difference in the manner in which the top players execute their shots. Some of them are stronger in one department than in another, naturally, but it all balances out in the end, and the man who thinks he can win is getting that little edge which frequently is the difference between winning and losing.

It stands to reason that when you are getting the breaks—breaks you naturally have to make for yourself—there's only one valid reason. You have the confidence that you can pull off a tough shot out of the rough or drop a tricky birdie putt. It's in your own hands in this game. Unfortunately, the average player often attempts shots that would make the tournament pros shudder. This tendency stems from a lack of planning, lack of evaluating capabilities properly, and that ominpresent bogeyman—wishful thinking. We've seen far too many high-handicappers who knock one into the woods, find themselves with a bad lie and no opening to the green, and then proceed to select a three-wood for their next shot. After knocking the ball back and forth among the timber, they usually end up taking a five- or a seven-iron and chipping out sideways. This is what they should have done in the first place. Instead of trying to play a career shot which he doesn't have one chance in a thousand of making effectively, the high-handi-capper should play a safe, sensible shot back in play. A tournament star would certainly chip out under such circumstances—so what's good enough for him should be good enough for the average golfer. This tendency to compound a bad shot by taking the short end of the percentages is the stuff of which eights and nines are made. We, at *Golf* magazine, have long felt that the main difference between 85- and 95-shooters is the double and triple bogies the 95-shooters make. We know it's human nature to want to make up for a bad shot, but, believe us, it's far better just to take the safe way out.

The man who is certain of his ability, the one who just knows that he can perform the job at hand, gets the maximum out of his talents. But one major cause of frustration on the course is that most players expect too much of themselves. They have not learned to play within their limitations. It pays not to set one's sights too high. A player should resign himself to a certain number of misses each round, no matter how superior a shotmaker he is.

Depending on his handicap, a player should determine what his par is for a course and for each hole. He should disregard the par on the card. A 90-shooter, for example, should consider his par to be 85 and try to shoot it. If he does this, he'll not only play better, but he'll be happier.

Another thought it might help to keep in mind is that golf isn't so much a game of good shots as of good misses. The better the player, the greater the percentage of good shots and good misses. Any play-er's objective should be to increase these two percentages, but no player is going to hit every shot well, no matter how good he is. There will still be a sizable percentage of good misses there. It might help to cultivate the following thought: "I can't hit 'em bad every time if I remain free of bad temper."

One of the best ways to avoid aggravation and frustration is to play safe, to keep away from trouble. But, if things do go wrong, it doesn't do any good to get mad. Sure, all of us burn inside when things start going wrong, particularly if we are in a position to grab first place. But in a gradual manner, we have learned that if you let yourself go up in smoke, there's only one person you're hurting—yourself.

All you have to do is start fuming over a putt that didn't drop, or a well-played approach that took a bad bounce and wound up in a trap, or a scuffed approach shot, and you're cooking your own goose. The first thing you know, you've lost your concentration, and right on the heels of that you've blown your biggest asset, your *confidence* that you can recover from this momentary disaster. Some players with magnificent potential never really realize the full extent of their possibilities simply because they never learn to control their tempers.

It's an old story, but a good case in point, how on one occasion, at a crucial point in a match, the late Walter Hagen sprayed his ball into an unplayable lie. When he walked up to his shot, a sympathetic spectator said: "Too bad, Walter."

Hagen looked at the spectator and grinned, "I put it there, so I'll just have to get it out."

And he did, with a marvelous birdie recovery shot. Old-timers who know Hagen at his best insist that this ability to forget the last shot, or the bad shot, and play the next shot with imperturbable concentration was one of Hagen's greatest assets. What that spells to us is *confidence*.

Get mad and go into a fast burn over a poor shot, or a bad break, and you're merely helping to whip yourself. Hold on to your temper and half the battle is won because, instead of turning a bogey into a killing double bogey, you just might turn that bogey into a par—or even a birdie.

In the modern era of golf, as we contended earlier, the differences aren't in the shots. This is an era in which the ball has to be mauled off the tee, and as a general rule everybody hits it long. There are many varieties of swings primarily because of the fact that you get all types of builds. Yet the basic mechanics of hitting the various shots in essence are the same. Some players cover the flag like automatons, and others have to scramble like mad, but you'll find both types putting for their share of birdies.

From a mechanical standpoint, therefore, the payoff is in the putter. But you're dead long before the caddy sticks the putter in your hand if you don't play with complete *confidence* from the time you tee it up until you pick the ball out of the cup.

Think Like a Champion

Many golfers we've played with would be ruined men if they used as little headwork in their businesses as they do out on the golf course. For instance, a lot of them have trouble playing a pitch over the usual slope on the sides of greens. Through lack of confidence, they try to "just get back on the green." Usually they "dump it," that is, only get it three or four feet up the slope. Upset by this, they will likely knock it clear over the green on their next try. Now if they had done a little thinking, they would have seen that their putter would run the ball up over the slope and onto the green for a good chance at a par, or a certain bogey. True, you may think your muscle reflexes are apt to be dependable after you have played for some time, but you will find yourself missing more and more shots, if you don't bother to think out each shot beforehand.

Thinking, of course, is something we do automatically every day. In golf, good thinking is just as important as a good swing. On the golf course we meet some serious and tough problems. Each shot depends mainly and basically on a person's ability to believe *within* himself and *in* himself. In fact, the ability to think out a shot and to realize your ability to execute that shot is one of the most important factors in golf. And this statement, in various forms, will be repeated often in this book.

How many times do you step up to a ball and feel, "I know this shot"? You get a feeling in your bones, and you have so much confidence that you know you can make the shot. You hit it, and it turns out all right. But there are a lot of times when you stand up to the ball with doubt in your mind and unsureness about the selection of the club. You try to gamble because of this uncertainty. Actually, most average players don't play within themselves. They are always trying to do something fancy. They might get away with a shot one time, but they can't do it every time.

It is necessary, in playing a good round of tournament golf, to hold your thinking powers together for approximately four hours. You must think out each shot as well as possible. Contrary to his flamboyance and his devil-may-care image, Lee Trevino, the 1968 and 1971 U.S. Open champion and *Golf* magazine's instruction editor, is a thinking golfer. Here is his story on how thinking like a champion helped him win the 1968 Open:

"I went into a fellow's office one day, and on his desk there was a sign you've probably seen too which read: ThiMk!

"Kind of funny, right? I'd have to guess there are all kinds of interpretations, but personally I figure it was a gag aimed at people who slop along without thinking most of the time, kind of doing everything automatically. Like, let's say, most people are guilty of 'thiM-king' on the golf course. Ninety percent of those I watch simply tee it high and let it fly. Let 'er go, daddy-o! But play it open—and pray. Well, that's no way to play golf if you want to save shots. And saving shots is the name of the game if you want to get the most out of your abilities. You have to thiNk before you swat it, and nobody knows it better than I do. Now, I'm not knocking my own game, which I happen to think is pretty good, but I have to admit that nobody is going to mistake me for the classic ghost of Harry Vardon. Ordinarily I can knock it out there straight, but when the pressure closes in—and it does on them all—the ability to keep thiNking is what will pull a man through.

"I know that thiNking and thereby saving shots was what won the U.S. Open for me. Whenever I think of that wonderful week at Oak Hill there are two holes that come to mind, the fourth and the thirteenth, a pair of rugged par-fives. The fourth is a dogleg to the right with a fairway trap in the driving area on the right side. Try to shave that corner in hopes of getting into position to get home in two, and you're headed for a certain six, at best. But it was a great temptation.

" 'Don't be a wise guy,' I told myself. 'This hole was made to get home in three, so play it that way.' It was no problem to hit my drive safely down the left side. Here, again, the snake peeks out of the apple tree and whispers that if you go with the cannon you just might pull off the miracle shot and get it home in two. But I'm thinking of saving shots, not of longshot gambling. So I thread a one-iron straight down the middle, which leaves me a little old wedge shot of 50 or 60 yards to get home safely in the regulation three. Playing it this way through all four rounds of the Open the wedge got me close enough for two birdies on the fourth hole. By the end of the tournament, I had played this hole two under par.

"My thinking was the same on the thirteenth hole, a good par-five

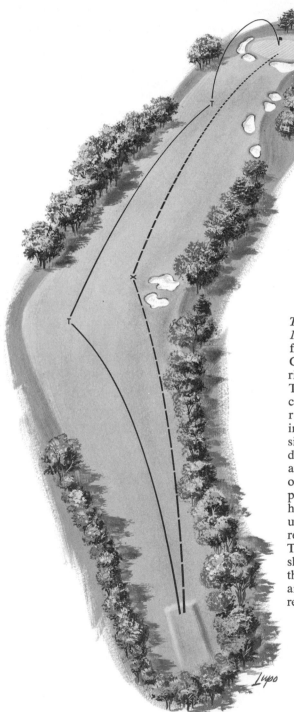

The two keys of Trevino's 1968 Open victory. The fourth hole at Oak Hill Country Club is a dogleg right, measuring 571 yards. The temptation here is to cut the corner, thereby running the risk of hitting into the traps. But Trevino simply played it safely down the middle each time and ended up two under on this hole. (Opposite page) Thirteen is the big hole at Oak Hill. It measures 602 yards, so there is really no reason to gamble. Trevino played a one-iron short of the creek and then hit a one-iron short and left of the traps. The result: one under par.

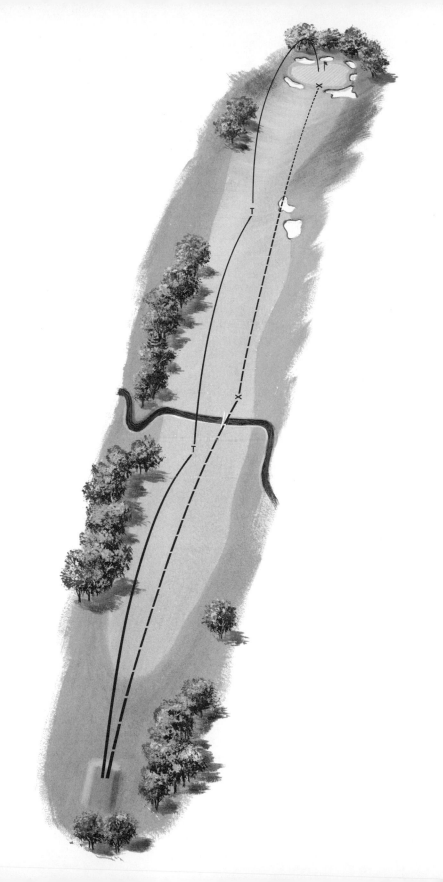

complicated by a creek and a fairway that chokes in near the green like a fat man's collar. Bust two-woods and maybe you'll get it home in two, and maybe you won't even make the cut. 'Keep the woods in the satchel,' I said to myself, 'and you got a good shot at keeping your sanity.' I hit a one-iron off the tee to keep it straight down the middle. I hit a one-iron second, because that's the club which for me spells straightsville. And then I knocked it comfortably home in regulation with a nine-iron. So for four rounds I finished up one under par on the thirteenth hole, and if you think that's bad you ain't never won the Open, and ain't ever likely to win it, either.

"What I'm getting at is that if you want to save strokes on par-fives, it calls for a special kind of thinking. Forget the birdies, and let them come when and if they will. Concentrate on managing the hole for a nice, safe, comfortable par. First of all, don't try to overpower the hole or feel that you have to bust the ball a solid ton off the tee. Instead, sell yourself on hitting your drive smoothly for good position. Next you want to lay it up in good position for a shot at the green, so you need the club that will give you accuracy first and maximum distance second. In my case, this club is the one-iron, and in the Open I never hit a wood on a second shot. The thing to do is to play the club that will do the job the safest way possible. *ThiNk of hitting the shots from tee to green that will keep you in the middle of the fairway and safely out of the woods, the rough, and the sand.*

"While the strategy of saving strokes is covered in greater detail in Chapter 6, let me get my two cents in about playing par-fours. The majority of them are not too long but are, on the whole, tricked up to murder the unwary guy who figures all he has to do is bust it a bundle and leave himself only a little old flip to the green. So he hauls off and knocks it into the woods or into the rough or a trap, and by the time he finally gets on he's lucky if he only has a 60-foot putt for a par. How much better to smoothly hit your best straight club, with me a one-iron and with you maybe a three- or four-wood, and sacrifice some of that distance for middle of the fairway accuracy. Now you've kept it in play, and your second shot is simple. On the long par-fours, of course, you've got to give it a riffle and hope for the best off the tee. Yet, in reality, those kind of holes are no worse than a hole on which you missed your tee shot. Way out there, beckoning to you through an opening which looks as big as the eye of a needle, is the pin. If you hit your absolute career shot you'll thread that needle and lay it on the carpet. So you wind up, nine times out of ten, and bust it with everything you've got. So what happened when you broke your shoelaces like that? Right! You wound up in the trap. How much better if you had shot smoothly for the opening—but safely short of the bunkers —and left yourself a little pitch to the pin. You still might get it close enough for your four but certainly shouldn't come off with anything worse than a five. But going for the cannon you got a six, and quite possibly a seven. Two strokes down the drain!

"Proper thinking also will save you a lot of strokes on the par-threes. On these, I would make an educated guess, the great majority of players always use too little club. That's why so many players wind up in the bunkers ordinarily guarding the fronts of most of these greens. I have to think that the average player should not use what he figures to be the "right" club. If he does, he has to hit the perfect shot every time. Thus, if you think you have a six-iron shot, take a five-iron and spank it. And don't shoot for the flag. Aim for the dead center of the green. It's a lot worse to be bunkered than it is to be just over the back edge of the green. In the end, you'll save a heap of strokes if you play within yourself and hit the clubs that will keep you straight and out of the rough and bunkers. Play it safe, even at the cost of distance, because a possible par but a sure bogey is always better than a possible birdie but a sure double bogey. *ThiNk! Don't thiMk!*"

2. Strategy and Basics of Golf

To be a thinking man's golfer takes more than just having a new set of clubs, wearing the most colorful clothes, or smoking the right cigarette. To play this game with any degree of success, you must have a varied arsenal of shots in your bag. And to execute these shots with some regularity and confidence, you must know what you are doing and why. In other words, you must have control of your game.

How often have you heard the words, "You can't score unless you keep the ball in play"? Probably too often. And not without good reason. Since every golf course is nearly always a test of accuracy and only occasionally a trial of distance, the key to better golf and lower scores has to be control. Obviously, any time you stray from the fairway you're in trouble. And if you're in trouble, you've sacrificed strokes that cannot be returned. Unfortunately, most golfers remember to "keep the ball in play" only after they've finished a round of golf—rarely before, and never during. Plainly, it's too late then. Control, or keeping the ball in play, is only sound preaching if you remember to practice it on the golf course.

Briefly then, the thoughtful golfer knows that *control* means more than just having a good swing. It also means:

1. Knowing where you want the ball to go.
2. How you want it to get there.
3. And being able to do it consistently.

Importance of Consistency

Possibly the greatest fault of the average golfer can be summed up in one word: Inconsistency. As a case in point, your editor was talking recently to what we might call an average player, a fellow who fluctuates aimlessly between 90 and 100. It was pitiful to hear him bemoan his latest round. "Imagine," he sighed, "I started birdie, par, par. Then the roof fell in, and on the next three holes I shot seven, eight, six."

The cause of the catastrophe was easy to understand. On the fourth hole his seven popped up when his drive caught water and then, trying to make up for it by attempting to get home with a wood, he buried it in a bunker. It got worse on the next hole when he did exactly the same thing but this time compounded the injury by three-putting. This so upset him that on the next hole, a long three-par, he had a triple bogey when he hit one out-of-bounds and then bunkered his subsequent tee shot by trying to get home on a hole that was beyond his range.

We at *Golf* magazine are convinced that the majority of what we might call average players are capable of playing much better golf without even the necessity of long practice sessions if they would learn to play the percentages and quit shooting for continued miracles. Consider the misplays of the fellow above. On that fourth hole he flailed away with his driver when he should have sacrificed distance for accuracy and hit off with either a two-wood or a three-wood. Trying to get home with a wood he was completely ignoring the percentages, just as he did on the long three-par. They were errors that cost him the good round he should have had.

Consistency means, of course, more than hitting the green in regulation or better round after round. It also means you have your game grooved and uncluttered, and are able to bounce back quickly from a bad hole or a bad break. Several years back, we at *Golf* magazine did a survey and found that the biggest problem for over 40 percent of our readers was the lack of consistency. We would even guess that if the professionals were asked what their game needed most, they would say the same. Remember that if you begin hitting the ball with consistency, if you start catching the greens regularly, and if your thinking is cleared, the planning of a round of golf is made easier and your scores come down. This is why we suggest you keep your thinking uncluttered and your golf game as natural and as simple as possible. These are the *facts* in the case: fundamentals, attitude, confidence, tempo, and simplicity—they spell good golf for everyone.

There are many ways to learn about golf. You can caddie, as many of the pros did, read, take lessons from a professional, struggle through a do-it-yourself program, or play hit-and-miss with the help of a well-meaning but usually poorly informed friend. (In the latter case, a good rule to follow is never to seek help from someone playing the game actively who can't beat you and/or who doesn't qualify as a proven instructor.) But a person doesn't have to have caddie experience or clinical training in order to play. However, to be able to consistently hit the ball a certain way and make it go according to *your* plan, not *its* plan, you definitely need the help of someone who has studied the *facts* and knows them completely.

To come up with effective shots consistently requires mastering, of course, the fundamentals: swing, stance, and grip. While this book was not intended to cover the fundamentals of the golf game—there are plenty of good books on the subject—let's take a look at a few important facts about them for a moment.

The vast majority of leading pros and top amateurs employ the Vardon grip, with a slight variation here or there, but it doesn't necessarily mean it is the correct one for you. Try it first. If it doesn't help you control the club, and that is what the correct grip will do, practice with the interlocking or the ten-finger grip.

Most pros recommend the square stance; that is, the line drawn through the hips, knees, and toes will be parallel to a line drawn through the ball, and in the direction of the line of flight. This is a good, basic, fundamental stance which can be used to go into any type of swing. At address, get as comfortable as possible, weight evenly distributed, body slightly bent over from the waist, without stooping, the knees flexed, and the toes pointed outward. Your left shoulder will be a bit higher than your right, of course, because your left hand is positioned on the club above the right, and you will have the feeling of being under and behind the ball, which is just the way you want to come into it.

Ordinarily, a stance with your feet just as wide as your shoulders would be about right, provided it lets your natural movements go into your effort smoothly. Once you're set, though, try to start everything together without being obvious that any one thing begins the action. If you wish to use a forward press, all right, but it certainly is not necessary. As the clubhead is taken back, the left hip turns and the left shoulder starts around until it is under your chin and almost pointing to the ball. It is important that this be so, and that your head remains steady.

The left heel comes off the ground just slightly. Be aware that it serves as an anchor. It can either roll or come up to show some breathing space underneath; but, regardless, keep a good portion of

The important parts of a good swing (left to right). To hit the ball high, play it more toward the left foot with your weight slightly on the right side, hitting the ball more on the upswing. Start of backswing; top of swing and start of downswing; impact—the moment of truth; and completion of swing.

the foot on the ground solidly. At the top of the swing, the left knee will point slightly back of the ball, and everything is coiled around to the right. Your hands should be well up over the shoulder, the back of the left wrist straight, both wrists cocked, the grip firm, and you will be in an excellent position to start the downward swing. Then, as the hands get below the hips and well into the impact area, you will unleash all the fury you have developed. But don't rush into it yet. Wait.

The start of the downswing is a little different from that of the backswing. It's begun with a move of the left hip. At least it is with many golfers. When the hip is turned back to the left as far around as it can go, it will pull the hands down into and through the ball, the shoulders will turn into the shot with the left elbow dead straight, the left heel settles back on the ground, the right knee breaks in toward the ball, and the right elbow brushes in close to the right hip and then continues across the beltline.

You should still be looking at the ball, your head having remained steady, and at this precise moment the wrists will uncock and snap the clubhead into and through the ball, and you should naturally and effortlessly finish nice and high with a full follow-through. Does this sound like too much for something that has to remain simple and uncluttered? It really isn't.

Just remember to swing within yourself and concentrate on developing consistency and timing. Whenever your balance is right and the swing is natural, the chances are extremely good that everything will fall into place and you will have hit the ball long and straight.

Overanxiety is the cause of the blinding flash of shaft that guarantees the complete ruin of your balance, tempo, and rhythm, all essential to the good golf swing. Slow down and take the clubhead back with a kind of reluctance. Speed and power are created on the way down to the ball. Remember the old axiom: no one ever went to the top of the backswing and left the clubhead up there. It will come down (see Newton's Law), but with greater success if done rhythmically and smoothly. And you'll be surprised how much more distance you will cover.

Work on these simple hints until you can get the feel of the clubhead going through the ball, shot after shot. When you have grooved your swing and have your timing and balance under control, you will eliminate or prevent practically every error that can creep into your swing, and you can be confident of the results. Rushing the shot anywhere along the line, or being too quick with one part of the body while delaying another, will cause the ball to go any erratic way it so desires, and you won't be pleased. We can't emphasize this too much: exclusive of the grip, tempo is the most important factor in the golf swing.

When you keep your swing simple, you not only develop the consistency everyone needs, you also reduce the number of checkpoints necessary to get the groove back should it stray away. Many of the touring pros employ two key points to check on: their right elbow and their head position. They keep the right elbow close to the side on the way to the hitting area to insure their right shoulder passing under their chin while their head remains steady throughout. Now when they get toward the top of their backswing, the elbow will come away from their body, but as they start down again, it will come back in close and shave across their body, almost brushing their beltline. When this happens, they know the ball is on its way to the target.

Needless to say, the head is the axis for the entire golf swing. If you keep it still, you can even shut your eyes and hit the ball solidly. Most golf teachers admit that the head moves slightly during the golf swing, and to try to keep it absolutely fixed will freeze other portions of the body that must remain flexible to hit a ball well. The head *must not move up and down;* however, a margin of an inch or two of lateral movement is acceptable, and in fact is unavoidable with the turning of the shoulders.

Undoubtedly, "peeking" is one of the worst faults with which golfers—and not just high-handicappers—are cursed. It derives from curiosity and the natural tendency to anticipate the result of the shot you are about to play. And in picking up your head, the whole swing is thrown out of its intended plane. As a result, just about anything can happen—and usually does. Our suggestion is to watch for the divot or the mark your clubhead makes on the turf in going through the ball, and let the swing bring your head up naturally.

Remember the facts that can strengthen your game: fundamentals, attitude, confidence, tempo, and simplicity. It can be done. Think positive, stay natural, and keep your game simple. It is our contention that if amateurs would take a more relaxed viewpoint on the game and try to think positive, they would be able to score better.

Proper Equipment

Winning golf is traceable to proper equipment, and the clubs of today are the finest ever produced. But you can be using a set like the pros', have the sweetest swing in the world, know and follow the basics, even plan and organize your game to perfection, and still, if those clubs aren't right for you, you'll be adding unnecessary strokes to your game, and not getting the enjoyment out of golf that you should.

Now we're not suggesting you rush out to buy a new set. Nor do we want to make you lose confidence in your present set. What we would like to do here is simply and sincerely make you more aware of what golf clubs are really like and what they can do for you. In fact, getting help from clubs that fit your swing is more than a psychological lift; it's an actual one. There's no feeling quite like the one of knowing that the club you pull out of the bag is going to do the job you want it to do. And this knowledge adds up to sheer pleasure. What is often overlooked is the fact that this feeling is or can be built right into the club. Today's golf clubs have more playability than ever before. The manufacturers, with their years of research and experimentation behind them, have incorporated their findings into the clubs you see on display in pro shops and stores, giving the pro more clubs to offer you, and you more variety to choose from.

The club that looks so simple is really a complicated bit of precision-built machinery. Hundreds of steps, a large portion of them hand operations, go into the making of a single iron, and a visit to a plant is always an eye-opening experience. Gone is the guesswork that was too much a part of clubmaking in the past. The manufacturers now follow a precise formula to pattern the correct combination of head weight and size, wall thickness and flex point of the shaft, along with grip size and club length. The club you purchased from your pro or store, especially if it is a registered model, is a beautifully made instrument. Such is its balance that if a piece of tape is used to patch up the whipping on the woods, or if so much as an eighth of an ounce is added to the grip, a point or more is added to the swing weight. And did you know that if your woods are of the vintage years before impregnation, the exposure to moisture, dirt, and sun has almost certainly added to the total weight and also affected swing weight? There's much more to the club than meets the eye, so let's get a bit technical and check out a few things.

The expression "swing weight" seems to be the most perplexing of all golf terms, while the "lie" of the club is the most overlooked phase of nomenclature. The location of the center of gravity is the latest improvement in design, and the shaft is the most noticeable change. Actually, swing weight is merely the feel the club has in relation to the hands. It is an arbitrary measurement, indicating the distribution of the weight of the club. It is the proportion of the weight in the head compared to the shaft and the grip, and is measured on a logarithmic scale reading from D0 to D9 (men's readings, normally) to C0 and C9 (ladies' readings, normally). The higher the swing weight, the heavier the club will "feel." (This is not to be confused with total weight, which is the actual weight, and which differs with the clubs within the set, especially in the irons that get heavier in actual weight as they go up in number.) Swing weight is extremely important because it gives the club its feel and balance. Any changes, no matter how small, can be spotted by those golfers playing regularly. Therefore, more attention is paid to it than to total weight.

At this point, we would like to caution anyone against tampering with clubs. The balance in the club is an expensive result of the manufacturers' matching shafts of correct wall thicknesses and strengths and flex points, in direct relation to the size and weight of both the clubhead on the one end, and the grip on the other. Harnessing this feel or flex point in each of the shafts in each of the clubs in each family of clubs so that all of them swing the same (true swing weight) is the greatest achievement by the makers. Do not risk changing this by messing around with your clubs. It isn't worth it. For any alteration or repair, ask your pro to return the club to the manufacturer. He knows best what to do.

Now a few words about the shaft. In looking back to the old days, one has to marvel at what was accomplished using clubs with the wooden, hickory shafts that gave different reactions according to weather, with different flex points in each one, making it impossible to get true balance with the set in use. That they did as well as they did, setting some records that still stand, is amazing. Now it's different. Today's shafts give the exact feel you want, with little of the uncertain twisting motion of those of yesterday. The shafts have come a long way from the days of Bobby Jones, and they go a long way toward producing the right shot at the right time, round after round.

Normally, there are at least three different flexes available in your store or pro shop: stiff, medium, or regular, and it usually isn't too difficult to select the correct one. Your strength, age, muscle tone, golf ability, and swing habits are among the characteristics taken into consideration before you are outfitted with a specific shaft by the pro. A person who swings easily and needs help in getting extra distance might find the flexible shaft just right for him. But if this person proves to be too strong for the flexible shaft, he will lose control of the clubhead and *not* get distance. He would be better off with the medium, or, if his swing is grooved and he is powerful, he could go the stiff. In turn, if the shaft is too firm, he'll find that his arms will begin to tire just above the wrists, he'll lose the use of his wrists, and the club will feel heavy and unbending. It'll then be time to accept the shaft with the medium flex.

Extra-length shafts are available on special order, also. Some golfers use drivers that are longer than normal so they can generate more clubhead speed at impact to produce more distance. While this theory is true, if the longer driver can't be handled, it won't deliver the goods and you'll be sacrificing more than accuracy—you'll be wasting good money, as well.

This brings up another point. We are often asked about the pros' clubs—are they unique, are they special, are they hand-made? Actually, those used by the touring professionals are not too different from those offered to you. It is not a case of their equipment being souped up for extra yardage and more accuracy. They wish it were. No, it is more a case of their knowing, from years of trial and error, what they want and being given what they ask for. But this is your privilege, too. Today's club pro is a businessman who not only carries a large inventory but also knows that all major manufacturers have special-order or custom-built departments where he can get the clubs for those golfers who do not fall into the average category.

Requests for clubs that are not standard in grip, shaft, or head are not too much to handle—if within reason. That is to say, don't expect to get a heavy head placed on a short shaft, or a heavy swing weight to go with a flexible shaft, because the total weight of the iron would then have to be abnormally heavy or the wooden clubhead unnecessarily weakened. But bona fide special orders are not uncommon, and the liaison between the craftsmen who do this special work and the pros who request these tailor-made clubs is good.

One of the new improvements to show up in golf clubs is the location of the center of gravity. It is now being concentrated lower and closer to the true center of the hitting surface, so that the "sweet spot" on the iron is really the spot to get that "sweet" hit.

All of this taken into consideration, today's clubs feel better, fit better, look better, and will play better. But the finest, most carefully matched set in the world will be no good at all unless the lie is right for you. The lie is that angle as measured from the bottom of the sole *back* to the shaft. A large majority of golfers can and do get along quite well with medium shafts, a D1 to D4 swing weight, and the prescribed lofts standardized by the manufacturers; but the correct lie will differ with the type of swing you have, and an upright swinger cannot use with ease and accuracy clubs having the same lie that fits a short person who swings in a flatter (not necessarily incorrect) plane. To do so results in more bad shots than is supposed, because it forces the golfer into making many hard-to-detect errors.

The lie is correct if the toe is slightly off the ground when the club is placed behind the ball as at address. The sole, therefore, rests almost straight, just a bit back of center, to allow a little air space under the front end. This one-eighth of an inch under the toe is needed because, during the swing, the shaft deflects and the lie tends to flatten slightly. But it should never be more than that. It is common to see golfers using clubs that toe up too abruptly, or to reach for the ball in such a way that they do not have enough blade with which to hit the ball. They are imposing too much of a handicap on themselves. Don't *you* minimize the value and importance of the correct lie.

Since balance and feel of the club are transmitted through the hands, the correct grip is important, also. Most manufacturers offer leather, rubber, composition, and all-weather types. Each pro has his own preference so we suggest that you test them all and make your own selection. But don't be careless on grip size. This is usually measured at a point 2 inches down from the top of the cap, and the standard size for men is usually .90 inches in diameter and .85 for ladies.

But, despite all advancements, many golfers still fight buying a new set for reasons that are either sentimental or financial. Some are convinced that only in their old set can they get the right kind of feel they need, that the people today just don't make them the way they used to. Even some of the pros think this way, as happened once during a tournament held near the site of a major golf manufacturing plant.

One of the company's golf consultants visited the plant and left his clubs there for repair and refinishing. When he learned they wouldn't be ready for two days, he agreed to use a new set featuring a later development of the firm. His first two rounds were in the 60's, and he was high among the leaders. On Saturday his old clubs were delivered to him, but he was asked to continue using those furnished as replacements. However, he was so anxious to get reunited with his regular set that he switched again.

At this time, another consultant of the firm reported breaking his seven-iron during practice. Since it was impossible to replace the shaft immediately, he was offered the same newer model set turned back in by his colleague. He tried them, liked them, and used them to come out of nowhere to finish in the top ten, getting himself a good chunk of the prize money. And the first professional, using his old clubs, which he felt he couldn't get along without, shot himself completely out of the running!

We all know golfers who hang onto their sets because they won a certain championship with them, or played so well with them many years ago that they wouldn't part with them for the world. Then, too, there is the guy who does buy new clubs but doesn't trade in his old, and every time he starts playing badly, he wishes he had his other set, and never gives himself the chance to get to know the ones he is using.

GOLF BALLS

The better golf balls come in various types of construction to allow for more or less compression. The compression factor is usually indicated by a number, symbol, or color printed on the package or stamped on the ball itself. If there is any doubt, your pro can tell you the compression of a given ball, and this is something that most golfers would do well to take into account. Anyone whose drives average less than 175 yards—including the vast majority of women golfers—should play a low-compression ball (often designated as 80-compression) or one designed especially for women. Such a golfer is not likely to compress a high-compression ball sufficiently to hit it as far as he should. On the other hand, a low-compression ball will not compress enough to give a big hitter his full distance. He should use a 90-compression ball or, in the case of a super-smacker, a 100-compression ball. The next time you buy a package of top-quality golf balls, check with the pro to see what compression he recommends for you. And keep in mind that weather has an effect on compression. The ball becomes less resilient when the air is colder, so that a golfer who plays a 90-compression ball in the summer might be advised to switch to an 80-compression ball in the fall.

Have Confidence in the Club You Choose

The late Tommy Armour had a point. Put the 90-shooter, he said, in the same spots on the fairway as Hogan, Snead, or any other professional, and the master will beat that 90-shooter by 10 strokes—and just because he knows which club to use.

Judging distance is a crucial part of golf. Few things are more discouraging than seeing a perfectly struck shot fall short of the green or carry over on the fly as a result of choosing the wrong club. The ability to gauge distance demands a certain amount of the innate skill of depth perception, but the tyro can improve his judgment by using a few techniques.

Practice is essential. It is the quickest way to arrive at a knowledge of one's potential, the surest way to achieve familiarity with the range of each club. Practice also develops a repeating swing so that the beginner can start to hit his shots the same length every time; he won't be crushing the nine-iron 180 yards one time, and patting it 90 the next.

Ben Hogan was probably the first golfer to make a science out of the art of judging distance. Hogan (and lately Jack Nicklaus with his cartographic, precision-notated score cards) perambulated about the course during practice rounds, amassing and mentally charting significant facts. So when Nicklaus says he is 156 yards from the pin, he *knows*. Using physical landmarks as guides, he has paced off and recorded all significant distances between points.

This surveyor's technique is fine for golfers who play most of their games on a very few courses, but there will always be times when he is face-to-face with a layout he has never seen. Or he may be in a place on his home grounds where he never expected to be. In this case, Gary Player and other pros use the progression system of estimating distance. The player picks an object (a tree or a bush) that is wedge distance from the ball. Such smaller distances are easier to assess. He then moves his gaze forward 10 yards and rests it on another landmark, calculating that he will need one more club for each additional 10 yards beyond the original marking point. By a series of such mental steps, he can visually work his way to the green—and choose the right club.

If somehow you cannot get a good perspective on the green, pick out something around the green such as a tree, and by focusing on that, estimate the distance from your ball to the putting surface. Greens are flat and lie horizontally with the land so they are often hard to distinguish from the rest of the fairway. A tree stands out against the sky, and its vertical silhouette is a better marking point. Also, if there is a sand trap in front of the green, it may be more simple to visualize what club you would need to land the ball in that trap, and then take one more so you can clear it.

If there are no hazards to affect your decision, and you are struggling to decide between one of two clubs, remember that most greens are three clubs deep—that is, you can hit one club to the front, one to the middle, and one to the back edge. There are two schools of thought on whether to choose the greater or the lesser club in a borderline situation. You should select the lesser club, one group maintains, so you will go ahead and hit hard and not try to baby the extra club and end up quitting on the shot. But other teachers say the opposite: use that extra club so you won't have to force your swing. Practice can tell you which error you are more likely to fall into.

However, most of our staff experts, from personal observations, are

Normal Distance for Average Golfers

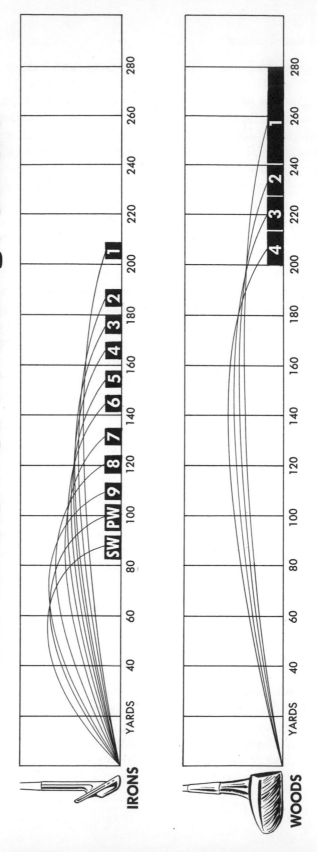

of the opinion that most golfers are guilty of underclubbing. It is a rare amateur who uses too much club. One reason, we assume, is that once having hit a perfect shot with one particular club, his expectation is to hit that same perfect shot every time thereafter. Another is pride, and it's an old saw that "pride goeth before a fall"—into a trap.

Let's say you are playing a medium length par-three (180 yards) where you think you need a three-wood to get home. But all the other members of your foursome are striding blithely to the tee with five- or six-irons. Chances are one player, probably bigger and stronger than you, will hit a perfect shot and get there with a five-iron. Another will fall far short with a face-saving excuse that he didn't really hit the ball. The third squeezes into the trap that fronts the green by really crushing the ball, but he'll explain that he didn't really hit it either. So you're conned into changing your mind. Forget pride! Hit your three-wood or whatever club you honestly think you need to get home. Just remember, it's better to be a winning David than a losing Goliath.

You can't mention underclubbing without talking about overswinging. This is a destructive and awkward method of churning up power. Yet, as soon as you underclub, the obvious compensation is to break your shoelaces with the most powerful swing in your arsenal. With this method you can only shoot blanks. Any time you try to stretch distance you throw yourself off balance, shatter your rhythm and timing, and undoubtedly wind up lunging at the ball. To have the best percentage going for you, (1) keep your swing contained in its groove and (2) take enough club to get the job done. So, size up your shot, select the first club that jumps into your mind, and swing away with confidence.

Even if they have the right tools at hand, the prevailing mood of most high-handicappers is to "help" the club lift or spoon the ball for more loft and more distance. Whether you're laying on with a two or a nine, let the club do the job and it will—that is, if you swing it and give it a chance. By the very nature of its length and loft, the two-iron, unforced, will deliver more distance than the three-iron, the four-iron, etc. As a case in point, consider the misuse of the sand wedge. Far too often the golfer tries to pick the ball clean. Actually, the sand iron, with its heavy flange, is ideally designed not to dig in but simply to slide under and through the ball.

The execution of the shot is as basic as wiggling your feet into an open and firm stance in the sand with most of your weight held on the left side throughout the swing. The second point is to choose the spot

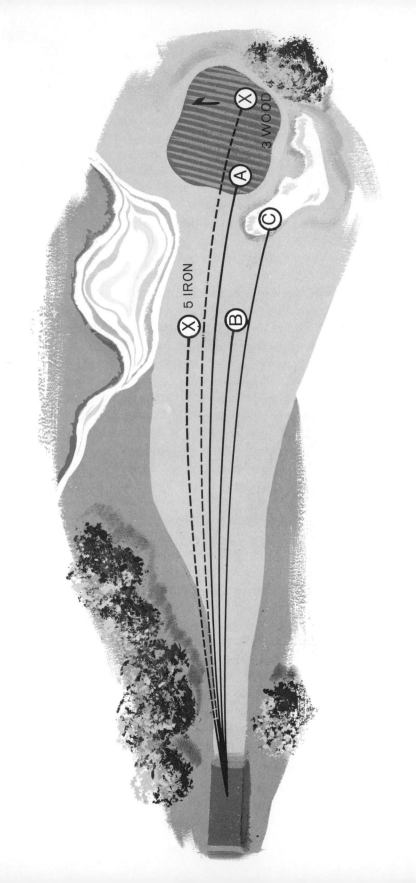

On a medium par-three, don't you (X) try to be a hero (A), (B), (C), with a middle iron. Be smart and take enough club (X, three-wood), to carry the green instead of falling short or straining for trouble and double bogeys.

that must be struck—an inch or so behind the ball. And lastly, hit through the ball, driving the clubhead right at the hole. It really works if you believe enough in the club's design to let it work for you. And the same is true of every club in the bag.

One of the most important facets of successful and consistent golf—and probably the least thought about—is the build-up to complete concentration at the ball. By this we mean all the preliminary thoughts and motions that take place just prior to actually hitting the ball. All good golfers have a certain routine they go through. In approaching a golf shot, this routine ultimately leads to concentration at the address and thus permits them to swing the clubhead smoothly through the ball and toward the target. The trouble with the average player is that he has no routine at all. Properly done, this routine starts with a realistic appraisal of the shot itself. Next is the selection of the proper club. After that comes the gripping of the club itself. Then you assume your stance. And, finally, you address the ball. Thus your concentration has narrowed to the ball alone.

Of course, nothing can be more exasperating than to execute a shot perfectly only to watch it sail off line into trouble. This failure to properly line up the shot happens when inexperienced players take their stance as soon as they step up to the ball—before placing their club behind the ball. Thus the ball is often incorrectly positioned in relation to the stance. The flaw could be avoided if they were to alter their procedure in this fashion: (1) Walk into the shot. (2) Sole the clubhead behind the ball, aiming the bottom line of the clubface directly at the target. (3) In the mind's eye, draw a line perpendicular to the line of flight from the clubhead to the correct spot between the feet for the particular club being used. (4) Place first the left foot, then the right foot into the correct positions for the particular club, keeping the clubface directed at the target. (5) Execute the shot. In other words, what we're recommending is that you don't jump into the shot feet first.

Strategy from the Tee

That first tee shot is highly important for it well may set the mental tempo for the day. Knock it off into the bulrushes and you get away in a grouch. Hit it down the fairway, even if it isn't too far, and the day looks a lot sunnier. That is, your tee shot sets the stage for the play of every hole on the course. How well you hit the ball off the tee also helps to set your mental attitude for the remainder of your performance on that hole. That is, a good tee shot will give you confidence. A poor one may put some doubts in your mind.

Par permits no more than three strokes to get on the green on any golf holes. On three-par holes, you should be on the green with your tee shot. A bad tee shot, therefore, can almost guarantee a bogey or more. On the other hand, a good tee shot will give you the position you need to play a golf hole in the least possible number of strokes.

In other words, in order to get the "jump" on any golf hole, it's important to position your tee shot. You want to put your drive in an area that will give you the easiest shot to the green. As a general rule, we would say that in trying to position your drive, and of course nobody does it perfectly every time, you should take your driving angle from the placement of the flag. In other words, if the pin is tucked in the left side of the green, play your drive to the right side of the fairway. If the pin is tucked right, then play your drive down the left side of the fairway. Usually this planning will give you the big part of the green at which to hit your approach shot. But let's say you foul things up by driving to the left side with the pin also on the left. Now you have a pocket handkerchief piece of green at which you can gamble, but there are traps in front of you and a big one to the right. Disregard any heroics, and lay the ball up safely for position on the next shot. If there is trouble, such as a line of trees or an out-of-bounds on either one side of the fairway or the other, a similar plan is necessary. Whatever side of the fairway the trouble is on, tee your ball up on the same side and play your drive to the opposite side. This way you are avoiding trouble by hitting away from it. Whatever the situation, it's important to position your drive. Always try to avoid trouble by hitting away from it.

Some teaching pros use the so-called highway system when giving instructions on position golf. That is, as you're on the tee looking down the fairway, in your imagination, visualize a highway running right down the middle of the fairway. Then visualize four lanes with four vehicles traveling side by side on the imaginary road. There is usually enough room on the average fairway for more than four cars to fit side by side, so there is plenty of room for your tiny golf ball to fit on the fairway.

Now in your imagination put a white line right down the middle of your fairway road. Figure out on which side of this white line the most trouble lies. When you have done that, play across the center line to the other side of the fairway road. Very rarely should you play for the center of the fairway. Always play for either the left side or the right side.

To carry this visualization process further, if the conditions are normal and there is not too much trouble on either side of the fairway, then ask yourself this question, "From which side of the fairway would it be easier to land on the green?" So on the tee of each hole use these three keys:

1. Mentally dissect your fairway by drawing an imaginary line right up the middle.

2. On which side of the fairway does the greater danger lie?

3. From which side of the fairway is it easier to shoot to the green?

After you have hit your tee shot and are now in range of the green, mentally cut your green in half right down the middle, and then dissect it horizontally in half again making four quarters. Now which is the easiest quarter to hit? Which is the quarter the flag is resting in? Is it wisest to shoot for the safest part of the green or go for the section in which the flag is resting? Use your own judgment. If you feel con-

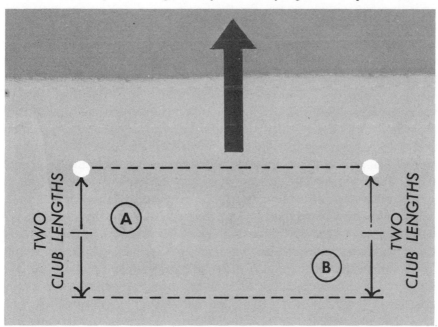

Intelligent use of the full teeing area can mean playing off a level rather than an uneven lie. By using the width (A) and depth (B) of a tee, you may even avoid going over a trap on a par-three. Avoid teeing up in a mess of divots. They can make you play down the line they are pointing, and most of them point the wrong way!

fident that you can hit the section where the flag is resting, by all means go for it. Don't be timid. But, for the players that aren't quite as skillful as the experts, go for the safest part of the green.

If it is the first time you are playing a course, play position on each hole as has been suggested. But for the golfers who play the same course repeatedly, at some time make a sketch of each hole. Dissect the fairway green of each hole, and then put a dot on the fairway and another on the green to indicate where to play positions on each particular fairway and green. More on how to chart a course is given in Chapter 7.

In addition to playing position, when playing from a tee, you must also consider the following: how far away the hole is; what clubs do you hit well off the tee; and how much distance you can get with each of these clubs off the tee. By the latter, we don't mean that you should try for maximum distance all the time. Actually, the best way to make certain your swing collapses is to hit as hard as you can all the time. No top professional does it, and neither should you. What you should do is to swing within yourself for the first few holes. You can then find out how you are hitting the ball—straight, slicing, or hooking—and take any steps necessary to insure you hit it straight—before you subject the swing to the strain of an all-out effort. By getting the swing into the groove early, you will be able to let out the stick successfully when it's necessary—on the long par-fours and par-fives. Many younger players are especially prone to be "club-conscious" and to belt everything from a drive to a nine-iron as hard as they can. Often they may outdrive you on the early holes and are tickled pink. Then on one of the longer holes—where it matters—you can send the ball past them. They get so worried they start overhitting everything, their swings collapse—and you've got them. Sometimes you will find that, no matter what you try, your swing won't get into the groove on those early holes. Those days be content to swing within yourself all day. Using maximum power then is pure folly. One time that it is helpful to hit all-out is toward the end of a match. Pressure is building up, and often you are becoming too tired to coordinate properly. You may find that hitting hard then actually keeps your swing in the groove.

Would you believe it if told that your slice was caused by the way you tee up the ball? It could be true. Teeing the ball upon the wooden (or plastic) tee is like putting styles: it's individualistic and varies as each person's perspective varies. Golfers who have the feeling of hitting under and through or on a high trajectory like to see the ball well off the ground. The high tee, then, is recommended for those who stay behind the shot well or remain a little longer on the right side. They sweep through, as compared to those who prefer to look at a ball just off the ground because they hit through. If you can move to your left side smoothly, or if you tend to hit down on the ball (and get away with it), then tee it low. Where does the slice come in? Low-ball hitters generally fade the ball, because they will open the face of the club at impact to conform to the terrain, as customarily happens when a driver is used from the fairway. Conversely, a ball that is teed high will encourage a hook. For those who feel that it helps to tilt the tee slightly when playing downwind, do so. Any idiosyncrasy is healthy as long as it is believed. But definitely use a tee on the par threes. Your "lie" will always be good, the height can be adjusted to personal taste, and uniform contact can be made every time.

Once you have learned to hit the ball straight, the ability to hook or fade the ball can be of invaluable assistance. There are times when you don't always gun for the middle of the fairway. Sometimes being in the middle can be a disadvantage, depending on the manner in which the hole plays and the hazards in the line of your next shot. For instance on dogleg holes, knowing how to hook or fade the ball can cut yards off the hole and put you in an ideal spot for the second shot. If you are now capable of hitting the ball straight, there is no reason why you should have any problems learning to maneuver the ball. To hook, or draw, the ball you simply close your stance a bit more than normal. This means that your left hip and left shoulder are pointing more to the right of the target. This will cause you to stay inside on your backswing and, if you concentrate on keeping that right elbow in close to the body, you will be assured of an inside-out swing that will produce the desired effect. In fading the ball, it is simply the opposite procedure. Here you take an open stance with the left foot drawn back from the intended line. This opens your hips to the target, and causes you to take the club back more toward the outside and helps produce the action of cutting across the ball.

There's nothing that will put a golfer behind the eight ball faster than driving the ball out-of-bounds. To the average golfer, out-of-bounds markers present a hazard that is far more mental than physical. By this we mean that most golfers are so afraid of going out-of-bounds with their drives that a process of negative suggestion sets in and the golfer hits the ball exactly where he doesn't want to hit it—out-of-bounds. He does this because he tries to steer the ball and does not

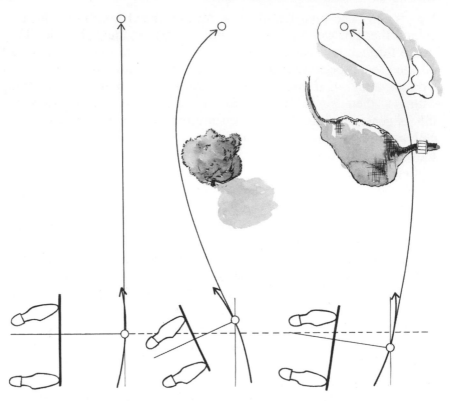

To intentionally slice (left), open stance by withdrawing left foot from line of flight and swing outside-in. To intentionally hook (right), close stance by withdrawing right foot from line of flight and swing inside-out.

use his normal swing. We feel that better results can be achieved for the high-handicap player if he forgets all about the out-of-bounds and takes his normal swing. The better-than-average player, however, can guard against going out-of-bounds by hooking or fading away from the trouble. In other words, if there is out-of-bounds to the right, he should start his drive toward the right side of the fairway and hook it away from the trouble. And he should do just the opposite when out-of-bounds is on the left.

If you've been having trouble with your driver, it is always wise to use one of the other woods. More and more tournament professionals are using the so-called fairway woods to drive with for the sake of control and accuracy. Remember the one-wood (driver) is one of the more difficult clubs to master. This is especially true for the average golfers during the first few holes. But they still will grab the big stick even if the hole isn't wide open—and even though all their muscles are cold. What they're doing is committing first-hole hara-kiri. Much better to take the more lofted two-wood, or the much lighter three-wood, and swing it easy to keep it down the middle and get you off to a good start.

When using a more lofted wood, the ball should be teed lower to the ground than normal driver shots. Don't make the error of teeing the ball too high to get extra height. You might merely sweep the clubhead under the ball and "sky" the ball. Tee it fairly low, with a little less than half of the clubhead appearing above the ball at address.

Irons have a definite place on the tee, disregarding the obvious short par-three holes on which they must be employed. If you play your long irons well, and in a situation where accuracy is more important than distance, use the one-, two-, or three-irons.

When hitting a tee shot, select a target in the background that you aim your shot at. This target may be a tree, house, etc. Run your eye back and forth from your clubhead to this target to give yourself the line of desired flight of the ball. In other words, train yourself to visualize your ball following this imaginary line you have picked out to be your target. For instance, if you're attempting a drawing shot or a fading shot toward your target, get squarely behind your ball and see through your mind's eye the shot executed the way you visualize it. Keep this same picture in your mind as you address your ball ready to start your swing. Remember the old golfing saying that goes like this, "You can't hit it unless you can first see it."

Make Those Long Shots Pay Off

Bobby Jones once said that the funniest thing that ever happened to him on a golf course occurred one day when he was playing his own East Lake course with a high-handicapper. They came to a very short par-four, and the hacker proceeded to hole out for an eagle.

"Wonderful," Jones congratulated his playing partner. "What club did you use?"

"A five-wood," the other responded proudly.

Jones's surprise showed in his voice. "A five-wood?"

"Yes," said the other. "What do you hit on your second shot here?"

"Well," drawled Jones, "usually a nine-iron. But if the wind's against me I might use an eight."

"Did you ever hole out here in two?" demanded the high-handi-capper.

Jones shook his head.

"Well," replied the hacker condescendingly, "maybe you're using the wrong club." Or clubs.

What we're getting at is that those in the eight-handicap-and-over class—which means the vast majority of those who play golf—actually would be far, far better off to throw away their two- and three-irons and replace them with a five-wood and maybe even a six-wood. And it makes even more sense, as we will try to show you, for those who have a handicap of 12 or more. There are four basic reasons for our suggestion.

1. The two- and three-irons are just about the most difficult clubs in the bag to use, and their usage is complicated by the feeling that you must swing harder to lift the ball.

2. Normally your trouble is in front of the greens and the five- and six-woods will carry you high over that trouble and let you stop the ball.

3. All players are short 75 percent of the time, and short woods, as compared with the long irons, will give you that little extra distance on the fly.

4. Very few average players ever take enough club to begin with.

Why then, you might ask, do they even bother to have the two- and three-irons in the bag? The answer is simply that the very good player can do more tricks with them. He can strike them more accurately than he can the woods, he can keep the ball lower in the wind and he can fade or hook the ball more easily and accurately. But let's face the fact that the two- and three-irons must be struck with precision and timing usually far beyond the ken of the high-handicap player. Looking down at those small heads, he feels that he has to hit the ball harder and that he must make a conscious effort to get the ball airborne. Thus he tries to really wallop the ball, loses his rhythm and timing, and completely ruins the shot. The result is that he skulls it or rolls it unhappily into a trap in front of the green.

If you took a picture of a player hitting a ball with a two-iron and then using the five-wood, you'd be amazed at the difference in the two swings. Nine times out of ten he'll jump at the two-iron, rushing his swing in an attempt to muscle the ball. Well, that's not golf. In most cases, we are convinced, the major difficulty is that mental conviction that he must hit the ball harder. Hand him the wood, and it is easier for him to convince himself that he must swing the club and let the clubhead do the work.

Try it yourself sometime. A 15-minute experiment should convince you of the truth of what we're saying. Hit 20 shots with a two-iron and then hit 20 shots with a five-wood. When you look out at a marker while holding that iron in your hand, it seems a mile away. But when you grip the wood, it seems to bring it a lot closer. But even more important, you'll be amazed at how much more smoothly you are swinging with the wood.

Remember that the five-wood will get you as much distance as the two-iron, on the average, and that where the two-iron is a low, running shot that must thread the trouble in front of the greens, the five-wood will give you the loft without effort and carry you over the trouble. It will stop a lot more quickly, too, simply because of its high trajectory. That last factor is, we believe, of great importance to the average player. Make a survey of your own golf course, or those you play, and you'll find that normally the trouble, be it water or traps, is in front of the green.

Right here let's take into consideration another factor that contributes to your woes. One of the major faults among golfers—professional as well as amateur—is underclubbing. From our observations, as we said earlier, all players are short 75 percent of the time. Take a month's survey of your own game, and we think you will be absolutely amazed at the number of times you are short of the hole compared with the number of times you are hitting past the flag. We doubt if the average player is past the hole three to five times during a round. The principal reason is that most players judge their approach shot on the perfect shot. In other words, you tell yourself, "I should get there with a five-iron." You should, if you hit it perfectly. But for the high-handicapper it seldom comes off perfectly. Thus he is leaving it short most of the time.

True, some average players, particularly those with strong hands and a relatively good sense of timing, find that long irons are a strong part of their game. Let's make one point clear—players who use five- and six-woods because they think these clubs have more loft than the so-called straight-faced irons and are, therefore, easier to hit are mistaken, not only about the actual degree of loft, but also about the type of shot the clubs produce. As proof, please check the chart on page 42. No, it is not the club. We should say it is more in the manner in which the ball is hit that produces the bad shots when the long irons

It is a glaring misconception among golfers that the long irons are too straight-faced and so are too difficult to be used from the fairway. And we dare say that even after consulting this chart, proving that even the six-wood does not have more loft than the four-iron, many will continue to ignore or fear the iron from within a range of 165 to 185 yards.

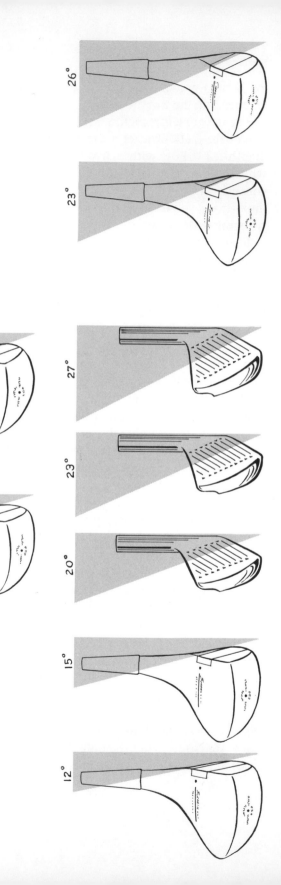

are used. For example, it would be true that golfers who swing in a flat arc would have more trouble with their irons than an upright swinger. Those with a flat plane tend to be fast away from the ball, their hands drop below and behind the shoulder, if that high, and they snatch the club away too quickly. Under such strain, they find they cannot get back to the ball with ease and comfort, and they will "wheel" the body around, causing the ball to be topped or pulled off line. Weak players also have a problem in that they incline to use too much body on the takeaway and consequently they, too, flatten their swing arc.

These errors are caused by the golfer, not the club he is using. To be a *low-handicap player,* you *must* learn to use your long irons. All pros use them, and *some* think the *average golfer* should too. Lee Trevino, for instance, says, "I don't buy the theory generally advanced that the average player is better off to leave them in the bag. I feel that all it simmers down to is lack of use. The average guy who even takes time out to hit a few balls before he plays, concentrates on warming up with his short irons, the seven, eight and nine. Then he gets out on the course, messes up two- or three-iron shots and growls, 'Hell, I can't hit those at all.' First of all, everybody is inclined to swing too hard with the long irons when he should be swinging easier and letting the club do the work. Second, I suggest that when you go to the practice tee you spend more time warming up with the four-iron than you do with any other club. If you can hit the four-iron, you'll be able to hit them all."

Yet the majority of our experts are of the opinion that the long irons are the average players' greatest bugaboo and they'd do a lot better to leave them in the bag. There was a time when the five-wood and six-wood were frowned upon or considered at best to be ladies' weapons, but not any more; and they'll do the same job without the necessity of hitting down and through the ball. Those shorter woods are real stroke-savers if you want to become a more consistent player.

It is in these long shots that we strongly suggest that for greater consistency you hit the shot you know you can pull off even if it goes slightly awry, which in most cases it does. Let's say that the five-wood or even with your longer middle irons—and certainly with your three-wood and four-wood—you "think" you can get home if you hit it just right. But let's say that it's a small, well-trapped green. The odds are that you're going to wallop away and hope for that once-in-a-thousand "miracle." So you put it in a bunker or wide of the green into the trees or the rough. How much better off you would have been to lay

WOOD
IRON

If you are not sure that you can reach the green, use an iron instead of a fairway wood, and play short to the opening away from the bunker.

up to the opening to the green, and definitely short of the bunkers, leaving yourself a little flip into the pin. Go back over your recent rounds and you'll be astounded at how many shots you would have saved.

Strategy and the Middle Irons

For out-and-out versatility, the middle irons (four-, five-, and six-irons) are undoubtedly the most effective clubs in the golfer's bag. Of course, versatility covers a lot of territory: tee and fairway shots, getting out of the rough (both for distance and accuracy), trouble shots, bunker play, and chip shots. When you think about it, that's quite a crowd of strokes to gather in any one round. With all those irons to choose from, it's only smart golfing to be able to pick the right club and to know all the ways the middle sticks can work for you—and save strokes.

Now let's take each of the situations just mentioned and see how the middle irons do the job in setting up pars or saving them.

The tee shot with an iron on par-threes is similar to the fairway shot but, nevertheless, there is a difference. The lie is better. Actually, it should be perfect, since the ball is placed on the tee. However, too many players all too casually stick the tee in the ground with no regard to the height. If it's too high, then more than likely you'll sky the shot or have to pull up—and lose control—to get the flat of the club on the ball. Either way, you've wasted a chance to strike a blow for par or birdie.

The grass on most tees is usually short enough so that if the ball seems to be resting just on the top of the blades, it should be perfect. If

LOW SHOT   HIGH SHOT
          NORMAL

A tremendous asset in golf is being able to maneuver the ball. For high or low shots the loft of the middle irons does all the work for you because less effort is required to bring the ball into flight. To hit low shots, the hands are held forward, and the weight distribution is canted to the left more than normally. A lateral movement in the legs rather than the usual turning insures and enables you to keep your hands lower through the swing. This action results in a slight hooding of the clubface and a low trajectory for the ball. Also, it is wise to remember that with the lower angle of flight the ball will exercise its tendency to roll more. To hit the ball high, play it more toward the left foot with your weight slightly on the right side, hitting the ball more on the upswing.

such is not the case, then rest the club behind the ball and see how much of the ball leaks over the blade. If it's more than one-quarter, then the ball is teed too high. So don't be overconfident and careless when you step up to that par-three. You've got the hole bagged only if you think before you swing.

Aside from the tee shot, the middle irons are more commonly played in the fairway where, although not all lies are perfect, the loft and length of these clubs when properly used can achieve wonders for your score. Of course, generally speaking, the ball is positioned near the middle of a square stance with the hands held ahead of the club-face from address through impact. And naturally, the ball must be struck first before the club touches the ground, which means hitting down and through the ball. Remember, one way you cannot hit a solid shot with the middle irons is to try to steer it.

Even if you haven't hit the fairway, the middle irons are versatile enough to get you out of most trouble more smartly than you think. For example, in thin short rough, the four-iron and five-iron will easily cut through and sail the ball out. Of course, you should allow for more than normal run, since the intervening grass, caught between the blade and the ball, will provide very little backspin. As a result, it's quite possible you'll get more distance from the rough than from the fairway.

Then again, in heavy rough you'll find the six-iron the most dependable of the middle irons. It's not what you'd call a gambling club but just an honest, deep-faced weapon with enough loft to cut in well, fly the ball out, and usually give plenty of distance to clear any trouble. But beware! Don't press the shot or try for a full flight or you may leave the ball right where you found it. In addition, the six-iron has enough depth of face to be invaluable when you're hugging a bad lie such as a divot, depression, or the like. It drives into the ball with authority and is especially handy when you want to throw a punch shot at the green and into the wind. Since the blade is deep enough to give you considerable control as well as distance, the six-iron (five-, or even four-) is ideal. To keep the flight low from, say, under trees, simply hood the blade a little, play the ball back farther and don't overswing. This last is easy if you restrict your pivot somewhat by making less of a turn. However, if you're tempted to try this short carry shot from trouble, be sure that sometime you have a little re-hearsal first. The punch shot (see page 55) doesn't fly like the regular shot, but will arch and drop with less roll, considerably short of your normal effort.

Among the many reasons most people fail to play golf as well as they would like is the fact that they are so wrapped up in the technique of hitting the ball that they tend to ignore the technique of playing the game—which can be another matter altogether. Take the problem of choosing the proper iron, for instance. Even low-handicap players often err in this respect, particularly on their home courses. They are so used to playing a certain iron on a certain hole that they often yank it out of the bag without even considering the possibility of using one less or more iron. Never choose a five-iron, for example, without first considering the possibility of either a four-iron or a six-iron. Let's presume that you are 150 yards from the green. We'll say that you ordinarily use a five-iron from this distance. If there is a bunker in front of the green, however, might not a wiser choice be your four-iron? To make sure you clear the hazard? If, on the other hand, there is a bunker (or heavy rough or trees) behind the green, might not the wiser choice be your six-iron? To make sure you fall short of trouble? After all, avoiding trouble is far more practicable for the overwhelming majority of golfers than trying to knock a shot stiff against the flagstick. Furthermore, by always debating your choice of irons, you'll soon find yourself hitting the ball with added confidence.

A rather startling yet key instance of mid-iron versatility is found in the unsettling (to your opponent), ego-pleasing (to you), and stroke-saving bunker shot. It's a proud golfer who can put a ball on the green from a trap 130 to 160 yards away. And rightly so. But most golfers think it's impossible or beyond them, that it's a pro shot or a once-in-a-lifetime gamble. Well, it's not always true.

To take a nine-iron or a wedge just to play out is a wasted stroke. First of all, confidence in the club will go a long way toward curing that hit-and-hope attitude. And there's no reason why you shouldn't be as confident with a mid-iron in the trap as with a putter on the green. A sand shot by the average golfer can be hit both for distance and accuracy.

Second, examine both the lie and the lip. If the ball has bounced or rolled in, chances are you have a relatively good lie. Now if you're also only a yard or so into the trap—and fairway traps usually come in large sizes—then the lip is probably well ahead of you, giving you plenty of room to maneuver with a four-iron, five-iron, or six-iron.

Remember, don't be intimidated by the lip if you know you can get to the ball. Of course, your best bet to begin with is a six-iron. If that works—and it should—then, in a similar situation, go to a five-iron or, if the trap is real shallow, a four-iron. You'll be surprised how fast and how high the ball rises.

Third, the style for hitting these bunker shots calls for some minor adjustments. Like other trap shots, settle your feet solidly in the sand for firm footing and balance. Then choke down slightly on the shaft to prevent overswinging. A successful shot will be impossible if you try to "turn it on" or "muscle it." With the ball played forward of center, which is more than normally, bring the club back low to the ground in a slow one-piece swing. Returning it in the same arc, let the clubface lift the ball—not you. The whole idea is that, even though you're still hitting down and through the ball, you'll leave a very shallow or thin divot at best.

One last point to remember is that the sand has a tendency to open the face of the club, so aim a little left of target to counteract the slight fade. More on sand play can be found in Chapter 4.

Chipping, the last example of mid-iron versatility, is as important as any of the others. The basic idea in the pitch-and-run, or chip shot, is to have the ball roll within one-putt distance of the cup or—better yet—in the cup. More on this is given later in this chapter.

And now you know why we believe the middle irons are the most versatile in the bag. The potential for low scoring is all there in the clubs. But they can't play the game by themselves or for you. So there's only one thing left to do—get out on the course and swing them.

Strategy and the Short Game

The short irons are definitely the clubs that lower golf scores. On the basis of their being used ten or twelve times in the course of a round, and figuring, as you should, on getting down at least one-third of the time with a pitch and one putt, and never more than a pitch and two putts the other times, you can reduce your totals at least three or four shots in eighteen holes. Often, among amateurs, this is the difference between average golf and excellent golf. Among the professionals it is always the difference between average earnings and excellent earnings.

The seven-, eight-, and nine-irons and the two wedges represent perhaps the widest range in distance of any club-grouping in the bag.

They are in use anywhere from a few feet off the green to some 135 yards from the pin. Yet they feature a length, loft, and lie that makes each ideal for the pin-pointing they are designed to do. The short irons have an individuality and accuracy potential none of the others have, and tournament golfers select the specific one that will do the best job of getting the ball up close under the circumstances.

Most high-handicap players use a favorite club on all their short pitches. This contributes to their high scoring because one club is not fitted for the continually changing circumstances. Where other phases of golf—driving, bunker play, putting—require the consistent use of the same club, few amateurs realize how much more difficult they are making the game for themselves by sticking resolutely to the one club when faced with the short chip shot. Just because you have a favorite stick is no reason to use it exclusively. Surely you don't select a club for your long shots simply because you like it. The choice is governed by the problems of distance, elevation, run, obstacles, and so on. If this is true of the long game, it should be even more true of the short.

On any short shot you must take at least three good looks: one, at the ball, two, at the hole, and three, at what lies in between. It's only after making these three observations that the right club can be selected with which the shot can best be executed. Of course, the professional is concerned not just with the green but with the exact position of the flag, and not merely with the roll of the green but the grain as well. To determine how hard or soft the green might be is not a matter of guesswork. A good player usually walks on the green and lets his feet give him the answer. This way he can judge how to play a pitch or chip shot with a fairly good idea of how the ball will react. Naturally, a hard green will provide more roll and a soft one will hold better and allow less run.

With "one-club chippers," the seven-iron is generally the favorite. But, normally and unfortunately, there are many situations when a seven-iron simply won't do. If the ball is above the green and you must hit short, running it to a tight flag, the seven-iron will usually impart too much roll. Since the blade will close a little faster and turn the seven-iron into something nearer a six-, the better club must be a nine-iron or pitching wedge. On the other hand, with a chip onto an elevated green or over a hazard, the seven-iron may not loft the ball sufficiently. The "scoop and dump" shot is the usual and unhappy result.

Plainly, then, the only method to playing short shots effectively is to first find a mental picture of the way the ball must be made to behave. It is this that automatically suggests the proper club selection. Whatever it is—four-iron, seven-iron, nine-iron, or sand wedge—this is the club to use. For example, there are many factors which must be taken into consideration when you make your pitch shot. You must check on the contour of the green to figure out the roll, note whether the grain is with you or against you, and the distance. Reading the green (see page 60) is one of the greatest talents the man who needs those one-putt approaches can have.

You might find it to your advantage on an exceptionally long chip to select a four- or five-iron if you are going against the grain and an eight- or nine-iron from the same distance when going downhill or with the grain or both. You must practice these saving shots, not only to understand them, but to determine how far each club is going to run for you. But, as a general rule of thumb, with the straight-faced clubs such as the five- or six-iron, pitch one-third of the way to the pin and figure on the ball rolling the other two-thirds. With the seven- or eight-, pitch about halfway. With the nine-iron or wedge, cover two-thirds of the way in flight and get one-third run. For a quick stop, get to know how to pitch with the sand wedge from varying distances.

In each instance, pick out a spot on the green where you want the ball to land and concentrate on hitting that spot. If judgment of contour and grain are correct, and you are using the right club to do the job, you should be up there for a saving one-putt green. Another factor to consider is that your shot should land *on* the green. Hitting on the putting surface gives you a truer bounce. If you hit short, you are taking the risk of the ball finding a depression or hole or bump, and ruining your shot. So the actual key, it seems to us, is practicing hitting to a certain spot and observing the distance of the roll you get with each of the scoring clubs. Notice we said clubs. Many foreign players chip with one club, changing the loft by the mechanics of their swing. It is my view that they are making the game a lot harder and, under pressure, might revert to the wrong swing. Most American pros don't believe in altering the swing. Let the right club do the work and you have this big battle half won.

Since chips from the fringe of a green are usually handled like a long putt, use a club with little loft: a three-, or four-iron. (Many of our top golfers use their putter—referred to in such circumstances as a "Texas Wedge"—off the edge of the green.) Don't try to loft the

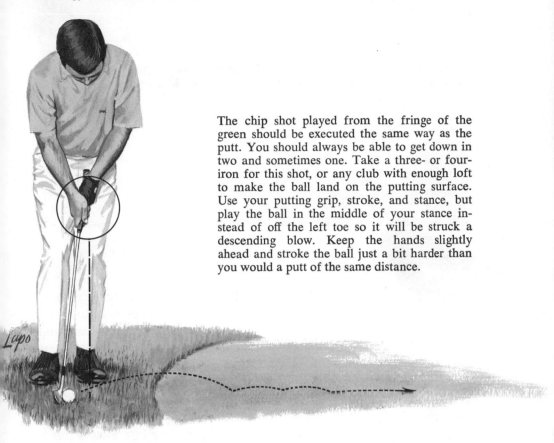

The chip shot played from the fringe of the green should be executed the same way as the putt. You should always be able to get down in two and sometimes one. Take a three- or four-iron for this shot, or any club with enough loft to make the ball land on the putting surface. Use your putting grip, stroke, and stance, but play the ball in the middle of your stance instead of off the left toe so it will be struck a descending blow. Keep the hands slightly ahead and stroke the ball just a bit harder than you would a putt of the same distance.

ball, but rather hit the ball with a crisp running stroke, relying on your sense of distance (and experience, which you gain after practicing this stroke) to tell you how hard to stroke the ball.

On uphill chips, the ball is played off the right foot, since you wish to hit the ball as solidly as possible. If you would use a six-iron from a level lie, use a five-iron when the chip is uphill; the incline will add loft to the ball to the extent that a five-iron shot will behave like a six- or even a seven-iron.

Downhill chip shots require the opposite approach for two reasons. First, less club should be used than under normal conditions. Second, the ball is played off the left heel. Because the green is sloping downhill, you don't want to hit the ball too firmly. Rather, you want to drop it onto the green softly.

When hitting *up* to a pin that is perched up on the back level of a split-level green, there are two choices available to you. One would be

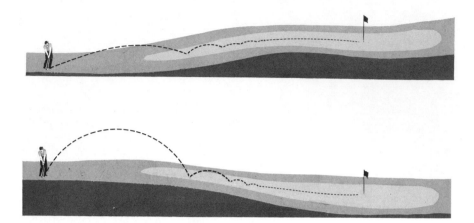

Top illustration shows how to chip to an uphill flagstaff, while the lower one shows how to solve a downhill situation.

to take a pitching wedge and loft it all the way to within three or four feet of the pin. The other would be to use a five- or six-iron, and run the ball up over the rise to the pin. What determines your choice is the distance the pin is from the ridge. If the distance from the ridge is at least 10 feet, then by all means loft the ball onto the upper level. The danger in using the wedge is that you're apt to hit the shot into the rise of the hill. If the pin is only a few feet from the edge of the rise, then run the ball up to the hole with a five- or six-iron. The safest shot (when in doubt) is running the ball to the pin. The ball always has a chance of ending near the flag.

Imagination can play a helping hand in determining how fully to hit a pitching-wedge shot to an elevated green. To obtain a feeling of how far to take the club back, imagine tossing the ball underhanded in a high lob toward the green, and picture as your target a bushel basket on the green. The basket image is careful in picturing the kind of high shot needed to hit, and stay on, an elevated green. Visualizing the shot in this way will give you a precise feeling for the amount of force you need in your swing with the wedge. Just take the club back with the same force and movement in mind, and you will be able to go for the green with confidence.

Hitting a short pitch over a trap to a tight pin placement scares any golfer. However, rather than try to hit his shot "stiff," the weekend golfer should be certain he gets the ball up on the putting surface. Don't look at the trouble in front. Concentrate on hitting

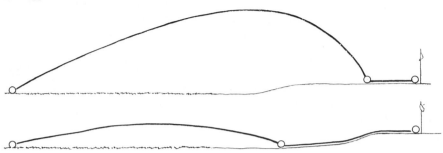

Two ways of approaching a terraced or split-level green.

your ball past the pin so you at least have a putt for your par instead of a dreaded trap shot. Hit this shot with authority. By this we don't mean a jerky movement, but more of a deliberate control action, with the left wrist kept firm throughout the swing. Select your most-lofted club and let its loft get the ball up for you.

Remember that there are two basic types of pitching shots: the high, soft pitch and the low-running pitch. The soft pitch shot, which is hit with a lofted club, flies high to the green, lands near the pin, and because of the backspin applied comes quickly to rest. This shot, frequently called a lofted pitch, is a "must" when you must hit over a trap or other hazard and stop the ball quickly. This type of shot is

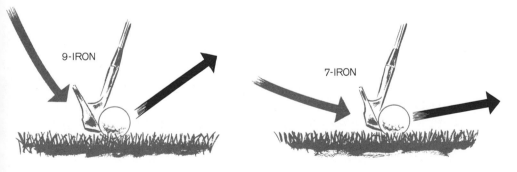

The nine-iron and wedge (left) secure "biting" action through an upright backswing and swift knees. In a one-piece action, using basically shoulders, arms, and stiff wrists, the ball is struck a sharp descending blow before the blade cuts the turf. The pitch-and-run (right) is just the opposite. If the blade is taken away low to the ground and returned in the same way, the ball will probably be met at the bottom of the swing. The result should be a low-flying ball with a good run and no bite.

good when the green is hard or when the pin is located close to a trap or forward on the green. It is also valuable when the wind is behind you, or when the green slopes away from your ball.

The pitch-and-run shot, though lofted to a degree, lands short on the green and runs up to the pin. This shot is generally employed where the opening to the green is wide and smooth, or where the flag is set on a plateau near the back and higher than the front of the green. It is also useful when hitting against the wind or when the lie of the ball is bad. When using the pitch-and-run shot, it's important to select the landing spot for the ball so that it will run properly toward the pin.

When making a pitch shot, it's sometimes wise to punch-stroke. This is true when you have to fight either a cross-wind or a wind blowing right into your face. The intention is to keep the ball low so the effect of the wind will be kept to a minimum. The important characteristic of the shot is that the ball will "bite" when it hits the green. Therefore, it's very important that you judge the distance you want very carefully.

To achieve a well-hit punch shot you must make some adjustments in your stance. Put all your weight on your left foot. In fact, many golfers find that they are actually leaning toward the direction they want the ball to take. Keep your hands well ahead of the ball. Play the ball more toward your right foot than normal. At impact you'll feel that your hands are going through the ball lower than for the full short iron. Take your divot well after impact, keeping your left arm and wrists firm as the club meets the ball and turf. Your follow-through will finish low, with your club pointing in the direction of the target.

Another shot that you should consider is the cut stroke, which is exactly the opposite of the punch shot. The result is a high, soft shot that sits almost immediately when it hits the green. You will find this useful when the wind is at your back or when there are tall obstacles you must hit over.

For the cut shot, play the ball slightly forward of the center of your stance. The key to getting the ball in the air is to open (lay back) the clubface. Also, open your stance a little more than usual. This will cause the clubhead to move in an outside-in path, cutting under the ball and giving it a clockwise spin. To counteract the slicing tendency of the ball, aim a little to the left of the intended target. If the ball bounces once it hits the green, it will move from left to right. Your swing is identical to the full wedge shot except that the open stance will make your swing more upright and get you completely under the

The club and hand action on the punch shot (left) should be crisper and less sweeping than on a full iron shot. The clubhead will come into the ball at a sharper angle, providing lots of bite.

ball. One important thing to remember: use the cut shot only when your ball is lying high in grass. Don't use it when the grass is not plush or on any type of hard surface.

The Art of Scrambling

Scrambling! It's a word that many golfers dislike. To be pegged as a "scrambler" somehow seems to imply, even if the player scores well, that he's actually a duffer and that sooner or later everything is going to catch up with him and his entire game will come crashing down. How many times have you overheard someone's badly beaten opponent explain his loss to the clubhouse crowd with, "Joe beat me with a 78—but he scrambled all over the course!"

Well, we'll tell you something that all the pros on the Tour know well. The player who is scrambling the best is the one who wins the tournament that week. In fact, as long as the emphasis is on power golf, any player who hopes to reach the top must be a super scrambler; and if this is true of the tournament performer (which it is), it would have to go double for the rest of the golfing fraternity.

This is an era in which longer golf courses are being built, and these new layouts usually don't have the heavy growth of the established shorter courses. Consequently, everybody is either banging the ball in a quest for birdies or going all-out just trying to keep up with par on these king-sized holes. But when you unload all your power, you sacrifice accuracy. Once you stray from the straight and narrow, you have to start scrambling.

The scrambler, be he professional or amateur, has the special talent to be able to get the ball into position for that saving one-putt. This requires great proficiency with the scoring clubs, from the five- through the sand-iron, so that you can chip and run, lob your pitch, or play a running shot as the case requires. We have said that the average player should be as good a scrambler as the better player for the obvious reason that he *has* to scramble more often.

We do think there is some confusion in many minds about scrambling. Scrambling certainly doesn't mean gambling. Most of the time it means just the opposite—it means playing safe so you might be able to salvage a "scrambling par." And it's funny how often that very thing works out. A player will be in trouble, say, for example, bunkered near a green, with the pin tucked in a tight corner of the green with a pond behind. Instead of trying a dangerous shot right at the pin, he'll play the ball safely out away from the hole toward the fat part of the green. Then, after holing a 20-foot putt, everyone will moan, "What a scrambler!" Actually he was just using his head, playing it safe and settling for a bogey—if he had missed the putt—rather than gambling and maybe ending up with a double or even a triple bogey.

Golf is designed so that if you make a bad shot, it's usually going to cost you a stroke, unless you get that infrequent long putt that everyone occasionally sinks, so don't try so hard to save that one stroke that you lose two more. You'll never get to be a good scrambler by taking reckless chances. They just don't pay off in the long run. Play it safe, and some days everything will drop. If not, then at least you'll have saved as many strokes as possible anyway, or at least you won't have thrown additional ones away.

This isn't to say that you automatically give up on every tough shot.

That's part of the challenge of golf. But look at the lie and hazards, and analyze the entire situation to figure if you have any chance of pulling it off. If not, then simply play safe, even if it means a probable bogey. Don't go for that "career shot" all the time. They just don't come that easy.

Actually, scrambling could be called the "art of golf." It also requires "heart." We have seen golfers actually throw clubs in anger for having missed a shot. We don't know why. No one is immune to making errors, even the best of them. When resorting to heaving a club, you're only berating an innocent party, your equipment, instead of the guilty one, you, yourself. You are the one who put the ball wherever it winds up. Instead of blowing up, devote all your attention and talent to figuring out how you best can get out of the situation you alone put yourself in, without wasting any shots.

Any golfer who hopes to win or score well has to be able to come up with the recovery shot that will save him from those bad rounds. A man, no matter how good his game is, cannot hit that many greens and play so many good shots in a row and never be in trouble. But yet, as true as this is, it isn't always what happens.

During the Doral Open in Miami a few years ago, Rex Baxter, in the final round, hit 18 straight greens in regulation, yet was able to make only one bird for a 71 total—higher than the last-day scores of winner Billy Casper's 70, runner-up Jack Nicklaus' 69 and Jay Hebert's 68, none of whom on that day was quite as consistent from tee to green. The difference in most cases was those recovery shots up close enough when the golfers got near the greens in two on the par-fives or when they missed on the others to one-putt for their birdies and pars.

As was stated in Chapter 1, there are two sides to every golfer's game. One is the physical, and one is mental. Naturally, no player is going to score well if he doesn't practice and, therefore, have the tools to get the job done. So the physical part is a tangible thing that can, to a good degree, be measured. Every player, unless he's kidding himself, knows about what he can shoot, and is aware of his own limitations of the golf course. But it's the mental side that can't be measured, and here's where good scramblers are made. You can practice trouble shots from difficult lies, and you can work until your swing is grooved. But that's about all you can do to physically prepare yourself to become a scrambler, because getting out of trouble is usually more mental than physical.

We realize that it's easy to describe the mental attitude a golfer should have, and not so easy to achieve it. But if we could list four things that will help your game mentally and make you more relaxed —and, therefore, make you a better scrambler—it would be these:

1. Concentrate on the shot. For the routine tee shot or approach shot, you can occasionally lose your concentration and get away with it, but not on the trouble shots. It's usually going to require a few solid minutes of uninterrupted concentration to pull it off.

2. Form a mental picture of how the completed shot should look. Visualize the trajectory of the ball as you want it to go and keep it in your mind. Then call on your physical tools to perform the shot as you see it.

3. Don't think too far ahead. As soon as you hit a bad shot, don't say to yourself, "I'm sure to get a six or even a seven!" Just think about and play the next shot as well as you can. It'll save you a lot of grief.

4. Don't expect too much from your game. You know about how well you can play, so don't figure on spectacular day-to-day improvement. Control your emotions and you'll probably score better—and certainly no worse.

Along the same line, we would have to advise the amateur golfer to relax more on the course. Golf is a great game, no matter what your score, so enjoy it.

3. Strategy on the Green

The average club golfer takes approximately 38 to 44 putts per round. Against a regulation 36 putts for 18 holes, this means he is taking at least *two to eight three-putt greens* a round. A good professional, on the other hand, is taking two or three less than regulation. To *win* a tournament on the PGA Tour today, you probably have to *average* around 30 putts a round.

How come the massive difference between the club golfer's performance and that of the tournament winner? Confidence? Practice? Natural ability? Yes, all these are factors in the development of a successful putter. But what about those players who practice their putting from dawn till dark, yet can't buy a putt? We submit their problem is that they have no real *system* of putting. They practice and practice in vain!

A system of putting will build up your confidence and, what's more important, can rebuild your confidence if you temporarily lose your touch. Even among professional golfers, however, it is generally conceded that there is no one perfect way to putt a ball. On the Tour, you will see men using 50 or 60 different kinds of putters. Some will keep their bodies as rigid as possible; others as loose as they can. Some will be quick; some will be distractingly slow. Some will stroke the ball smoothly; and others will jab at it every time. But all of these touring pros have one thing in common: they putt very well. If they didn't, they wouldn't be touring in the first place. What, then, makes the pro so much better at putting than the average golfer? Practice, of course. But practice generally develops only one aspect of good putting, namely a good stroke. Expert knowledge of the various types of greens and contours completes the picture of the good professional putter. Naturally, there are other considerations such as confidence, concentration, temperament, and strategy on the green.

Any putting stroke that will consistently hit ball after ball approximately the same distance every time can be considered a good stroke. Try this on a living room rug or out on the green. Draw an imaginary line about 15 feet away and stroke each ball as close to that imaginary spot as you can. If some balls pull up a few feet short or long, your stroke is faulty and needs immediate repair. Try this experiment at longer and shorter distances. It must be repeated several times before you can draw any conclusions.

Assuming then that your putting stroke is a reasonably good one, that your stance and grip are comfortable, and that your putter is fine—remember that putting is a personal thing—there are a few basic fundamentals which must be observed. The most important is keeping the face of the putter square behind the ball—at exact right angles to your line—at impact. If you don't come through dead on line, you can't conceivably hole the putt. Mechanically you must also keep your head absolutely still, so that there is no movement of the body to jerk the putt off line, and you must see the blade of the putter make contact with the ball. Even before this is done, you have had two important jobs to do if you are going to putt well. You must determine your line to the cup by "reading" the green, and you must determine how hard the ball must be struck under the conditions at hand.

The Strategy of Reading a Green

The ideal golf green is one where every blade of grass is as clipped and straight as a GI haircut. On this perfect grass, the direction of a putted ball depends only on how it has been hit. If a straight-in putt goes straight into the cup, the ball has been struck with the blade square to the line. The grass has not been a deviating factor. This is the ideal putting green, and over the years man has devised new strains of grass to provide it. But even the newer grasses, and certainly the older ones, very often bend irresistibly to the forces of nature. An inherent property of grass is that it grows horizontally and creates what is known in golf as grain.

Grain on greens is something too many average golfers fail to consider, mostly because they are not sure of what it is and how to find it. Grain is important and quite simple to figure out. It is the direction in which the blades of grass grow. When enough of them line in one direction between your ball and the cup, the roll of the ball will definitely be affected. When you see the pros walking down their line

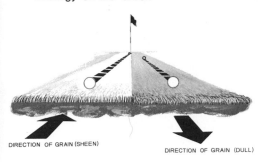
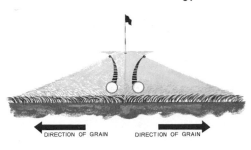

DIRECTION OF GRAIN (SHEEN)

DIRECTION OF GRAIN (DULL)

DIRECTION OF GRAIN   DIRECTION OF GRAIN

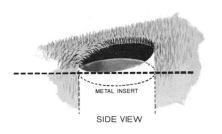
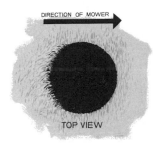

DIRECTION OF MOWER

METAL INSERT

SIDE VIEW

TOP VIEW

(Top left) Putt against the grain must be hit harder or it will pull up short. (Top right) Cross-grain can cause a straight putt to swerve off line. (Bottom left) Damage to the cup and a lower soil layer indicate the bottom side. (Bottom right) Direction of mowing grain is disclosed by grass pulled into hole.

of putt with heads bent low, as though searching for a lost contact lens, they are "reading" the grain of the green—looking at the tips of grass to see which way they are pointing.

Actually, analyzing the grain is the most refined part of reading a green. The simplest way to understand the concept of grain is to look at a piece of firewood that has been split in half. The grain streams out from a center and runs in several directions. The grain of a putting green, though it is more consistent, affects the rolls of a ball across its surface.

Over cross-grain, a golf ball will always roll toward the tips of the grass blades. Thus if the tips are pointing to the left in relation to your putting line, the ball will break from right to left. If you're coming from the opposite direction, of course, the ball will roll from left to right. How much break to allow for grain is a matter of judgment and experience. There can be no specific guideline. Generally speaking,

though, if you have a putt 20 feet long or less over level terrain, with
the grain going right to left, you might allow for perhaps an inch or
two of break to the left.

The grain on some courses has more effect than others. It's been
pointed out, for example, that in South Africa, where the grass is very
coarse and exceptionally grainy, the ball will actually break uphill if
the grain runs that way. This is rather unusual. For sidehillers on

On this naturally banked green, the grain (broken line) is running up the hill.
This is unusual, but must be noted and considered. The undulation is enough to
create a left-breaking putt, but as the ball slows near the cup, the grain will
retard the downhill roll. So, take a line less to the right.

normally grainy greens, if the bank is right to left, and the grain is in the same direction, play the ball a couple of inches farther right than if there was no grain at all. If the grain goes against the bank, don't play for quite as much break, as the grain will retard the ball's roll in that direction.

The speed at which the ball rolls has a lot to do with how much effect the grain will have. On longer putts, then, where you must hit the ball harder, the ball's course will not alter much because of grain *until it begins to slow down.* So it's a good idea on lengthier putts to examine the grain two or three feet from the cup, which is where you expect the ball to begin stopping.

When you have the grain going with you, down your line of putt, the ball will roll more freely, and faster, so you must allow for this in the force with which you hit the ball. Conversely, if you're going against the grain, into the tips of grass, the ball bumps into those tips and meets resistance, and you must give the ball a firmer rap.

It is, of course, illegal to roughen the grass on a green to find out which way the grass lies. Generally, however, the grass just off a green, on its fringe, will have the same grain as on the green itself. And it is legal to brush your putter across the fringe and thus determine the direction of the grain. That is, one way or the other, the putter will stroke the surface against the grain, causing it to brush up much in the same manner that you might comb against the natural lay of your hair.

A safer method of determining the grain of a green, however, is to look for its shine. When looking toward the hole, should you notice a shiny reflection of the sun on the green, you are usually looking with the grain, and thus your ball will roll a great deal more freely and much farther than you might normally expect. This sheen is caused by the mowers clipping the fibrous runners of the grass. Conversely, if the surface of the green appears dull from where you stand, you are looking against the grain, and you must hit the ball much harder than you might generally consider necessary.

Another way you can determine the grain is to study the growth around the edge of the hole. When you look closely at it, you notice that the grass around three-quarters of its circumference is sharp, distinct, and cleanly cut. On the remaining portion, the grass will be more ragged and inconsistent. This is because the grass on the side of the cup toward which the grass lies will readily die due to the fact that more of the root system is severed on the "down-grain" side of the hole when the green is cut. It means that when standing on the same side of the hole as the rough edge and looking across the cup, you will be looking into the grain. Should you have to putt over this rough edge, you are stroking against the grain and will have to hit harder.

When you putt with the grain, your ball meets little resistance from the grass, which already bends in the direction of the putt. Such a putt must be hit approximately 15 to 25 percent more softly than a putt rolling against the grain. In like manner, the grain that runs directly across the line of your putt will have a similarly strong effect, and you must allow for some right or left roll even on an almost absolutely flat surface. For example, a long putt breaking right on a green with its grain growing left to right would probably require you to allow for 2 or 3 more inches of break, depending on the amount of slope.

The type of grass employed on the green also has an effect on your putting. There are two basic types of grass used on golf courses: Bermuda and bent. There are almost infinite varieties of these two, but these are the fundamental strains. The easiest way to tell the two apart is to remember that bent grass does exactly what its name implies: it bends. Bent grass is allowed to grow longer than Bermuda, and the tops of the leaves curl over and lie flat, so that the length of the blade is bent almost double. Bermuda grass, on the other hand, looks like a crew cut. It is much shorter than bent, and it is bristly and stubby to touch. The two grasses have very different putting characteristics and, in many cases, their own geographical location.

Bermuda greens are found mainly in the South. Bent is popular in the East, Midwest, portions of the Southwest, and on most of the West Coast. Of the two, the most difficult to become accustomed to is the Bermuda. If you have never played it before, it might take a month or so just to get used to putting on it. Its most distinctive characteristic reveals itself on breaking putts. More so than bent, a Bermuda green will either accent or hold a breaking putt. This is simply because the amount of break is determined largely by the direction in which the grain grows. For example, a 20-foot putt against the grain might require a stroke you would normally use for a 25-footer. Whereas a similar putt *with* the grain might call for a 10- to 15-foot putting stroke. In like manner, a long putt breaking left on a green with its grain growing right-to-left would probably require you to allow for two or three more inches of break, depending on the amount of slope.

Bent grass, having a thinner leaf, does not affect the roll of a putt as much as Bermuda grass. However, it is wise to make a slight allowance for this factor when you are putting.

It takes skill and practice to read the green—there are no short cuts. The great Harry Cooper at one time tried a special pair of glasses that made the hole look elliptical and as big as a bucket. For a while he couldn't miss, and all his green-reading problems seemed to be solved. But the effect wore off, and Cooper was left with only his naked eye, and the normal human problem of reading a putting green.

The Strategy of Judging Distance and Break

To line up a putt, try to picture in your mind just where the ball is going to have to go to reach the hole and at what speed it is going to have to travel. Look over the ball position from all conceivable angles. Even the beginner knows how to crouch behind the ball to study the line, but he should also appraise the putt from behind the hole. A front and rear view will help him catch any hidden breaks he might otherwise have missed. Looking over a putt from the side may also help him to visualize the proper path. Reading distance is an uncertain art, but walking the length of a long putt can give the feel for how much power is necessary. Some pros like to stand halfway between the ball and the hole on long putts, estimate the amount of force they would need to reach the hole from there, and then mentally double that stroke for the real putt.

On long putts, it is a good idea to pace them off. In fact, if you will work at the habit of pacing off your putts, you will be surprised at the subconscious manner in which you develop a feeling for the speed of the putt. Because the normal stride is about three feet, you can tell almost exactly whether your putt is 27 or 35 feet and quickly develop a tempo suited to various distances.

When considering distance, remember it's important to give your ball a chance to go into the hole. As a rule, try to stroke the ball so as to send it a foot or two beyond the cup. As a result of such boldness, we must admit you may frequently leave yourself some fairly long putts coming back. Under such circumstances, the tendency of most golfers is to be timid on the return putt. In nearly every instance, however, boldness will pay off. Your line, of course, is your chief concern, since on a short putt distance is an almost negligible factor. *Actually, the line has been indicated for you by your first putt. Naturally, it will follow about the same line coming back. All you have to do, then, is line up your putt along this line and stroke it with confidence.* Keep in mind that the grain will be just the opposite on your second putt from what it was on your first. If, therefore, you putted with the grain on your first putt, be sure to putt the ball very firmly on the return putt.

The possible exception to this boldness concept is when you have a downhill birdie putt on a fast green. Before putting in such a case, concentrate on the putting surface, speed, contour, and grain of the green. Then decide whether to go for the birdie, or just lag it up to the hole to get your cinch par. It's generally wise to play such putts to die at the hole. In this way the ball can fall in from the front or from either side. A hard-hit putt will fall only if it is dead center and strikes the back of the cup. Also, the lag putt on a downhill green, if planned to die at the hole, will end up just below the cup, giving you an easy uphill putt back. But everything depends on the conditions. Remember, don't turn a birdie into a bogey.

As we have said, the purpose of lining up a putt is to give the player a mental image of the line to the hole so that when he is actually putting—and looking at the ball, not the line—his eidetic memory can take over and guide his stroke. If the player is to be armed with this mental picture of the correct path to the hole, his preliminary study of the putt must not be desultory. Perhaps the best way to get this mental picture is to do as Jack Nicklaus does: look over the putt very carefully as you stand upright next to your ball, ready to putt. Nicklaus has always advocated standing up straighter on long putts in order to pick up the line, but his new method is an enlargement of the old system. The principle makes sense. It is best to study the line of the putt from the position where you will be when you *actually make the stroke itself*.

There are several other ways to determine the break on a green if the preliminary survey leaves you confused. Gary Player, and other pros, looks into the hole before putting. They check to see whether one side of the hole is damaged, worn, or roughed up, reasoning that, if so, that side will be the low one. As they reach the hole, most putts tail off and strike the low side of the cup. Player and the others are also looking to see if there is a deeper layer of earth on one side of the hole. That side will be the top or high side, and the golfer can plan accordingly. Nicklaus uses a trick that works best on hilly courses where the greens are difficult to read, and a putt looks like it may break either way. In such a situation, Nicklaus studies the slope of the ground surrounding the green, notices which way it lies, and figures that it is probable that the green will run the same way.

The plumb-bob technique of break and distance is becoming more and more popular. Al Geiberger and Mickey Wright used it to their advantage, and it is a good system for putts of under 30 feet when you want to verify your original impression of the break. You must first determine which is your dominant eye. Take a normal-sized sheet of paper and cut a hole in the center. Place a penny on the floor, and holding the paper at arm's length with both hands, look at the penny through the hole with both eyes open, then alternately closing each eye. The eye that still sees the penny is the dominant one. After this bit of detection, refer to the illustration on page 68 for the method.

Once the player has located the break on the green, he still must take into account the exigencies of each individual situation. Wet greens, or greens that are thick and uncut, will not break as much as normally, and a putt over a completely soaked surface may only have half the usual borrow.

How a putt will take a break depends largely upon where that break is in relation to the ball, type of grass, and the hole. If most of the bend is near the ball rather than the hole, the player should allow for less curve than a reading seems to call for. The ball will be traveling at its top speed just after it leaves the putter. A fast-rolling ball slides over the grass, ignoring bends and dips. However, if the break is close to the hole, the player should allow for the maximum borrow, because the ball, as it loses its momentum in the vicinity of the cup, is more susceptible to the slope of the green.

When putting on a green with a slope or slant, you must be able to judge the break of your ball as it comes toward the hole. Generally, you can determine this break by getting well away from the ball and taking a good over-all look at the entire green surface. If this doesn't answer your break question, examine the cup itself. If one side looks lower than the other, the green does slope toward that side.

Keep in mind that the putt which must break twice is going to break much more sharply off the second turn than the first. This is again due to the fact that your ball will have slowed down sufficiently so that it will be affected more by the contour of the green. For this same reason, a putt that has to roll across a slant at the near conclusion of its roll will break more sharply at that point than if the slope is met shortly after the ball was stroked. In other words, on putts that must roll over several slopes, be sure to allow for more of a break nearer the cup than at the beginning of the stroke.

If you are putting with the grain on Bermuda greens or any type of green that is fast, putt more toward the center of your stance. Putting

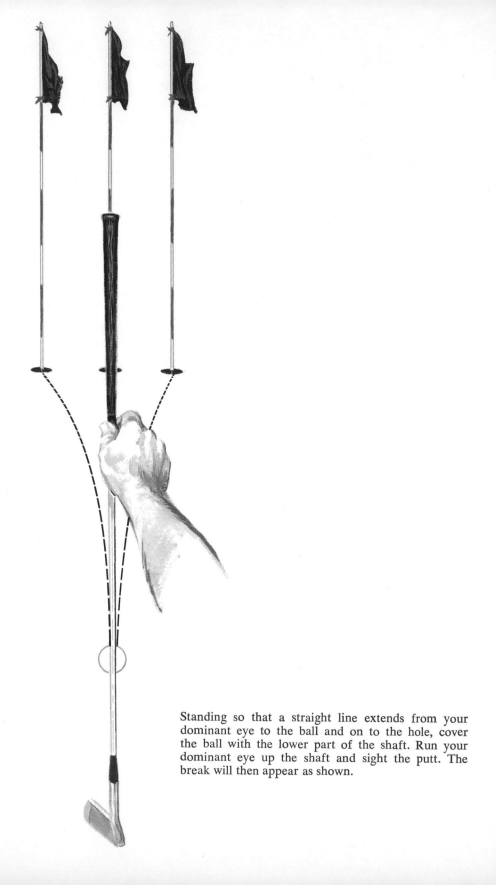

Standing so that a straight line extends from your dominant eye to the ball and on to the hole, cover the ball with the lower part of the shaft. Run your dominant eye up the shaft and sight the putt. The break will then appear as shown.

off the left toe tends to put overspin on the ball and makes it move considerably faster. Playing it more toward the center of your stance gives you more control over the speed. Against the grain, you're better off putting off the left toe since you will want overspin to help the ball toward the cup.

On putts breaking from right to left, it also helps to putt more from the center. Whether you realize it or not, the stroke has a tendency to turn in with the contour of the green. As a result, the ball hit opposite the front toe will frequently be hit with a slightly closed clubface, thus pulling the putt to the left of the hole. The opposite applies with putts breaking from left to right. It should be played opposite the toe, thereby giving you a better chance to hold the line.

A few words about uphill and downhill putts. Straight uphill putts, on any type of green, have a tendency to fade or slide off to the right. This is caused by the fact that the putt is hit with a sharp stroke, with the blade often coming into the impact area slightly open due to the quickness of the downstroke. Since the wrists will roll ever so slightly, the face opens at the top. Thus a firm start with the downswing will frequently result in a slightly open blade at impact, causing the ball to slide off to the right.

To overcome this, try playing the ball opposite the left toe on uphill

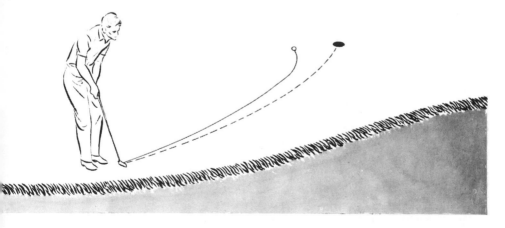

The sidehill putt is one of the most difficult to judge. Factors to be considered are the degree of slope, direction of grain, and the stroke. When the green slopes in the same direction as the grain, the amount of "borrow" is at its greatest. Also remember that the stroke has the tendency to run in with the contour of the green. With a break from right to left, putt more from the center of stance.

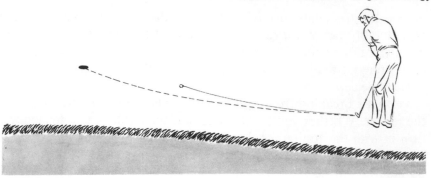

The uphill putt on any green will have a tendency to fade or slide off to the right. This is caused by the fact that the putt is hit by a sharp stroke with the blade often coming into the impact area slightly open due to the quickness of the downstroke and a slight turning of the wrists. On Bermuda greens, the grain is so thick that even firmly stroked putts pull up short.

putts. This will insure a square blade and solid impact and promote the needed overspin.

With straight downhill putts, a golfer will frequently pull the putt to the left. In this instance, the player will generally try to "baby" the putt. This turns the clubface in at impact, the exact opposite of an uphill stroke. Putting opposite the center of the stance will correct this tendency because it will enable the player to hit the ball squarely before the hands can turn in. To summarize, uphill putts are played opposite the front toe and downhill putts nearer to the center.

In his eagerness to collate information about the green, even an expert can begin to "overread" and start to see imaginary breaks between his ball and the cup. He will then baby a short putt, and allow for a break that isn't there. On a putt of under three feet, never aim outside the hole. There is never much break on a putt so short, because the speed of the ball will nullify even a substantial borrow.

On extremely fast, slippery greens, as previously stated, sometimes putt cautiously and with a lot of thought. A "charged" putt may leave you in a more difficult position than you faced originally. If, however, you do putt boldly on fast greens, allow for less break because the faster the ball is moving the better it will hold the line. And you probably will make quite a few of your short putts this way. On the other hand, though, you always are taking the risk of leaving yourself open to three-putting, even from a very short starting distance. Course management, conditions of play, and the type of competition come

Distance is the key to putting, because even the worst putt will probably not be more than a foot off line. Therefore, avoid charging too far past the hole. If you're a foot wide but the right distance, you'll only have an easy tap-in remaining.

into play more than ever on fast greens. However, in all events, it will be more advantageous to leave yourself with more uphill or straight-in putts, even a few sidehill putts, rather than those dangerous downhill putts. Downhill putts on fast greens can slide away from the hole too easily and put you in a precarious position for three-putting. The point is, then, to attempt to stop your shots on the putting surface somewhere below or beside the hole, rather than above it.

Wet greens are slower as a rule than dry ones; therefore you must stroke your ball more firmly. Remember that putts will not break as far as normal on a sloping green when it is wet; also, you are permitted to move your ball on a green if casual water impedes the line of your putt. More on putting under adverse conditions can be found in Chapter 5.

Always keep in mind the fact that greens, regardless of their type, will always be slower in the morning than in the afternoon. But when the early dew evaporates, the greens will be at their fastest. Later in the day, the greens are very difficult to putt, particularly when they have had a good deal of traffic. Divots, footprints, and scuff marks all contribute to rough putting conditions in the P.M. hours. To really see how much punishment a green takes during the course of one day's play, focus the headlights of your car on a green some Saturday or Sunday evening. Every mark on the green will be accented by the lights and shadows and it will give you a good idea what you are up against.

Additional Points of Putting Strategy

Here are a few suggestions that can definitely improve your putting. Most of them are what you might call universally accepted rules of on-green strategy. A few are ideas and opinions that we at *Golf* magazine have found to be extremely helpful in getting that little white ball into the hole.

One of the first things you should do when you get to the green is check your ball. According to the rules, you may remove any foreign

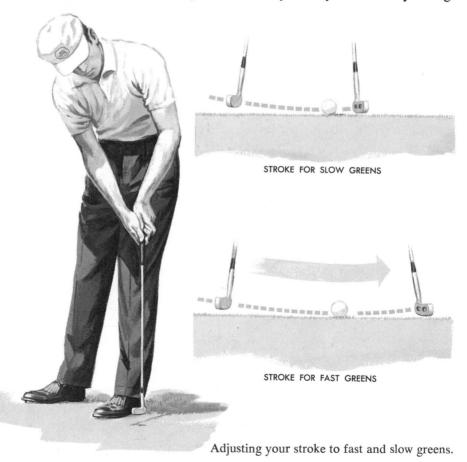

STROKE FOR SLOW GREENS

STROKE FOR FAST GREENS

Adjusting your stroke to fast and slow greens.

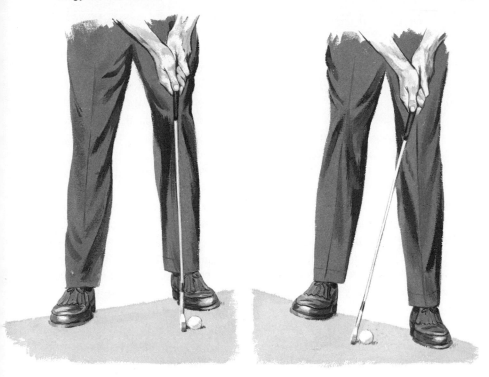

Adjusting weight placement and the position of the ball at address for up and downhill putting.

particles from your ball, repair ball marks on the green and even replace your ball if it has a damaged surface. Also carefully check the area between your ball and the hole for any bumps, divots, or scuffs that may accumulate through the course of play. USGA rules permit you to repair ball marks and flatten the surface with the base of your putter. However, you are not allowed to use your foot to level the damaged area.

Pay particular attention to the area around the cup. There may be spike scuffs, footprints, or ragged edges that could seriously hamper the line of your putt. Since the ball is traveling slowly near the cup, it is subject to the slightest imperfections on the green. When such imperfections exist, it is usually a good idea to putt more firmly, hoping that the ball will be able to resist the rough spots. That is, hit the ball harder and don't allow for as much break. Irregular greens are next to impossible to read, so it's hard to determine the exact break (or bounce) you're going to get. Even if you do have the ball breaking toward the hole, if it's moving too slowly the ball will be easily knocked off line by one bump or another. On this kind of green, it's best to take your chances of banging the ball at the hole, never "giving up the cup" unless the break is so severe as to dictate it.

When putting on rough, thick, or "hairy" green, your major problem is to get the ball "up" and rolling. Our first suggestion, if you must play under these conditions for any length of time, is to switch to a putter with more loft. This will mechanically help you to do the job. We know that most people prefer to master one putter and use it come hail or high grass on the greens, and we firmly believe in this under ordinary conditions. But what we are discussing here is exceptionally rough greens where the grass may be ragged and the ball settles down into it more than normal. In this case, it is essential to position the ball slightly more forward than you usually play it. If you play the ball off the left toe, move it as much as an inch ahead. This means that you will not hit down on the ball and cause it to squirt off line. Instead, you will be catching it on the upswing, giving it that rolling action necessary to bring it out of the grass smoothly. There are two other important points to remember when putting on "hairy" greens. Since the grass is longer, you will have to hit the putt harder, with a good follow-through. Second, the long grass will prevent the putt from breaking as much as it would on faster greens. Therefore, don't play as much break on a putt when the grass is long, and hit it harder! Putting on perfect greens can be tough enough, but under ragged conditions, you have to make alterations to give yourself the best chance.

Leaving the pin attended or taking it out is mostly a matter of your own preference. On long putts, we find that most pros prefer to have the pin attended. This gives them a background to hit at and, often, a place to aim. If your caddie is positioned properly, you can aim for his feet if it justifies the line. On short putts, the majority of the touring pros have the pin removed. They want that cup to have as much room as possible for their ball, and leaving the pin in doesn't help the situation.

Make up your mind before you putt whether you are going to stroke boldly for the hole or just lag it up. When you have a long putt that you intend to lag, try to leave the ball in a good position for your second putt. It's generally much better to have a five-footer uphill than a three-footer downhill. If you are going to stroke a putt firmly toward the hole, remember not to allow for as much break as you would if you were lagging. A ball hit firmly tends to resist breaks and bumps more than a lagged putt.

Concerning the short putts, it's again usually wise to hit the ball firmly. Never send the ball to find the hole. Don't try to feel it in. Select your line and stroke it firmly.

There is an art to "aiming" your putts on the green, and most pros are convinced that 90 percent of the average players hit their putts outside of the cup more than is necessary. First of all, consider the fact that the cup is 4¼ inches wide, which means that you have 2 inches on either side of center. Thus a putt stroked to the left side of the cup has 4 inches of leeway. So unless you are certain that there is more than 4 inches of break, never putt outside the cup. Now let's say you see a 6-inch break. In this case you need only to putt 3 inches wide of the cup. Overallowing on the expected break causes more missed putts than almost anything we can imagine. Use that 4-inch cup in your calculations and you won't be moaning, "It didn't break as I expected it to."

While in this book we have paid little or no attention to actual technique, there's a common mistake golfers make on the green that our experts feel should be mentioned. That is, many golfers use the same putting stance whatever the break on the putt. Our experts have come to the conclusion that three stances are necessary on the green: (1) that for a straight putt, (2) that for a left-to-right break, (3) that for a right-to-left break. To demonstrate the point let's take an extreme example—a left-to-right break of six feet on a putt right across the green. If you take your normal stance with, say, the ball off the inside of the left heel, you will have to allow the full six feet—assuming that this ball position enables you to meet the ball with the clubface square to the line, with, therefore, no side spin imparted to the ball. However, if you were to place the ball farther forward, say off your left toe, you would be contacting the ball later in your putting stroke and, therefore, with a slightly closed face, imparting a slight hook spin to the ball. This spin will fight against the break and enable you, say, to take only half as much break as with your regular stroke. You will putt much nearer the straight line between you and the hole. Should you miscalculate the strength, you will be that much nearer the hole for your second putt. The same principle applies to the right-to-left break. Play the ball back toward the middle of your stance. You

When aiming your putts, be sure to use all the cup.

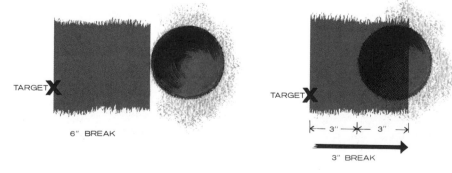

TARGET X

6″ BREAK

TARGET X

|← 3″ →|← 3″ →|

3″ BREAK

will then contact the ball while the clubface is still open, imparting a slice spin to the ball. This will hold the ball up into the break and give you good control.

Finally, a word or two about putting on the practice green prior to your round. As is stated in Chapter 9, plan to spend at least 15 minutes on the practice green. Try a couple of 20-footers, a few 40-footers, then plenty of short ones. Let's face it. The toughest putt in the world for the average player is the short putt which suddenly isn't conceded. No putt should be conceded, but you'll seldom see a "friendly" round in which the shorties aren't knocked away by an opponent. Then, all of a sudden, he'll just stand there and wait for you to can a little old two- or three-footer in which he sees hidden trouble. Two feet isn't long, but sometimes it can look like two miles. So concentrate from 10 feet in during practice, and those suicide shorties will lose their terror.

If you have more time, one of the simplest methods of achieving both accuracy and stroke is to take about 10 to 12 balls onto the practice green and start by knocking the first ball in the hole from no farther away than one foot. After sinking that one-footer, place the second ball about six inches farther back and knock that one in. Keep moving the remaining balls back about six inches at a time and don't leave a spot until you knock that putt in. By the time you get eight to ten feet from the hole, you probably won't be making the putt on the first try, but you should be certain that you are hitting the ball with enough force to get it past the hole if it does not go in the cup. This will teach you distance. Then concentrate your entire efforts on taking that putter blade straight back and straight through the ball and you will soon have the necessary distance and accuracy to become a good putter.

All these strategy theories, ideas, and suggestions aim at one specific thing. They are practiced, conceived, and designed to put you in a confident frame of mind. Uncertainty tears down a golfer's confidence, particularly on the greens. Once you have carefully decided exactly how you are going to play the putt, you'll find that you have gained a great deal of confidence in the putt itself. Unfortunately—all the putts won't drop for you. But it is some comfort at least to miss a putt and fully understand why you did.

4. The Strategy of Getting Out of Trouble

Every golfer has those days when even his well-hit shots find trouble or difficult lies. How many, though, can cope with these contingencies and finish such a round within a stroke or two of their handicap?

The trouble is, the average golfer learns the fundamentals of the game and is reasonably competent from tee to green when the ball is kept in play down the center of the fairway, but is not sufficiently knowledgeable of the finer points to adapt his swing and his thinking to golf's many trouble shots. Yet all of these shots have a logical solution, and as we run through the most common of them we shall try to give you a thought or two to dwell upon which may help you when you are out on the course.

In fact, trouble shots are surprisingly easy if you activate your imagination. If you can't visualize a shot, you can't possibly play it. You simply must be able to imagine exactly what flight the ball will take before you can play any shot, regardless of how erratic that shot may be. Let's suppose you are deep in the woods, way back in the jungle. Either you clear a certain limb in your path or you remain in the woods. If, in your mind, you can't see the ball clearing that limb, you have no chance of escaping. Consequently, the procedure is to analyze your chances of clearing the limb and then to force your imagination to visualize your best chance of clearing it. Then forget everything except hitting the ball. And keep your head down. Many golfers ruin a trouble shot by looking up to see how successful they were before they actually have played the shot.

In addition, a great many troubles fail to come off because golfers, when they're faced with a tough situation, start feeling sorry for themselves and, when a person feels he got a bad break, the chances of pulling off the correct shot become slimmer. The proper attitude, of course, is to say: "Well, I put it there, now I'll have to hit it out." The unusual lies, the unlucky bounces, and the difficult situations are all part of the game, and if you know your golf pretty well, then knowing how to hit the so-called strategic type shots will make you a better, more consistent player.

Slope Strategy

Success on uphill-downhill shots requires a little more swing strategy than usual. The uneven stance of hilly lies creates a push or pull that must be counteracted if the shot is to come off properly.

In general, maintaining balance is the key factor throughout the swing—and achieved most easily by not swinging hard. Also keep the swing smooth and uninterrupted, let the clubhead follow the ground's contour, and hit down on the ball without raising the body at impact. Especially the shoulders, the hips, and the head. The hilly lies may not seem like real problem shots, but it would be well to prepare yourself for these eventualities in advance of your round, because, unlike the straightaway conditions of the practice area, the course you play is seldom level, and these situations, which may not be your personal problem when you're reading about them, might suddenly confront you.

In reality, slope, or uneven, lies usually fall into four categories: uphill, downhill, standing above the ball, and standing below the ball. Here's how each should be played:

UPHILL LIE

An uphill lie means the weight will be a little on the right side. Therefore, the left side is naturally withdrawn a bit. To play this type of shot, open the stance, take the club straight away from the ball, and hit down and through as you would for any other shot. The club and the hands will almost be in a normal position. The hands may be slightly forward if you want to keep the ball down, and slightly back if you want to hit the ball into the air. Keep the head in a steady position and swing through the ball. But if you are hitting to a green from an uphill lie, remember that the ball will tend to travel a higher trajectory and not as far. So compensate by using a little longer club.

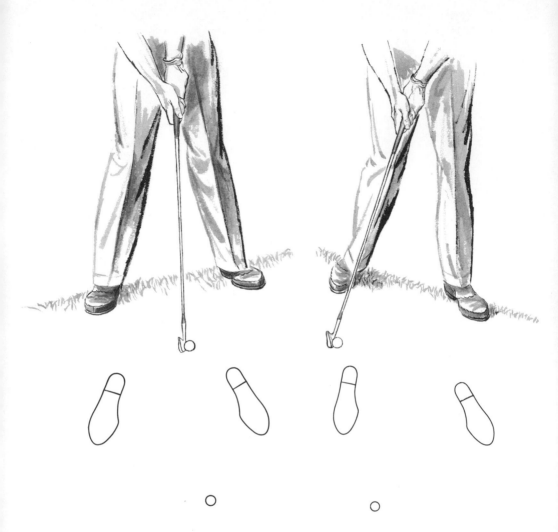

(Left) Hitting from uphill lie similar to normal fairway shot, except weight is more on right side, and left side is withdrawn. Open stance, keep head steady, swing through. (Right) A downhill lie calls for leveling of hips by bending uphill knee. Keep swing smooth, uninterrupted: let clubhead follow ground's contour, without raising body at impact.

DOWNHILL LIE

A downhill lie means that the center of gravity is forward. To offset this bit of unbalance, bend the uphill knee so that the hips are level, and play the ball a little to the right of center of an open stance, with the hands ahead of the ball. The club might be a little less than one used on a level lie, because with the downhill swing we come into effective contact with the ball sooner. Unless the fairway rises abruptly behind you, the takeaway can be fairly normal. On the downswing let the clubhead follow the ground's contour, and hit down on the ball without raising the body at impact.

STANDING BELOW THE BALL

Sidehill lies can be perplexing. When the ball is higher than the toes, use the same club you normally would for the length of the shot involved. Play the ball opposite the center of a square stance, flex your knees slightly, and keep your weight forward on the balls of your feet. The ball, being higher, will be closer to you, so compensate by shortening your grip on the club so that the clubhead rests on the ground without the arms being bent more than for the normal shot.

(Left) When the ball is lower than the toes, the tendency to fade or push the shot to the right must be overcome. Open stance, put weight more on the heels, do not rush swing, keep your balance. (Right) The sidehill-uphill lie will tend to hook because of the flatter swing. Select a longer club, shorten up on both grip and swing, play ball back toward right heel, keep head steady.

Since a hook is probable from this position, allow for it by aiming to the right of your target, and play the ball naturally.

STANDING ABOVE THE BALL

When the ball is lower than the toes, the reverse is true. That is, the tendency is to push the shot off to the right or, even worse, hosel it laterally. To play this troublesome lie, aim a bit to the left of target to offset the inclination to fade and keep the ball in the center of a square stance. However, the stance should be slightly wider than normal to help maintain your balance, and the knees must be bent more than usual, with the weight kept back on your heels. Stand closer to your ball, and stay low through the entire stroke. Do not take a full swing, but rather take a club one number lower (for example, a three-iron instead of a four-iron) if the lie permits, and employ a three-quarter swing. This will give you better balance on this shot.

Rough Strategy

From the first tee through the last green it's possible to play golf quite well with one basic stroke. You take a club and play the same shot, make the same swing, every time. However, golf doesn't always come up roses—it all too often grows rough. By definition, the higher grass that parallels every fairway from tee to green is called *rough*—and it's supposed to be. But not so rough that you have to be hasty, select the wrong club, swing extra hard, hit, hope, and sacrifice shots. Here, of course, is where repetitiveness breaks down; where more is required than grooved swinging efficiency. To overcome this common hazard demands adherence to certain rules of the rough strategy:

1. Careful study of the situation,
2. Accurate assessment of what sort of club is necessary,
3. Constant acceleration of the clubhead through the ball,
4. Confidence in the method finally chosen to execute the shot.

The first rule requires an understanding of how varying conditions will affect the behavior of the club and the ball. Distinguishing between the various kinds of rough and how the ball sits in it depends a great deal on experience, and the professional golfer is especially qualified on the ways to attack this problem because it's a notable habit for the rough to be grown higher for us in tournaments.

The first thing to do then in sizing up your lie is to evaluate the height of the grass, the thickness, and how well the ball is perched in

4 WOOD   6-7 IRON

Sometimes it's better to play safe from the rough by hitting a six-iron or a seven-iron rather than a gambling four-wood. If the grass is heavy, the wood has a tendency to smother the ball, leaving it in the rough.

it. And basically there are two types of lies in the rough—the *flier* and the *floater*.

If at any time the ball is sitting up, you've got a fairly good lie or what is called a flier. The grass here can be two to four inches high but thin, and you can get to the ball without a solid wall of grass piling up between the blade and the ball. What you can expect from this lie is run and lots of it. The ball will probably rise out of there like a knuckle ball, giving you added yardage because of the overspin imparted to the ball when the grass gets between it and the club. This makes a shot with a nine-iron react like a seven-iron, a seven-iron like a five-iron, and so on.

With the second type of lie, the floater, the grass is not just high but thick. The ball, in other words, is buried—almost out of sight. Again, what can you expect from this lie? Well, obviously, it's not going to fly

Three types of rough: (left to right) Heavy rough, packed down rough, and soft rough which will cause a popped-up ball.

too far. And when it does come out, it won't have too much roll because the grass piling up between the blade and the ball has cushioned the blow. The ball reacts like it's been hit with a pillow.

According to rule two, after surveying your problem with care and golfing intelligence, you must then select the proper club. Usually the amateur golfer uses more club than the lie will allow, instead of getting to the green without taking too much of a chance. Just like the smart club decision in the fairway trap, where you must decide whether to take a four-, five-, or six-iron to get the ball over the lip, the first thought in the rough should be not on distance but on getting out. So if you can't reach the green, it is important to realize that you can't.

We're going to create a typical situation to demonstrate how you would go about selecting the proper club. Let's suppose you've hit your drive about 210 yards on a straightaway par-four measuring 410 yards, but you're in thin rough and the ball is not sitting up. Since you have a good 200 yards to go, you might grab for the three-wood. Right away, this is a bad choice. The three-wood doesn't have a good cutting edge and only makes the rough shot even rougher. A four-wood has a smaller face, a deeper angle, and a slightly better cutting edge. It will go as far as a three-wood, and it is safer, too. We can honestly say that it's a rare occasion when a three-wood is chosen for a rough shot. You might chance it, but, in general, unless you have a really fine lie—where you can see the ball above the top of the club-face—you'd be better off forgetting the woods. A two- or three-iron choice, on the other hand, is almost as dangerous as three- or four-wood because the face is small, the shaft long, and, besides, if it's a hard club to handle when the ball's in the fairway, it's even harder to handle in the rough.

Now you're still in the rough, and you're not concerned any more with going for the green. What you're looking for is a club with a double function. First, one that will get you out safely and, second, will give you some distance. Whatever you do, you don't want to muff the shot and leave it there. Probably the best club in this situation is a four-iron, which has enough loft to cut through the grass and get down to the ball. Remember, because the grass will get between the club and the ball, it should fly out of there. In fact, by sacrificing a little distance for safety, more often than not, you'll get that flier and all the distance you were planning on with the longer iron.

Remember that often you can achieve accuracy and greater dis-

From deep rough, play ball off right heel, take club back high, hit down on ball.

tance, even with a more lofted club, by hooding the club or closing the face at address. The reason for this is that the rough ordinarily will cause your clubface to open as you drive it in to make contact with the ball. Thus if you toe in the clubhead more than normal, the clutching action of the rough automatically will cause a square position of the clubhead at contact. This technique applies with a wood as well as with your irons, provided that the rough is not so severe as to preclude the use of a wood. Hooding that clubhead in the rough will give you square contact and keep you from popping up or leaking off to the right.

As a second example, assume you are within six-iron distance of the green, but in heavy rough three to five inches deep. Since the six-iron will impart less length than normally, you may select a five-iron. But —and here's the second factor—if it's so deep that a five-iron will not get it out (as in this case), then it's time to sacrifice distance, go with a lesser club, and drop down to a seven- or an eight-iron. Getting out must always take precedence over "gunning" for the green. Of course —and it's only natural to look for the most from the worst of lies —you should take the club that will hold some promise of distance and still get you out. The point, however, is to play it smart. If the rough is so deep that you can't escape with the expected club, admit you can't get there, pay the distance penalty, and drop back a club or two.

Although club selection in the rough area bordering the green is not as difficult, it does have its moments. If the grass is heavy and thick, you should usually take a sand wedge because it is heavy enough to plow through the grass and has plenty of loft. On the other hand, if the grass is thin, then you might go to a pitching wedge, and an eight- or a nine-iron.

Once the lie has been examined, and the right club selected, you

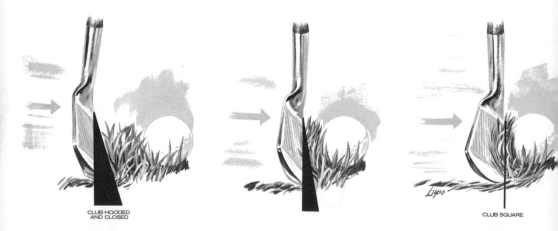

CLUB HOODED
AND CLOSED   CLUB SQUARE

Playing safely from the rough often requires that you take a club with more loft, sacrificing some distance for a sure out, but there is more to it than that. Learn to hood your iron or wood when hitting from the rough.

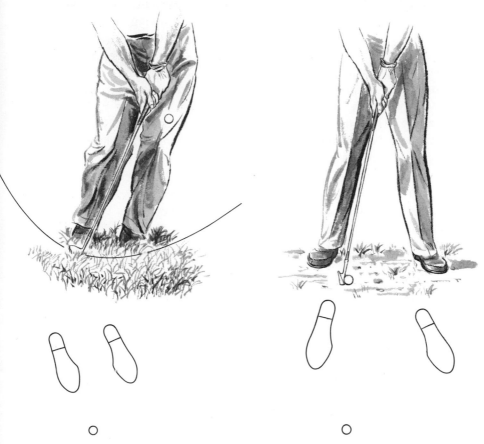

(Left) From the rough alongside an elevated green, position the ball back near the right foot to make quick and clean contact. Let the loft of the club do the necessary lifting. (Right) Hitting from tight lie or from hard ground, play the ball more toward right heel, take club well back, hit down into and under the ball. Stay with this shot all the way.

still face the task of hitting the shot. And, as a rule of thumb, you need to make a better swing out of the rough than anywhere else. As we know, a good golf swing is one in which the club is accelerating at and through impact. But this is even more true (if that's possible) when you're in the rough. The average golfer, if he is hurrying his backswing, fly-casting, hitting from the top and wasting energy on his tee shots, will be in even worse shape in the rough because he will be consciously trying harder and enjoying it much less.

Therefore, in swing technique, the following advice is most important. First, the ball should be played in approximately the same position as in all other normal shots, although moving up on the ball slightly (very slightly) may help in assuring that you hit down on the ball. However, if you play the ball back too far in an effort to chop down on it, it will probably nose over instead of rising up and out. Second, the backswing should be slow and controlled, not jerked away. And third, on the downswing, always keep the clubhead accelerating. This constant increase of speed on the downswing is especially crucial in heavy grass since any letting up or slowing down allows the grass to grab, causing the ball to spill off the face to the right or, by trapping the clubhead in the clutch of grass, forcing the ball to scurry back down into the rough. And you are right back where you started from. A shot has been lost, and there is no relief in sight yet.

It helps, too, to take two or three practice swings in the rough in order to get the feeling of how much resistance you're going to encounter and how fast the club cuts through. Never just stand up to the ball and swing. This is especially true around the green, where touch is so vital. Your surprise at the ease or thickness of the rough is hardly a fair exchange for a shot blown over the green or left in the high grass. Surprise in golf is a virtue only when it lowers your score.

Of course, in any shot from the rough around the green, the problem is to know how far the ball will go. Even the pros don't always know. But, in general, the more firmly you go through the shot, the more it will come out basically the same each time.

As far as swing technique around the greens is concerned, the long arc is not much good. You have to chop through too much grass, and this impedes clubhead speed. The shortened and more upright arc is a great deal more effective. (This especially when shooting to an elevated green.) Here the hands are used more on the takeaway but only for the purpose of keeping the arc shorter and sharper. If you take too long or too big a swing, the tendency will be to slow down in order to hit the ball, and slowing down usually means pulling up. What you are looking for in the swing—and we repeat this deliberately—is firmness and acceleration at and through the ball. This prevents the blade from opening—an error that is the direct result of slowing down instead of accelerating.

For anything less than a full shot, say a 20-footer to the green, choke down on the shaft a little. This adds firmness, prevents any flippy wristedness, and puts more club in your hands. Remember to keep the blade square since the ball has tendency to squirt or slide off and what you want here is a solid, firm hit.

The sandy lie in the rough, a situation that threatens golfers who play seaside courses, does not mean a stroke has to be wasted just to get the ball back out onto the fairway. It does, however, mean the swing will be slightly different. Unlike grassy rough, where the ball sits up on roots that offer little or no resistance to the clubhead, the ball in sandy rough is tight, with no room for the club to cut underneath it, and sand has less give. This calls for hitting the ball first and swinging the club through after impact. You cannot afford to stop or chop or hit on the ball too high or low. Firm up your stance, especially if the sand is too loose to hold your weight. Never try to hit the ball hard, because you can be thrown off balance. Select a club longer than normal to allow you to reduce your backswing and still get distance, and grip the club a bit tighter in the left hand. The sand doesn't give the way grass does, and a firm left hand grip is necessary to keep the clubhead from stopping or turning. Take the club back a little more abruptly, play the ball back to center to insure your hitting it first, then hit it squarely on the nose. Keep the clubhead going through and you'll burn the ball out of the tight lie, with plenty of distance and good action.

When pitching from lies in sandy, scrubby rough, you can play it with a seven-, eight-, or nine-iron, depending on how much green you have to work with once the ball lands. Position the ball in line with your right instep and your hands forward toward your left leg. Use an open stance with the weight on the left foot. What you must do is hit the ball first, driving it down into the ground. The clubface is kept straight and the right hand pushes the club through and toward the pin. This action keeps you from hitting into the sandy ground behind the ball and coming up short. It is a one-piece hands-and-arm shot made with a very slight weight shift. Always remember to keep your head down through the complete swing, because this shot requires good, clean contact. The ball should be struck a little harder than if you were pitching from fairway grass.

Finally, we come to the fourth rule and the word *confidence*. There is no special technique or swing theory for this word. There is only playing the game and the shots. Confidence is knowing that the club you have pulled from the bag and the club you've got in the middle of your backswing is precisely the club that's going to do the job. And in line with confidence, we would strongly suggest that the average golfer

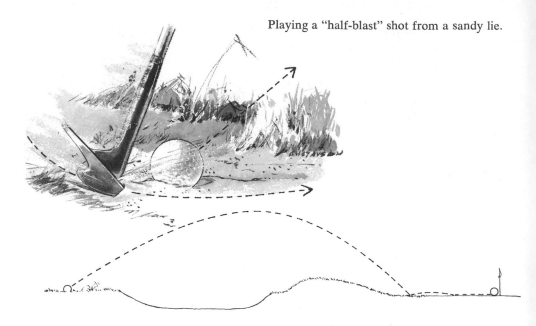

Playing a "half-blast" shot from a sandy lie.

spend as much time practicing shots from the rough as he does on the putting green and at the driving range. That's one way to make sure this game is not as rough as it seems to be or you think it is.

Other "Rough" Situations

Although trees add beauty to a golf course, they certainly spell trouble for the golfer's game. When you are confronted with trees, you have only three choices: go over, around, or under. To go over trees you can use the pop-up shot described on page 93. To go around a tree, employ an intentional hook or slice (see page 37). To go under a tree, you must keep the ball low. To do this, play the shot with a straight-faced club, usually a three- or four-iron. Choke up on the club according to the distance you need, but never grip it full length. (If you swing too fully with a full grip, you cannot expect to keep the ball low.) The ball should be played slightly back of its normal, long-iron shot position and the hands kept ahead of the ball on the address. The ball should be punched rather than hit, and, in order to accomplish this, use no more than a three-quarter swing with the right elbow close into the side and with little or no pivot, or wrist action. Be sure to hit down on the ball with the body weight well through on the left foot. Like the backswing, the follow-through should be kept to three-quarters that of the normal swing.

Occasionally on a fairway, you may find your ball in a divot hole. To get the ball out, concentrate on hitting right down into the ball more firmly than you would in the average fairway shot. If you do this with authority and confidence—and you should—you will be amazed how often the shot will come off better than if you had a real good lie in the lush grass of the fairway. It is necessary to stay on the shot and to hit down and through with confidence.

A heavy clover lie on the fairway can cause some trouble if not properly played. Actually, the difficulty here is that you will hit a "flier," a ball which skips and runs because it has no stop action. The clover is "greasy," and when it gets smashed between the face of the club and the ball, it can give you a lot of crazy, mixed-up action, shooting off at a tangent or "flying" right on over the green. In this case, you must concentrate on hitting the ball before you take your divot so that the scored face of the club can do its work without interference. But if it looks impossible to hit the shot without catching the clover, the best thing to do is to play a little short of the green, allow for some run, and hope for the best. That is, if a lie is so bad that you feel you cannot help but hit a flier, take one club less to allow for the additional run. Also, try to uncock the wrists sooner than usual, giving you almost the feeling that you are hitting from the top. This will enable you to avoid a cutting action and come into the ball at a shallower level.

When your ball is precariously sitting on a bed of pine needles or twigs, you must be extremely cautious. First be careful when placing your club behind the ball; if you disturb the lie, the ball is apt to move resulting in a penalty stroke. The better choice is to place the clubface behind the ball with the sole of the club slightly off the ground. Take the club back without breaking the wrists, and allow your left shoulder to turn slightly under and toward your left chin. The most important phase of this shot is coming into the ball. You must meet the back of the ball first, then after impact the club can strike the road—with no detrimental effect to the shot. If possible don't allow your right hand to overcome your left at impact—keep the blade square. Remember to strike the ball first and the twigs or pine needles last.

As for hitting a shot from a bare lie or from hard ground, the real problem, especially with a wood or long iron, is getting the ball into the air. For this reason, many pros play a little bit of a cut shot from a bare lie. They open their stance by pulling the left foot back slightly so they're aiming a little left of the actual target, and they also open the

Three ways to handle tree problems: (above left) an intentional hook, (above right) an intentional slice, and (left) a low punch shot.

The pop-up shot is valuable when you have to clear an obstacle such as a tree and yet make the ball stop quick. To hit this shot, play the ball from the center of an open stance. Keep the hands slightly behind the ball and let the club work through and under the ball by using a bit of wrist action.

clubface a bit. Then they take a more upright swing and hit down sharply, more directly on the ball, playing for it to move left to right. The key is not to sweep the ball, as you might on an ordinary lie. Hit right down on the ball, striking it first and then the ground. You can actually get a very crisp action on the ball if you contact it correctly. On hard ground, because you can pivot normally, it is not necessary to use more club. Be sure to hit down on the ball. If you hit behind the ball with no turf there, your club is going to skid, and so will the ball.

When your ball lands in a bare spot or tight lie near the green, don't

Hitting a ball from a deep divot lie. Note the ball is played back toward the right foot.

throw up your hands in despair. There's an easy and safe way to play it and get down in one putt. Address the ball off the right foot, with the hands slightly ahead and the shoulders and hips lined up a little left of the target with most of your weight on the left foot. Hood the clubface of the pitching wedge and strike down on the shot, making sure to contact the ball first and then the ground. This will produce a very low shot—so allow for about 50 percent roll. For no reason should you try to open the clubface and hit a cut shot. Nine times out of ten you'll either hit the shot fat or skull it. With the low pitch-and-run, you'll get a better degree of control and accuracy when playing off a bare spot or from a tight lie.

There are times when your ball can get into some very "unlikely" parts of the course. Often, the golfer will make an ineffectual attempt at the shot, then curse his luck, or tamely take a drop and a penalty shot. Of course, there are places from which no one could recover— and you must learn to recognize these—but what many people fail to realize is that every shot doesn't have to be played by the book, that ingenuity and know-how can save the day in many seemingly "impossible" situations.

Suppose your ball is nestled up near a tree or a wall or other obstruction and the only way you can swing at the ball will send it to the right of your objective into deep rough, or even out-of-bounds. What you do here is to stand up to the ball so that you can take a clear swing, then close the blade until it faces the direction you want to go, and swing away. Take a higher-numbered club for this shot, as closing the face will reduce the effective loft of the club.

Another stroke-saver under some circumstances is the "between-the-legs" shot. When your ball is lying in a spot where you cannot stand or get your club back to hit the ball in the desired direction, such as near an out-of-bounds fence or post or tree or rock or on the edge of a deep trap where you would have to stand several feet below your ball level, this shot will save the bacon.

First, draw an imaginary line from your ball to your objective. Study the distance to the objective so you will know how hard to hit the ball. Now straddle the ball with a fairly wide stance, having the leading edge of the clubface turned down so that it is square to the imaginary line through your legs. Use a nine-iron or a wedge and chop down on the ball with a vertical stroke. The clubface will have enough loft to hit the ball away from the trouble, and you will find

(Above) When overhanging branches make the kneeling shot the only one to play, spread knees wide apart, keep wrists firm and be content to just get the ball out. Remember that because your plane of swing is flat, ball will curve to left. (Below) Here it is impossible to put ball on green, because severe downhill slope will reduce the loft of even the highest-numbered club. A sand wedge was used to send the ball over the trap into the bank in front of the green. Ball bounced off the bank onto the green to salvage a par score.

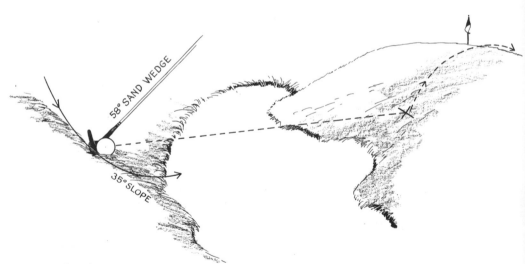

58° SAND WEDGE

35° SLOPE

that it takes very little talent to hit the shot. Try it a few times before you find yourself faced with this kind of situation.

Sometimes an obstruction will prevent you from making any sort of a shot right-handed. In such a case, you can make the stroke by turning an iron upside down and hitting with a left-handed swing. Remember, however, that a club with the least loft has the narrowest blade which will diminish your hitting area. For this reason, we find that a six- or a seven-iron will produce the best shots. You must also be aware that the loft on the face will angle the ball to the right of target. Take care of this when lining up your shot.

There are several pointers which the player should keep in mind when executing this unfamiliar action. Play the ball back toward your left foot, and be sure to keep your head steady over the ball during the swing. A restriction of the weight shift is also desirable, for any excess motion can ruin the shot.

If you're not up to hitting a left-handed shot in the manner just described—or haven't practiced it, which is essential—then consider using your putter from the "wrong" side. As long as your putter is of the blade variety, this shot can be very useful.

Another type of shot which is "different," but highly effective, is the "carom" shot. If your ball lies up within a couple of feet of a wall and you want to hit directly away from it, consider bouncing the ball against the wall and getting it to go where you want on the rebound. Be careful to study the surface of the wall—if it is very uneven, the ball might bounce back and hit you, which can lose you the hole in match play (two strokes in medal play), to say nothing of possible injury.

The rewards, of course, for learning to play these "double-trouble" shots—and the satisfaction—are immense. So next time you have a couple of hours to spare, go out somewhere quiet and try out a few of the shots mentioned here. Chances are that before you're too much older, you are going to surprise the life out of the other members of your foursome!

Strategy from the Sand Trap

The sand trap shot is *not* to be feared, but it's to be respected and it must be learned. Most traps are located close to the greens, protecting that 4¼″ hole everyone aims for, on the only area on the course where all golfers are allowed two strokes to negotiate whatever distance they find themselves from that spot. Therefore, if a golfer misses the green and is faced with a recovery shot from sand, the only way he can save par is to blast out close enough for one-putt.

True, there is many a stroke in golf lost in trap and trouble shots. Many of these useless strokes are the result of a mental barrier which the player conjures up when he finds himself confronted with trouble.

That is, the major problem with trap shots is tension and fear. The trap shot itself is really no more difficult than any other shot in golf. It is just that people think it is.

Most trap shots are missed because the golfer has no clear idea as to how to play them. First, perhaps, he'll try to "flick" it clean off the top of the sand with his wrists, only to have the ball catch the lip of the trap and roll down to his feet again.

For his second try, perhaps he will take a wild, full slash that results in the club being buried four or five inches behind the ball, which goes all of a couple of feet. Need we go on? These golfers treat the sand as their enemy although, in fact, it is the medium through which they can control the length and trajectory of the shot.

While the sand-trap shot can generally be accomplished with a nine-iron, the sand wedge is a better choice. Actually, most average golfers don't appreciate how well designed the sand wedge is for its job. Compared to a nine-iron it has more weight, more loft, and a much wider flange. It also is appreciably deeper from the top to the bottom of the face.

The sand iron's extra weight enables it to cope more easily with the sand's resistance. Its extra loft makes it easier for the golfer to get the ball up and out of the trap. The wide flange makes it skid rather than dig deep into the sand and stop. And its extra depth from the top to the bottom of the face gives a good safety margin for making contact with the ball.

To illustrate the merits of a sand wedge in an explosion shot, let's take the case where you're trapped around 10 to 15 yards from the pin. The ball is lying fair, with no more than a quarter of its surface beneath the sand. The sand is of average texture—not hard or wet, nor extra-soft and fluffy. Here's how you play the shot:

Take a slightly open stance, as on any other short iron shot, with the left foot withdrawn a little from the line of flight. The ball should be off the left heel. Keep the stance narrow, with your heels not more than six inches apart. A narrow stance keeps you "over the ball" to deliver a precision blow. If the stance were wider, you well might sway to the right on the backswing. As a result you would hit too far behind the ball on the downswing to be effective.

As on every other shot, the right foot is at right angles to the line. The left foot is turned 45 degrees toward the hole in order to enable the body to make a full forward pivot, forcing the club to a complete finish. On this 10- to 15-yard shot, aim to enter the sand two inches behind the ball. It is generally considered by most golf teachers that the clubface must be laid open for sand shots and in *Golf* magazine we advise this always.

Your swing naturally will be on a more upright plane than for any other club because the sand wedge has the shortest shaft of all the irons, and this dictates that the ball be played closer to the feet than on any other shot. The arms and hands should be close to the body at address with very little daylight showing between the body and the hands.

The "feel" of the swing is that it is more "straight up and down" than for any other shot, but this is due entirely to the naturally very upright action with a short-shafted and extra-heavy club. Emphasizing the "cocking" or bending of the right arm on the backswing will help you get the right action. The tempo of the swing should be a little more leisurely than on a nine-iron pitch. This in turn dictates that the backswing will be of sufficient length to keep the entire stroke smooth. Remember, no stabbing at the ball, or chopping. Your backswing should be around three-quarters of what you normally make on a full shot. The stroke must be completed with a full follow-through. With all the best trap players—exceptionally fine examples are Julie Boros and Sam Snead—most of the action *appears* to take place from the moment the clubhead enters the sand until the full, free finish of the swing. Although this is an illusion, nevertheless it is an indication of the importance of completing the shot.

The club must pass through the ball on all normal trap shots to keep the ball on line, and assure getting it out of the trap. The sand wedge stroke must be definitely thought of as a *cutting* action into the sand, under and through the ball. The cutting action, combined with the angle of the clubface as it passes through the impact area and the amount of sand taken, produces the various spins and trajectories vital to ball control from the trap.

Now let's examine in a little more detail what happens to the club and ball in the impact area. When the wedge enters the sand two inches behind the ball, the clubhead passes *under* the ball, with a cushion of sand about three-quarters of an inch thick between club-face and ball. Because the club flange is about three-quarters of an inch below the ball, the striking force of the club will have to come from the top portion of the blade. The heavy weight of the club flange at impact is *underneath* rather than behind the ball—as with a sand iron shot off the fairway. This gives a higher trajectory to the shot than normal. The large amount of sand between the clubface and the ball prevents the grooves on the face from gripping the ball. This means there will be little or no backspin—the ball will come out softly and fall like a feather on the green, rolling very little.

The result, therefore, of using the standard sand-iron swing and hitting two inches behind the ball is maximum height and minimum backspin. Using the same stance and swing formula, the golfer can add an additional five yards to the carry by simply entering the sand one inch instead of two inches behind the ball. As the club comes into the sand one inch closer to the ball, it is not below the ball as much as before. This means that the ball will be struck a little lower on the face of the club and that the weight of the flange will not be so far underneath the ball as in the first case. Therefore, the trajectory will not be quite as high as when the club enters the sand two inches behind the ball. Hitting one inch behind the ball will now impart some backspin, because there is now less sand between the face and the ball. However, it will not give as much backspin as when the club strikes still closer to the ball.

An interesting thing happens when you strike half an inch behind the ball in the sand with the standard three-quarter stroke. This application of the clubface will find a very thin layer of sand between the face and the ball. You will notice it increases the abrasive action of the clubface on the ball, producing maximum backspin. This is how the experts make the ball bite and jump back from its landing point on the green. Hitting half an inch behind the ball also means that most of the flange weight strikes on the *back of the ball* rather than below it as in the case of the shots already discussed. The weight coming in on the back of the ball will drive it forward on a lower trajectory and for a greater distance.

To produce the maximum distance and the lowest trajectory, the ball should be contacted first and then the sand. Here the backspin is caused by the ball simply being squeezed between the clubface and the sand, much in the same fashion as in a normal iron shot off the turf. A good amount of stop can be expected from this shot—although not quite as much as when you enter the sand half an inch behind the ball and have the extra backspin caused by the abrasive action of the sand. The trajectory of the shot is, of course, the lowest of the four shots we've described, because the weight of the flange strikes on the back of the ball, more so even than in the case of the "half-an-inch behind" shot. Note that we haven't said a word about changing the standard

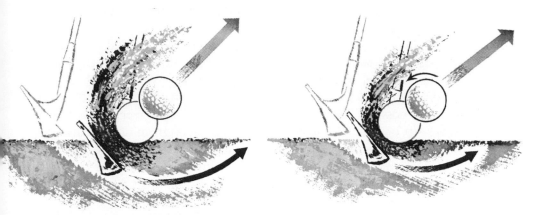

(Top—left to right) *Hitting two inches behind ball.* Clubhead passes under ball with thick cushion of sand between face and ball. This will prevent backspin. Heavy flange of club goes through under ball; striking force of shot therefore comes from top portion of blade, giving high trajectory. Distance 10–15 yards. *Hitting one inch behind ball.* This sends ball another five yards farther than hitting two inches behind. Flange is not so much below ball, so that club meets ball lower on face and ball has slightly lower flight. Because there is now less sand between face and ball, there will be some backspin.

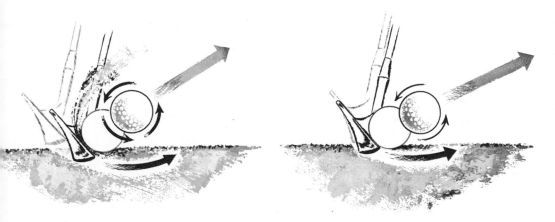

(Bottom—left to right) *Hitting half an inch behind ball.* Maximum backspin due to abrasive action of sand between clubface and ball. Most of flange weight strikes on back of ball, rather than below it, as in the shots described at left. This will drive the ball forward on a lower trajectory and for a greater distance. *Hitting ball first.* Weight of flange strikes on back of ball. This sends ball forward the maximum distance and on the lowest trajectory of all shots described. Good backspin is caused by ball being squeezed between clubface and sand, but not quite as much as in hitting half an inch behind ball.

three-quarter length swing. This is quite deliberate, as the only change necessary to send the ball the desired height and length is the different distance you hit behind the ball.

When blasting from a sand trap, it is a good idea to read the greens (see page 60) beforehand. If the green runs down and away from you, for example, allow for some roll. The slope takes much of the bite off the ball. If the green slopes upward, carry the ball as close to the pin as possible. The ball will not only hold the green but is liable to back up on you. Right and left breaks on a green should also be considered. On left-to-right breaks, remember that the normal spin on the ball will make it "kick" to the right, so play the shot more left than usual. On a right-to-left break, the slope will diminish the amount of spin to the right.

With a buried lie, the clubface should be slightly closed since you want to take maximum advantage of the force of the clubhead. Closing the face assures a more pronounced explosion, while opening the face provides more of a cutting action. The buried lie is the only type of explosion shot that requires more sand to be taken behind the ball. Sometimes it is wise to hit as much as four inches behind the ball so that the clubhead will be able to dig in and scoop the ball out of the depression it is in.

One of the hardest shots from the sand is the so-called fried-egg lie. This occurs in soft, powdery sand when the ball comes in with a high trajectory, hits, and then stays in its own crater. The player can see all of the ball, but it's down in a little hole, and the tendency is to skull the ball—often clear over the green and into another trap.

Actually, the fried-egg lie is tough for most players because of their hesitancy to hit down to the ball deep enough to get under it and knock it out of the trap. Too many golfers try to scoop the ball out and end up blading it—or hitting nothing but sand. It's important to get a mental picture of this shot; so visualize how you want the ball to react before you hit it. Because you have to cut down and through the sand to get under the ball, close and square the clubface a little more than with the standard trap shot, and play the ball in the middle of the stance. The rounded crater tends to make players think they have to do something different, but other than making the blade cut deeper into the sand, the swing is the same—a sharp takeaway, a smooth, unhurried downswing and a full follow-through. We have found that most pros like to have the clubface enter the sand at about the back edge of the crater where the sand starts to go down to the ball, and

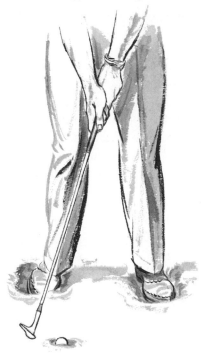

One of the more difficult shots for the average player is the plugged ball in the sand trap. The common fault is to quit on it. Ordinarily, the sand shot around the green should be simple, because the swing is slow and easy and the target is the sand a couple of inches behind the ball rather than the ball itself. Normally, the ball is played forward, opposite the left heel, with the blade of the sand wedge slightly open. The slow, deliberate swing is from the outside in and, with practice, you'll find it a lot easier to get close to the pin from sand than from rough. In playing the buried ball, square your stance and close, rather than open, the face of the club. If the swing is strong and uninterrupted, if the sand is hit a few inches behind the ball, and if the club follows through, the ball will pop out of the embedded lie onto the green.

then follow the slope down and under the ball. Don't chop down on top of the ball on this shot. Keep the blade going on a line to the target throughout the shot. The ball will come out rather low and rolling, so play for the front of the green to allow for this.

On a normal downhill lie in a trap, use the standard explosion shot, but the clubhead should enter the sand a little farther behind the ball—about a half inch—than it would if the lie were on the flat. This is necessary because the downhill slope affords less sand resistance between the ball and club. Also place a slight bit more weight on your right foot to prevent swaying forward. As a rule, a shot from a down-hill lie produces less loft than is normal. If you require loft, open the clubface slightly and compensate for it by pulling the forward foot farther back from the line of flight.

A downhill lie from the back edge of a trap can be a difficult shot. Even the pros are happy to get the ball out and on the green from this position. The reason for the difficulty of this shot is because it is nearly impossible to get under the ball and pop it up with backspin, as with a standard trap shot. The shot from a downhill lie comes out of the sand low and hard, and is difficult to control. But there is never any reason to leave the ball in the sand. You might occasionally trickle it over the edge of a hard green, because of the excessive roll imparted on the ball, but at least get it out of the bunker. On this shot play the ball back in the stance. You have to pick the club up quickly on the backswing in order not to touch the sand, which would mean a penalty. The clubhead should follow the contour of the bank behind you on the takeaway, so choke down on the grip to allow for this. You must come into the ball a bit farther behind the ball on this shot in order to get under it, so it is important to finish the shot. Most people feel as if they're going to skull the ball from this type of lie, and the sharp takeaway destroys their tempo and makes the swing seem unnatural, so work on maintaining as smooth a swing as possible. Because of the slope, the weight is forced to remain on the left side, so the body will be solidly in place. Go down and through the ball firmly, entering the sand about one and one-half inches behind the ball (de-pending on the texture of the sand).

When playing a normal uphill lie in a trap, employ the basic explosion technique except that the clubhead should enter the sand a little closer to the ball—approximately a half-inch—since the sand is usually deeper at the club's point of entry. Place more weight on the left or forward foot for this shot, and remember that the deeper sand will slow up the clubhead, necessitating a slightly more deliberate follow-through.

An uphill lie from the front edge of a trap is a rather easy shot and is played as a normal uphill lie. If there is no overhanging lip on the trap and the side of the green is smooth, it may even be possible to get out with a putter. To do this, keep the weight on the left foot, and try to hit the ball without first contacting the sand. Make sure to hit the shot squarely, for if you contact the ball too much on top, it can bury the ball in the sand. Incidentally, this shot should not be attempted if the sand is powdery or soft, making sure the clubhead strikes the ball before hitting the sand; otherwise it will be caught in and slowed down by the sand.

If the ball happens to embed itself under the lip, first determine whether staying in the trap, but with a more suitable lie, or hitting the ball to either side away from the green, might be better for you. You can base your decision on the texture of the sand, the depth of the trap, the nearness of the pin, how deeply the ball is embedded, and the circumstances of play. If you choose to blast it out, follow the same procedure for the regular explosion shot, except make certain you anchor that back foot and be careful not to pop the ball up into the air. If it hits you, it's a two-stroke penalty.

Another note of caution. When you are faced with an uphill lie as well as a plugged ball, your back foot is quite deep in the sand. To compensate, shorten your grip correspondingly. This will give you more control and also help restrict the backswing. If you go back too far, you'll lose your balance and your body will sway. The clubface will remain square as long as the hands do not turn.

The ball that is not quite in, yet not quite out of the trap calls for a proper decision, good judgment and positive execution. First, you must determine just how firm the ground is under the ball. Ordinarily you can tell by noting the amount and texture of sand surrounding the ball. Unless the ball is clearly in grass, in which case you can play the regular approach-type shot, chances are that an explosion shot is required.

To digress for a moment, one of the most difficult shots to handle around the green is the sandy lie. Specifically this is a lie in the rough where the ball is lying on a combination of soft sand and tufts of grass. If you could hit a full shot from this lie there would be no problem, but when you need to carry the ball just a few yards over a hazard to a tough pin placement, you've got trouble. The danger is, if you hit just a fraction behind the ball, you'll never make the green, and if you swing full and take little or no sand, there's a good chance you'll skull the ball—the latter being a result of the flange bouncing off the sand and grass into the ball. The technique that many pros employ is very similar to a trap shot. If the ball is sitting well, use your sand blaster. Play the ball more toward your left heel, with your weight concentrated on your left side. Take the club back halfway, a little beyond waist high. Make sure you take a little sand behind the ball, how much depends on the texture of the sand and what is below the immediate

In front of you looms the steep bank of the sand trap in which your ball is nestled. Just over the trap lies the green, with the pin so close that the flag is practically fluttering in your face. How do you achieve enough loft to clear the bank and enough "stop" to keep the ball from scooting past the pin? Try the cut shot. Play the ball off your left foot, open your stance, open the blade of the wedge, and swing the club on an outside-in path that cuts across the ball. Strike the sand behind the ball—but no more than an inch behind or you will leave the ball sitting there. Your swing should be upright, resembling a wood-chopping action, but don't force it and don't hurry. Swing in a relaxed, easy manner, letting the club go as far back as it seems to want to go and as far forward as momentum carries it. That should result in a fairly full follow-through. You can use the same shot to float the ball over an obstacle and plop it onto the green from the rough. In that case, play the ball off your right foot and hit the ball itself rather than hitting behind it.

surface. The fact that you're not in a hazard gives you the opportunity of grounding your club. How your club sets at the ball can reveal the nature of your lie. We can't overemphasize hitting through the ball—don't quit at the ball—hit it firmly and finish.

Back to traps. Now, let's remember that sand that is wet is usually sand that is heavy. Under the wet layer in many cases is hard ground. If this is the case, not as much power is needed to hit the ball from this type of lie as from soft sand. The most common fault seems to be hitting too far behind the ball: the clubhead enters the sand too quickly, and the wetness prevents the blade from getting to and through the ball. Another error is bouncing the club off the packed wet sand into the belly of the ball, ruining the shot and, in all probability, the ball as well. Concentrate on a target two inches behind the ball. Using a three-quarter swing, with the ball played opposite the instep of the left foot, get the clubhead into the target area with a natural, smooth swing and follow through. This is not too difficult a shot, but practice is recommended to learn exactly how much sand should be taken. More on hitting from wet sand traps can be found in Chapter 5.

The pitch shot from a trap 50 to 75 yards from the green is performed almost exactly as a pitch shot from the fairway. The swing is the same; however, because you cannot ground the club in the trap, you have to address the ball from above the sand. To be sure you make contact with ball first, play it back of center, toward the right foot. The swing is motivated by the hands, which are advanced slightly ahead of the clubhead. Using either a wedge or a nine-iron (or longer club if distance demands), contact the ball first, the sand afterward, with a one-half or three-quarter swing and a solid follow-through. This action will displace sand in the same way a fairway divot is taken. Do not look up until the shot is completed. Practice this as you would other approach shots, and you'll be pleased with the results.

One of the most difficult trap shots is with the ball below the level of the feet, which is generally the case when the ball is in the sand and the feet are on the bank of the trap. Here you require an exaggerated knee bend to get the hands into hitting position. Hold the club on the end of the grip, and, to maintain balance, shorten the backswing. The reason for this is that the more body movement, the more you are likely to miss the shot.

Another demanding trap shot is one where you want to carry the ball some distance, say 20 to 30 yards. The problem here is judging how much sand to take. As a general rule, as previously stated, the longer the shot, the less sand you take, and vice versa. Square up the blade, consciously keep more weight on the left side than on the shorter bunker shot, and take a three-quarter swing. Try very hard not to lean forward or backward or sway during the swing. Because you're taking a fuller swing, you are apt to slide around in the sand. This could cause a skull or, worse, leave the ball in the trap. Don't stop the clubhead at impact, as this can be disastrous. Swing down and through to a high finish.

Fairway bunkers usually are signs of good golf-course architecture. Strategically placed, they add character to the hole, keep the long hitters honest, and dictate how the hole should be played. If you get caught trying to steal those valuable yards, or if the attraction is too great to resist, the immediate concern is not why you're there but how to get out without sacrifice of distance. Hitting a wood or a long iron out of a fairway trap obviously requires a good lie. If the ball is not sitting up, or if the lip of the bunker is too pronounced, concede the distance and use whatever lofted iron is needed for clearance. It is extremely dangerous to use any straighter faced club than a four-wood. Since this shot demands a body pivot, get a firm sturdy stance which gives you both support and freedom. Take the clubhead back as low to the sand as possible without its touching. This encourages the downswing to return along the same path, allowing the loft of the club to take the ball off the sand with a normal trajectory and full distance. If the sand is loose and you must dig in for support, remember to keep your swing level by shortening your grip. Keep your head steady and still, because there is no room for error on this shot. While the swing is similar to the fairway shot, if an error is made, the penalty is much greater. If you hit the ball too low, you can lose as much as 100 yards; if too high, you will hit it into the lip of the bunker. It's a hard shot, but it can be mastered.

We have made several references to the texture of the sand. Actually, the kind of sand in a trap critically affects the strategy of shot that must be made. This is because of the two basic principles of the explosion shot: (1) The clubhead never touches the ball. (2) Varying the shot requires that the golfer make an adjustment either in the distance behind the ball that the club strikes, or in the power of the swing, or a combination of both. Golf teachers have inculcated the mechanics of the simple explosion so thoroughly that even the beginner should know them, but unless he is aware of these two underlying principles, he will not be able to adjust to the varying resistances of sand used in traps.

The rules of golf forbid testing the sand with your hands or any part of the club. You must try to judge the texture and depth as you assume your stance, digging in, wiggling and fidgeting with your feet to learn all you can.

Dry, powdery, deep, fine, and artificial silicon sands are usually the toughest to get out of. In extremely fine sand, the ball tends to bury itself in its own depression. The player should hit a spot about an inch behind the ball, and it will help to close the blade of the wedge so that the flange will not bounce and keep the clubhead from digging deep. Even hooding the face of the club will not prevent the clubhead's tendency to lose much of its speed as it ploughs through the heavy sand, so the golfer should concentrate on not quitting on the shot. Because so much sand gets between the face of the club and the ball, it is almost impossible to produce backspin on this full explosion shot, so expect your ball to roll a good bit after it hits the green. Surprisingly, you will have to dig your feet very deep in order to get a firm stance in a powdery trap, because although you slide into small-grained sand very easily, the stance is slippery and not secure. All of these tips apply even more strongly to the ersatz sand made of silicon compounds. It is finer than the most powdery real sand.

In coarse, wet, or shallow sand, the best shot is usually the half-explosion. Very coarse and well-soaked sand is like a cushion below the ball—a cushion that will resist the clubhead and may make the flange of the wedge bounce up and into the ball. To avoid this tendency to skull the shot, hit about three inches behind the ball. You will get more distance out of wet or coarse sand, but because there is less sand between the ball and the clubface, you will get more backspin, too. In the gravelly sand that is sometimes found in New England, the ball will sit up nicely, and you may be able to play a chip from the trap; in any case it will be easy to produce backspin. The dirty, clotted, compacted sand that is sometimes found in the Southwest is most conducive to the half-explosion. In very shallow traps, where there is only a thin layer of sand on top of a hard base, play a very soft explosion so that the club will not dig too deeply and strike the base. Two bits of advice on wet sand: (1) When you assume your stance, check to see whether the sand is wet below the top skin—it may be dry two inches down, and this can make the shot play more like one from dry sand. (2) If there is no lip on the bunker, you may be able to putt out of drenched sand.

In any case, there is only one way to improve your skill in all kinds of sand. Once upon a time, a spectator was watching Jerry Barber practice his sand play. Shot after shot rolled up to within a few inches of the hole, until finally the inevitable happened and one ball went in. The man laughed, turned to Barber and said, "Jerry, you sure are lucky out of the sand." Barber smiled and replied, "Yes, and the more I practice, the luckier I get."

And so will you.

Strategy and a Water Shot

Everyone fears water and rightfully so—many a good golf shot has ended up in the drink much to the dismay of the player. However, there is not much that can be done about it once the ball leaves the club. The problem is: what to do about the next shot? If the ball is an inch or more beneath the surface of the water, take a penalty of one stroke and drop out to where you can take a good swing at it. It is tempting indeed to see the ball sitting quietly there just beneath the surface and then not be able to move it at all. Keep your head and evaluate the situation thoroughly. You never want to gamble on any shot unless the odds are well in your favor. When a part of the ball is above the surface of the water, you can take the chance of extricating it—providing you know the technique of hitting a water shot.

Playing the shot from water is much the same as playing from a buried lie in a sand trap. Like sand, you must be prepared for the resistance the water will exert on the clubhead upon striking the water. For this reason, it is advisable to take a firmer grip than usual. Also be a bit more conscious of following through. There is a definite tendency to quit at the ball through the fear of the lie. Open your stance slightly and then hood the clubface at address, because the resistance of the water when the club makes contact with it will square the clubface immediately. Break the wrists early on the backswing and take the club outside the line of flight. The clubhead should enter the water one to three inches behind the ball, with the leading edge of whatever club you choose. This is the thinnest part of the clubhead and has the best chance of getting to the ball. The sensation should be one of slicing through the water, not splashing through. This is done by allowing the left hand to hit down and through the ball. When properly played with a sand or pitching wedge a great deal of backspin can be imparted to the ball, allowing you to hit boldly to the pin.

Remember that it's not advisable to try to hit the ball more than 100 yards from a lie of this type. And last, but not least, be extremely careful about moving. If you lose your balance and move even slightly, the shot won't come off. The clubface will either hit ineffectively behind the ball, or you'll land right on top of the ball driving it deeper into the murky depths. In regard to the water shot out of a hazard, remember it is just as much a hazard as a sand trap, so be very careful not to touch the water with the clubhead (which is called *grounding the clubhead*) in the address position or the takeaway. The penalty for touching the water or sand is severe—*two strokes*.

Everyone gets into trouble in the course of a round, but if you prepare to cope with it, you'll think and play better. There are two ways to tackle the problem beforehand. One is to practice the technique of getting out of difficult situations; the other is to plan ahead to avoid the trouble in the first place. When you keep the ball in play, golf is naturally much easier and much more pleasant than when you're continually in the rough. Therefore, always consider where the best positions are and where you want to be if your tee shot or approach shot doesn't quite come off. Good strategy is a must, whether you're playing a practice round on a strange course or plotting your home course. Should you err once you are out on the course, make the best of it. The sooner you forget about how you got into trouble and the more determined you are to get out, the better you will be. It may even spur you to play shots you once thought impossible.

5. Strategy and the Weather

Let the rain fall and the wind blow, and you will notice that even among your tournament stars the scores will rise accordingly—except for those who stand steadily in the top echelon.

The answer is that those who have earned ranking as masters of the mashie necessarily over the years have had to learn to change their thinking, or strategy, to meet changing conditions with maximum efficiency. In other words, you can't put your game strategy into one set pattern and hope to pull off the same shots you would under normal conditions.

Let's say, for example, that pitching to the green from in close with a wedge is your favorite shot. Ordinarily you can drop this shot and stop it within one-putt range. But what is going to happen to that high-flying wedge shot if the wind is wailing and the green is sodden and possibly has a film of water on it? The answer would seem to be obvious. Put it up into that wind, and it can veer in any direction. Then, when the ball plummets down, in all probability it will bury itself right where it hits.

Your answer here is to forget your favorite wedge and keep that ball as far down as possible out of the wind with—despite the wet surface—a running nine-, eight-, or even a seven-iron shot.

Wet-Weather Strategy

To beat his worst enemy—rain—a golfer must have the ability to adapt his strategy to wet-weather conditions. Beating the rain, we feel, depends largely on maintaining a firm grip and selecting the proper clubs. Unless consideration is given to these essentials, no effective shot, short of an accident, can be made.

One thing is certain. If you play in the rain, you're going to get wet, and there isn't a great deal you can do about it aside from the common-sense precautions to keep your hands and the grips of your clubs dry. Wet hands, besides causing slippage, also promote a feeling of insecurity that could affect the rest of the swing. About all you can do, actually, is wipe the grips with a towel before playing your shots, and keep your clubs covered as much as possible.

An umbrella is almost a must for wet-weather play. You can carefully grip your club under it. But, before handling the grip, wipe it dry with a towel kept in the umbrella ribs for that purpose. Then, without wasting any time, address the ball and make your shot as fast as possible so that the rain doesn't have time to affect your grip. Immediately afterward, the club is replaced in the golf bag and a cover placed over the clubs. This cover should be kept over the clubs at all times to prevent water from dripping into the bag while moving from shot to shot. Once the grips become saturated, good golf is seriously hampered.

A person who plays with gloves cuts down the possibility of slippage. Many golfers keep a pair of plain cloth gloves for that purpose. It seems that they grip best when the club handles are wet. A handkerchief wrapped around the grip can accomplish the same purpose. Use these alternatives, however, only when the grips become too wet to grasp with an ordinary golf glove.

While it's not necessary to keep the ball dry, it's a rather important consideration for the face of the club you're using. When there is a film of moisture on the clubface, problems could result. The face scoring lines (the horizontal grooves on the face of the club) are there to help keep the ball on its desired path of flight. But when water fills the face scoring the ball will fly off without the controlling influence of spin. That is, the ball slides at the moment of impact, and is likely to shoot to the left or right, usually to the right. This is not a slice or a hook; the swerve is much sharper than that. So dry the face of the club you're using before every shot. Of course, sometimes this effort won't have great effect. The clubface will get wet again before you can hit the ball.

Before teeing the ball, select a firm spot to take your stance. It's important to have your feet set so they will not slip during the swing. Also, have the caddie stand over you with an umbrella when teeing the ball to prevent your hands from getting wet. Remember that while wet-weather golf may be uncomfortable, you should not let it ruin your score. A windless rain need not be disruptive. Swing as you normally would, but concentrate your efforts on remaining *solid*. To facilitate this, start with a slightly wider stance to brace yourself against slipping on the wet grass. The stance will feel stiff, but it provides a sure foundation, and will keep you from losing your balance on sloppy ground.

Check the spikes on your shoes occasionally and clean them if they become clogged with bits of grass and mud. This will insure a firmer stance, which is necessary when playing in wet weather.

One thing to keep in mind when playing in the rain or on wet fairways is that the course will play longer because the roll will be less than under normal conditions. Accept this fact and hit your drives as you would normally. By trying to hit the ball higher or differently to get more distance, you'll only get into more trouble and make more mistakes.

The wetness of the grass has a tendency to keep the ball low when hit off the fairway. For this reason, it usually is best to avoid using the less-lofted clubs. It's more difficult to use clubs like the two-iron or three-wood under these conditions. Most golfers prefer a four-wood off wet grass because it's easier to get the ball into the air than with a two- or three-wood.

There are two essentials that must be kept in mind when hitting fairway woods from wet grass. One, that the ball must be picked more cleanly than under normal conditions. The other is that you keep your feet firmly planted to avoid slipping. In connection with picking the ball more cleanly, you must not go too deep after the ball. This is because the water will fill the grooves of the clubface. Water will not compress, and if you go too deeply the ball will squirt, or fly, meaning that it will shoot off to the right or to the left. By this we don't mean the ball will hook or slice. The grooves being filled with water will simply shoot the ball off to one side or the other, as previously explained. The head and body, under these conditions, must remain over the ball throughout the swing. This, of course, is what you should do on any shot, but on hitting a shot as delicate as this, any lateral movement forward or backward (sway) could spell instant disaster. You've got to catch the ball just right. If you hit it a fraction too heavy, or too thin, the addition of wet will magnify the error.

When you are faced with a long iron shot from a soggy fairway and the ball is sitting cleanly, don't beat down on it. Try to clip the ball off neatly. To accomplish this action, play the ball a little farther forward and try to make contact slightly on the upswing. Remember, avoid changing your swing to play under wet conditions. You'll be better off selecting a more suitable club for the shot.

While on the subject of club selection, it is wise to use at least one more club than normal for longer shots since you can't expect your normal distance. That is, use a four-iron instead of a five-, for example.

If the course is soggy, you will probably be given relief from having to hit a ball that plugs into the fairway. The lack of roll takes away distance, to be sure, but it also has a benefit: you can swing with less fear of the ball bouncing off the fairway into the rough or behind trees. And, unless the ball is being played out of thick, wet grass, which produces those "flyers," you can pitch directly to the pin. Not having to hold back on those short approach shots can be turned into a definite asset.

Should your ball come to rest in a patch of mud, be sure to take a club with enough loft to get out in one shot. Mud on a ball will often affect its flight. Unfortunately, there isn't much that can be done about this problem except to hit the ball as usual and hope for the best. If the ball is embedded in the turf or lies on the green, it can be lifted and wiped without penalty. The exception is when the ball is embedded in a hazard. Then it must be played as it lies. Make certain you know the rules which govern such situations and the allowances given under "Casual Water." They have been framed with only the golfers' interests in mind, and two of the most famous golfers in the world, Jack Nicklaus and Arnold Palmer, owe Masters victories to their knowledge and application of this particular rule. To think you are taking unfair advantage of a situation is not the proper attitude. For example, the USGA Rules provide a lift from casual water, which it defines as: ". . . any temporary accumulation of water which is visible before or after the player takes his stance and which is not a hazard of itself or is not in a water hazard. Snow and ice are 'casual water' unless otherwise determined by Local Rule."

When your ball lands in casual water—not in a trap or other hazard—you're entitled to a free drop. The drop must be made to the closest point of relief, no nearer the hole. Whenever you have a free drop, as previously advised, take it. It's to your advantage, unless, of course, you have to drop behind a tree.

Wet sand results in many interesting, unwanted situations. The sand may be soft or mushy or packed hard. But, remember, the *Rules of Golf* do not allow you to test the sand with your club, so try to get an idea of the conditions that exist when you walk into the bunker to take your stance.

There are two basic methods of recovering from a wet sand trap, each dictated by the lie of the ball. If the ball is buried in the sand, address the ball—as you should with all trap shots—with an open stance and with your weight distributed mainly toward the left side. The clubhead is lifted abruptly on the backswing and then struck in the sand, without any conscious effort at following through, four inches behind the ball. Since the follow-through is restricted, this method will require some practice in order to get the feel of how hard to hit the ball, which will come out of the sand much faster than normally and with little or no backspin. If the ball is lying cleanly in the sand, on the other hand, your method of recovery will be dictated by the nature of the sand itself. If the sand is soggy, you should play the shot with your sand wedge. If, however, the sand is hard, use your pitching wedge, the sharper blade of which will encourage digging; the flange on the sand wedge would simply bounce ineffectively. In either of these two cases—contrary to the method of exploding a ball— make a definite follow-through by accelerating the clubhead to the finish of your swing.

In some real sloppy lies—say a buried ball in wet sand on the edge of casual water—it is generally best to chip the ball out of the trap. The important thing here is to hit the ball first. As in all chip shots, put more weight on your left leg, to put a little cut on the ball by opening your stance so that your body is facing the hole slightly. In a similar situation, except where the ball is sitting cleanly, you would be wise to play the ball off the surface of the sand as if it were on the fairway. The long semiblast is really a gamble. However, if the pin is located close to the trap you have no choice but to use your sand club. Be certain, in this shot, that you strike down firmly under the ball. In wet, packed sand the club bounces up and out fast, causing inexperienced players to skull the ball.

Generally, short irons cause the most trouble. A clubhead striking a wet ball in wet grass will cause a "flier" in which the ball leaves the face without spin and travels farther than normal. Under such conditions, it's advisable to use less club, a nine-iron instead of an eight-, for example. Some players even prefer to chip rather than pitch when they're near the green. They're better able to judge distance with a chip from wet grass, and they're more accurate, too. They can punch the ball right for the cup. There is no bounce and little roll when the greens are soggy.

Putting on greens that are wet is dangerous, at best. Sometimes the rain is not heavy enough to penetrate the surface, and the ball will skim along rather than slow down. Only experience will warn you of this phenomenon. But when the green is soggy, you will need to stroke the ball firmer to overcome any drag caused by the water, and you will putt straighter to the hole, figuring on the wetness to take away the normal "break." While you must hit a putt harder than normally, step up the force of the blow. Avoid lengthening the stroke more than is absolutely necessary. The farther the putter blade has to travel, the

Skip shot, below, is important in battling the elements. Use an open stance, keep hands ahead of ball through hitting zone. Lower body by flexing knees and hit ball with sharp, descending blow. The swing is a one-piece action of the shoulders, arms, and stiff wrists.

70 – 80 ft.

more opportunities it has to waver off line. For a short cut, play the ball a bit more forward in your stance. This new positioning will enable you to catch the ball on the upswing, there will be more over-spin on the ball, and the putt will automatically roll farther—all without having to make a major alteration in the putting stroke itself.

Before putting on a wet green, there are two precautions you should take. First, check the line of your putt for particularly damp spots which often develop when it rains. We don't mean visible water because this constitutes "casual water," and you do not have to putt through casual water. But some spots on greens will become more damp than others and, if you have to putt over them, they will slow up the ball and your putt will come up short of the hole if you don't allow for it. Second, after you have taken your practice strokes on the green before actually addressing the ball, check the face of your putter to be sure its wet surface has not picked up grass cuttings or other small impediments. Any such object on the putter face can either deaden the putt and bring it up short or throw the putt off line.

There are two points to remember if there is casual water on the green. Coming off the apron, it's best to chip over the water since the ball stops rather quickly. If the ball must be putted, the stroke should be much firmer to get it through the water. At no time are you required to stand in water or putt from water on the green. The casual water rule applies on the green as well as on the fairway. So remember, don't hesitate to move the ball or yourself to a drier location, provided it's no nearer the hole.

The enjoyment of playing golf in the rain will be increased if you dress properly. There's nothing more annoying than playing in wet clothes. Besides, there is always the danger of wetting your hands on a wet piece of clothing. For that reason, many golfers carry a rain suit.

Golfers who wear glasses have the added problem of keeping them clear of water to maintain good vision. They'll find it helpful to wear a long-billed cap. One other thing. Keep several towels in your bag as replacements for the one in your umbrella. They'll come in handy if the going is really wet.

We've noticed one peculiar thing about those who carry umbrellas. This is, that they always seem to carry them in their left hand. We would suggest that you be sure to alternate the hand in which you carry your umbrella so that the left hand doesn't tend to get overtired. After all, the left hand is the key to your shots and if you put too much strain on it, the odds are that it will collapse on you without your knowing it.

No one really likes to play golf in wet weather, but the fickle elements are such that we'll no doubt have to contend with an occasional moist day now and then. Thus, to keep your score, be sure to follow wet-weather strategy.

Playing in the Wind

Playing in the wind always calls for a certain amount of luck, and yet there are certain sensible precautions you can take to lower the percentages which nature is putting up against you.

In discussing basic shots into the wind, we'd have to say that on the whole, the average player never takes enough club. He always seems to be looking for the perfect shot but seldom manages to pull it off. When hitting a shot into the wind, be aware of balance. Take a sturdy stance and play the ball back toward your right foot. Playing the ball back allows you to hit it more on the downswing, resulting in a lower trajectory. If the shot normally calls for a six-iron, drop down to a five-

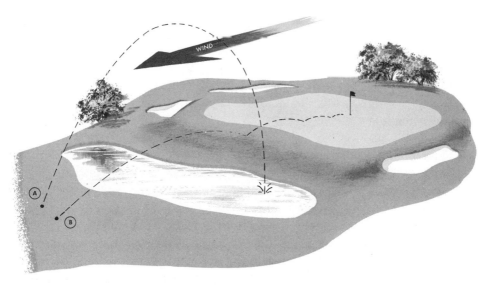

Always consider course conditions before selecting your club. Never just pull out the regular club you use for a shot, without giving it a thought. Here, "A" did just that. He took his nine-iron, up it went in the air, the headwind against him got hold of it, and he wound up in the water. "B" took a straighter faced club than normal and played a pitch and run close.

or maybe even a four-iron depending on the velocity of the wind. Remember, when hitting into the wind, the ball will stop practically where it lands, so hit your shot right up to the flag.

Playing downwind, or with the wind behind you, unless it is a howling gale, you generally can figure on taking one less club than you would normally. When hitting approach shots downwind, it is best to select the club that will drop the ball short of the green. The wind will probably carry the ball on, and even if it is short, it will usually run up onto the green.

The big mistake most players make regarding the wind is that they try to fight it by swinging harder than normal. This merely forces a player out of his usual groove and will get him nowhere. When you swing too hard there is a danger of scooping the ball into the wind. That is, as a rule the harder you swing at the ball, the higher it will tend to go. Consequently, when hitting against the wind or into a cross-wind, swing easily. And when the wind is with you, swing a little harder than you normally would.

The ability to hit a low, boring tee shot is essential when driving into the wind or when playing on hard ground where you want a lot of "run" on your ball. Hitting this shot is merely a matter of angles. On your normal tee shot, you play the ball off your left heel, and hitting straight away, you come in under the ball for loft. To hit the low, boring wind-cheater, position the ball an inch or even an inch and one-half farther back toward the center of your stance. Tee the ball lower than usual and keep the hands well forward at address. You should have this feeling of the hands being forward as you move through the ball with a strong left side which stays ahead of the ball. The total effect is that you are reducing the loft of your driver at impact, thereby causing the ball to take off on a lower trajectory than normal. To summarize, the three things to remember are: tee the ball low, position it back more toward center than normally, and address the ball with those hands forward.

When playing fairway woods into the wind, do not play the ball in its usual position—off the left heel. We would advise moving the ball back more than you normally do toward the right foot. This does not mean you should play the ball off the right foot. It is simply an adjustment that should be made in terms of an inch or three; but never back past the middle of the stance. There is no alteration in the swing aside from keeping the club low to the ground on the takeaway and returning in the same low arc. Grip the club slightly lower down the shaft in

To increase loft (left), play the ball more toward the left foot. Open clubface or use the more-lofted club. *To decrease loft* (right), play the ball more toward right foot. Close face or use less-lofted club.

order to shorten your swing and increase your accuracy. On all such fairway shots, as previously stated, we would suggest that you take one club longer, further reducing the loft of the shot and redeeming the distance lost to the headwind. This will help you assert much more control without the feeling of hitting so hard.

The secret of keeping your iron shots under control when the wind gets up is to keep the ball down where the wind can't affect it. This means taking straighter faced clubs than you would on a windless day. For instance, playing into the wind, for a distance where you would normally play a five-iron, use a four-iron and choke down a half inch or so. This reduces the length of the shaft on the four-iron to that of the five-iron, so that you're getting the same force in the swing, but the straighter face on the four- gives you the lower ball you want. As you will get much the same distance from the choked four- as you would from a five-iron, swing within yourself, and don't try to hit too hard. The harder you try to hit, as we stated previously, the higher the shot is likely to go, and the more a headwind gets the chance to balloon the shot. The only other changes most pros make are to play the ball an inch or two to the right of where they normally position it to encourage a low flight. Second, they put a little more weight than normal on the left foot at address and keep it there throughout the swing. Playing an iron shot with the wind, again take a lower club and choke down a little. Remember, the wind can't affect a low ball as much as a high one. Downwind, the wind tends to take the backspin off an iron shot, so allow for a little more roll on the shot than usual. Anytime you're in doubt on club selection in a wind, take the lower club and choke down.

If your course offers some protection like dunes or trees, use them to advantage, but do not get lulled into bad judgment: Remember, once the ball is beyond this "wall," it will again be at the mercy of the wind, so frequently check wind direction and velocity.

As strange as it may seem, wind can affect your putting. When the ball nears the hole and is traveling at a very slow speed, the ball is very much at the mercy of a strong wind. Carefully take this into consideration, especially on the long putts that you might want to lag up to the hole.

On cross-wind shots, use one more club and don't swing hard. For example, a shot normally calling for a seven-iron should be played softly with a six-. To get extra distance off the tee if there's a right-to-left cross-wind, close your stance a little and try to pull. Do the opposite if there's a left-to-right wind. That is, on left-to-right cross-winds, you naturally aim to the left side of the green and vice versa, and under fairly severe conditions this is where it is valuable to be able to hook or fade the ball. In other words, if you have a right-to-left wind, set yourself up a yard or so to left of the pin and cut it in there. The ball should hold its line, and will only drift a bit at the end of its flight.

If you have right-to-left cross-winds, aim the ball to the left of pin and fade the shot. If the wind is from left-to-right, aim to the right of the pin and play a hook. If unable to hook or fade the ball at will, remember that wind will not affect a well-hit shot too much. So if you are hitting a ball solidly, hit directly at the pin.

If the wind is left-to-right, try to hook it in there and, again, start the ball a few yards right of the pin. The wind will keep the ball from hooking too much. Now this is all well and good if you have the ability to hook or cut the ball at will. If you can't, remember a well-hit shot will hold the line—unless you're playing in a hurricane. So if you are hitting the ball solidly, simply go ahead and bang it hard at the pin.

Hot-Weather Strategy

When the temperature goes way up, the chances are good your scores could go way down. In hot weather muscles stay free and loose and usually coordinate the best. But to reap the full rewards, take these few precautions. Wear light-colored clothing so as not to attract as much heat, and wear a cap or hat. If you habitually use a glove, take at least two spares along to permit a change when the one in use gets too moist. Removing the glove between shots will keep it drier longer. Salt tablets, the coated kind which can be taken without fear of nausea, are a must. We would suggest taking two before going out and two more at the end of nine. This will help prevent that weak feeling that could occur around the fifteenth hole. Stay in shade when possible, and walk rather slowly to conserve energy.

To avoid hand perspiration and the consequence of the club's slipping, use a good hand spray, any one of the several fine ones now on the market. This is generally preferred to treating each individual club for slippage. Watch out for perspiration running down from the forearm as you address the ball. A towel will do the trick provided you use it to dry your forearm as well as your hands before making the shot. An absorbent band under the peak of the cap or hat is very helpful in keeping perspiration away from eyeglasses.

When playing in hot weather, eat lightly beforehand, and don't overdrink. Keep pre-game practice to a minimum. Thus you'll be ready for both the hot weather and the hot round.

Cold-Weather Strategy

Golf played in cold weather can be just as enjoyable as golf played in the warm sunshine—if you employ the proper strategy. Playing under cold-weather conditions, of course, is certainly more challenging, and offers several additional hazards to overcome, such as:

1. Your muscles are not as elastic, and sometimes are quite stiff.

2. The golf ball loses some resilience, and this makes distance a problem.

3. Warm clothing can restrict freedom of movement, and cold

numb hands may cause the grip of your trusty wood to feel like a frozen lead pipe.

4. Normal inactivity of the winter months finds many a golfer in less than his best physical condition.

With all these handicaps it is little wonder that at the first sign of the birds heading south, many golfers pack their clubs in for the year and become content to spend their time sitting by the fire just telling old golf stories and dreaming of spring. If you are one of those golfers who feels that the discomforts and higher scores experienced in winter are not worth the effort, here are some stratagems that may help.

The first step to winter golf efficiency is warmth with comfort and freedom of movement. Wear wool trousers and thermal ski underwear. Several layers of lightweight clothing are preferable to one heavy sweater or bulky jacket. A lightweight wool long-sleeved shirt, lightweight sweater perhaps a turtle neck, and nylon windbreaker with a collar that buttons around the neck are usually ample. Keep your head and ears covered and your feet warm. Try golf rubbers. Winter golf gloves which protect both hands from the cold, yet are light enough to allow hand "feel," are available. You might also take along a handwarmer to serve the added duty of keeping a spare golf ball warm. Whenever possible keep your hands in your pockets or under the armpits for added warmth. It is much easier to keep the hands warm than to try and warm them up once they become numb. When playing, remember: don't tarry—not only is it improper as etiquette, but moving briskly between shots also helps you to stay warm, and makes the game more enjoyable for everyone.

In cold weather, the most important part of the club is the grip. Care should be taken to see that grips are clean and soft. Cold weather tends to make all types of grips slick, and a dirty grip is nearly impossible to hold. Have your professional check your clubs and replace worn-out grips, for if the club turns in your hand, a missed shot will probably occur. About grips, Gardner Dickinson, Jr., once stated, "In cold weather, I think the fellow with rubber grips on his clubs has the better of it. When it gets cold, leather tends to get slippery."

Since cold weather reduces the resilience of golf balls, most golfers should use a lower compression ball. High-compression balls become rock hard and practically impossible to compress, besides giving a hand-stinging sensation when only slightly missed. Distance is directly connected with a golfer's ability to compress the golf ball; thus the lower compression ball usually proves more satisfactory. As an experiment next time you play in cold weather, try both a low- and high-compression ball and judge for yourself which is best for your game. A warm ball will go farther than a cold ball, so use three balls. Keep two warm in your pocket or near your handwarmer, and exchange balls on every hole, placing a warmed ball in play on every tee. It's against USGA rules to carry a device specifically designed to warm golf balls.

A pre-game warm-up session, important at any time of the year (see page 215) is doubly so in the cold. Hitting a few balls is also a must. Just because you feel tight, never try to overswing in order to loosen up. Use a normal swing.

Perhaps the most important thing to remember when playing in cold weather is to take a little more club than usual, for you can expect less distance than you would get under warmer conditions. Don't force your swing, but try to meet the ball solidly. If winter rules are in effect, and they should be, give yourself a good lie and hit the ball well into the air. When the fairway is narrow—and the wind is not to be reckoned with—go to a lofted wood rather than a low iron. The resulting high wood shot will produce less run and will minimize the chances of the ball's scooting out of play. When the wind is a factor and you have plenty of room to hit to, make a slight adjustment in your swing and go to a flatter plane. The consequent hook, lower trajectory, and extra roll will make up for any loss in distance your winterized swing forces on you. Even if you were to hit flush on the screws with mid-season power, it will fly out on a low line, then rise and fall with little roll. Although the fairways may be frozen, get all of the wood or the iron into the ball. As a rule, you should use one or two clubs extra—a four-wood, for example, in place of a three- or four-iron—depending on how cold it is.

Hitting the ball improperly off frozen turf or hard ground can hurt more than a golfer's pride. It can hurt his hands as well if the clubhead strikes the ground with any force. A wise golfer will avoid hitting the frozen ground with his club by developing a sweeping motion through the ball rather than a descending blow that would be used under normal playing conditions. When playing the long second shot to the green, for instance, it is usually best to play the ball directly off the left heel and keep a little weight on the left side to promote this motion. If the weight stays on the right side, you're apt to hit behind the ball and hurt your hands in addition to hitting a bad shot. By sweeping the ball off the turf, you minimize the possibility of having the clubhead deflected and affecting the ball's direction. That is, make certain you strike the ball first, and move the ball forward slightly in your stance. This will enable you to catch the ball on the upswing and diminish the chance of hitting behind the ball. The first bounce on frozen turf will always be a big one, so play all your shots about 15 yards short.

When the weather's chilly and the greens are hard, knocking the ball on some part of the putting surface becomes a golfer's nightmare. To cope with wintry conditions, you can make the following adjustments: take one more club, get the ball high in the air and, if possible, cut it a little. In the case of medium-length par-threes, let's say about a six-iron shot, choose one more club, a five-iron, to compensate for the restricted swing and loss of distance. If the green is hard, and chances are it will be, try to hit the ball as high as possible with a slight fade. The object is to have the ball land softly with a minimum of run. If you have difficulty fading the ball, just work on getting plenty of height on the shot. To do this, move the ball farther forward than normally and open the blade a bit. When there aren't any hazards in front, hit the ball to the apron (well short of the pin), and allow for some run.

From 10 to 30 feet off the frozen or hardpan green, a pitch shot, even one with terrific backspin, will not react properly. The ball will not bite, nor will it bounce correctly. The best shot, we believe, is a pitch-and-run or chip shot. The idea is to keep the ball low and, if possible, land just off the green. The lower flight should give you a more even bounce, whereas the high shot has a tendency to kick off at severe angles. Of course, the normal club for this type approach would be one of the middle irons, a four-, five-, or six-iron. In some cases, if you are close enough, say somewhere inside a few yards, you might even select a putter. The middle irons are fairly straight-faced and just what you need for a punch shot. Grip the club much shorter than normally, about two or three inches down the shaft. Play the ball to the right of center, your feet close, and your hands and hips open a quarter toward the hole. Above all, keep your hands ahead of the ball both at address and at impact. Since no divot should be taken, the ball must be hit or nipped cleanly. With a minimum of wrist action, take the club back close to the ground. Try to think of the downswing and short follow-through as a firm left forearm stroke with the back of the left hand facing the hole and the right hand keeping the clubface square to the target.

There are two important factors in cold-weather putting. One is the stroke that starts the ball rolling on the proper line, and the second is the amount of force used to make the ball travel the required distance. Both force and distance are tied up with such names as "feel" or "touch." Changes in "feel" requirements can take place on your home green between morning and afternoon, not to mention the particular changes that occur only in winter. In such seasons the greens are very hairy, coarse, and stiff (see page 74). Some basic advice, of course, is to keep your hands warm and make every effort to hit the ball squarely. However, this is not enough. Like death and taxes, some loss of sensitivity in your fingers is inevitable. Rather than worry about this absence of feel in your hands, concentrate instead on a firm but smooth stroke that starts the ball rolling with some overspin. Getting the ball to roll on top of the grass and not against it requires moving the ball a bit forward in your stance. This will help you to catch the ball slightly on the upswing, giving the ball some run.

There wasn't a better cold-weather player on the Tour than durable, aggressive Doug Ford. This he proved time and again. How did he do it? "I was more or less brought up in cold and wet weather around New York City," explains the former Masters and PGA champion, "so I guess I have developed an ability to get along with it. My normal game involves hooking the ball. I try to do this even more in cold weather by changing my alignment as I address the ball. I aim more to the right, close my stance a bit and roll my wrists slightly as I come into the ball. I find that a hooked ball produces better results in cold weather and especially in the wind, because it stays down more."

During the summer months look ahead to the cold weather by practicing and learning to control the height of the ball in flight. A golfer who can hit the ball high or low on command has a definite advantage during inclement conditions. When practicing in winter it is important that you swing "within yourself," because keeping the ball under control is essential. Practice whenever possible in your cold-weather golfing clothes. Practicing off hard ground is very similar to playing off frozen turf.

When playing winter golf, accept the fact that the ball won't travel as far. Holes are going to play longer—accept it. Scores tend to be higher—so what! Everyone else's will be, too. This is caused by weather conditions. If you don't believe it, check the newspaper for scores in the professional tournaments. Even the pros' scores rise when the temperature drops.

Winter golf can improve your game. Anyone who can play well

under difficult conditions has a real advantage in tournament play. Think about it. In most four-round tournaments—even in the summer—you usually encounter at least one day of rain or wind. An experienced winter golfer will usually excel on those days. One out of four is a nice advantage to have. Besides, the later you play each fall and the earlier you begin in the spring, the easier it becomes to keep your game constantly sharp all year round.

The Strategy of Spring Play

Coping with spring conditions is a combination of the strategies of wet-weather, windy, and winter play.

One of the difficulties involved in playing during the spring is wet, heavy sand in traps. For the average player, the trap shot is hard enough. Having soft or caked sand to contend with makes execution of this shot even harder. Normal trap-shot technique should be used in hitting this shot. By this we mean the usual "blast" or "explosion" shot, with the sand iron hitting the sand approximately two inches behind the ball. If the sand is wet and soft, be sure not to let the sand iron bury too deeply in the sand. If the sand is caked or hard, open the clubface more. The important thing to bear in mind when hitting a shot off wet sand is to explode the shot, hitting through the sand and making certain you follow through.

Quite often as a result of heavy and sometimes continual spring rain, sand is washed from traps onto fairways. Or sometimes, fairway grass is washed away, leaving a dirt or sand base. Playing a shot from sand in the fairway is a pretty chancy business, calling for great precision. The main idea to keep in mind in hitting such a shot is to hit the ball first, sort of pinching it. The clubhead should strike the sandy area right after hitting the ball.

Muddy areas always present a problem in early spring. Should you have to take a stance in such an area, anchor yourself well, working your feet down into the mud as far as practical. It's best, when standing in mud, to limit your body turn slightly, employing more of an arm swing. And, remember, always strike the ball first. In addition, remember having mud on the ball makes its flight unpredictable. When confronted with this problem, most pros generally take one less club than is required and try to keep the ball lower in flight than usual. This can be accomplished by hitting down slightly on the ball.

Incidentally, sometimes the mud will be in an area where casual water interferes with either the lie or your stance. If this is the case, you are entitled to drop the ball on a dry (or drier) spot not nearer the hole. Such a drop should minimize the mud problem because when you pick the ball up to drop it you are entitled to clean it.

Quite often in the early spring, you'll find your ball on hardpan near greens or in areas where the grass hasn't started to grow yet following the rigors of the winter. If you find your ball a few feet from the green and in an area where there is little grass, it's a good idea to use a putter. The thought behind this is that it pays to simplify the shot as much as possible.

If you use a lofted club when your ball's in a comparatively bare lie, you have to pinch the ball just right for best results. Such a shot calls for a great deal of precision, sometimes more than the average golfer can muster. It's a much simpler shot (and one with a great deal less margin for error) if you putt from off the green in this situation. This is not a difficult shot provided you gauge the distance to the hole properly and there's little grass between your ball and the green. Try to impart a little more overspin to the ball when putting from off the green. This enables the ball to run over any obstacles between it and the cup and helps the ball hold the line better.

Strategy, when putting from off the green, should be very much like what it is when you're hitting an approach putt. You must consider both distance and roll. The former is much more important. Lack of grass on certain parts of the green, sometimes a consequence of winter, makes putting more difficult, of course. Certainly, a lack of grass is going to cause your ball to roll faster, so this must be taken into consideration when you're planning the putt. A complicating factor is that sometimes patchy greens are left uncut, with the result that areas that have sufficient grass are slower than usual. This, too, must be kept in mind when you are planning your putt.

Sometimes after the winter, you'll find depressions in the fairways. It's very difficult for mowers to cut grass in these depressions and as a result, if your ball goes into one of them, you'll have a heavy lie. Location of your ball in the depression determines the type of shot you should hit. If your ball's on the upslope, take one more club; if it's on the downslope, take one less club and play the ball closer toward the right foot than you normally would.

If the ball's on the upslope, you should play it slightly more forward than usual. If the ball's in the bottom of the depression and the grass is heavy, you are going to get more topspin than usual. This should be taken into consideration when you are planning the shot.

Clumps of grass, uncut portions of the fairway, and patches of clover, all prevalent in the spring, contribute to what the touring professionals call flier lies. Sometimes a shot hit out of a flier lie will travel 20 to 30 yards farther than a shot hit with the same club from a more conventional lie. How do you guard against this?

If you have only a remote chance of hitting the green from your flier lie, take a more-lofted club than the distance to the green requires and play to the fairway for good position. If you have a chance of hitting the green from the flier lie, take one club less—a five-iron instead of a four-iron, for example. Be careful when addressing the ball in a flier lie lest you accidentally move it and suffer a one stroke penalty.

Most northern golf courses during the spring months permit "winter rules." But, in a strictly practice session, don't tee up in the fairway just because these rules are in effect. Always play the ball where it lies unless the lie is very bad. Even then, avoid extremes in teeing it up on the grass or selecting the spot to hit from. Taking preferred lies does a player's game more harm than good because this practice encourages a scooping action that is bad for one's game.

In the spring, the course may be sloppy, but that doesn't mean your game has to be. Actually, adverse conditions may make a better golfer out of you. Since the adoption of winter rules, many people have neglected to profit from the lessons to be learned from playing under adverse conditions. Don't feel if the ball isn't sitting pretty, what's the use? Learn to play the shots where they lie, if possible, and turn the unusual playing conditions to your advantage.

6. Par and Your Strategy

Every golfer, no matter what his handicap, goes out on the golf course looking to shoot or beat par, or, at the very least, to better his best score. Unhappily, all too few succeed. And it's not because they can't get the ball in the air. The amateur is usually too concerned with power and muscle. Power in golf is not a matter of great strength, it is a matter of timing. Take a look at Dean Refram, Chi Chi Rodriquez or Gary Player. These are all short or slight golfers who put a big stick to the ball. Essentially, power comes from utilizing what muscle you do have at the right moment. And it is usually acquired through exercise and practice. And yet, lower scores are less a matter of muscle power than brain power.

As we said in Chapter 1, golf is largely a mental game, a game played mostly between your ears. For example, a touring pro never just walks up to the ball and hits away. Then, again, neither do they freeze over the ball in confusion about what they want to do. Usually, they first go through a little examination. They think about the shot. They spend a little time deciding what type of shot they need, based on the distance, the obstacles (trees, traps, water, wind, etc.) and the lie, whether in the fairway, rough, or sand, sitting-up or buried. Only then do they select the club they think will do the job.

At this point, no matter what kind of shot is planned, have confidence in the club you choose. Don't second-guess yourself. To continually debate whether to hit a three-iron hard or to ease up on a four-wood is to guarantee disaster. Our advice here is simple—once you pick the stick, stay with it.

Of course it doesn't all end here. Once you've made your club choice, no matter what the shot, you picture what you want the ball to do, what it should look like, and where it will land. Then you let your swing produce that shot.

Now this may sound strange at first, but it really has a lot to do with maneuvering the ball on every shot you make. If you need to hit a hook, a slice, a high or a low shot, you must first change your imagination. Second, you must never think of the obstacles that may destroy the shot or of any trouble that might menace the successful execution. The clue here to pulling off the shot you've pictured is positive thinking.

This does not mean that the unskilled golfer should be encouraged to attempt professional gamble-shots—this is asking too much. And yet, where the professional plays with an eye on the percentages, the average golfer is out there swinging away, hitting, and hoping, and irrepressibly seeking to pull off that career-shot—the one he can brag about at the nineteenth hole. The plain fact is that most triple-figure golfers shoot these astronomical scores not because they can't get fours and fives, but because, in gunning and gambling for threes and fours, they take sevens and eights. Mr. Average Golfer scores like Mr. Average usually because he has forgotten the cardinal rule of keeping the ball in play. He has gotten himself in trouble because he's playing someone else's game and not his own, sacrificing the lower score he would have shot if he had played safely and within himself.

"Playing within yourself" means you must know your own game and its limitation. In golf, there's no point in fooling yourself. If you're not a professional, you're an amateur; and if you're an amateur, you're probably an average golfer. And an average golfer simply cannot be expected to play scratch golf. If you can admit that fact to yourself, you're on the way to knowing your game and playing in character.

One good method to genuine improvement and knowing your game is to estimate your own par before you step on the first tee this weekend. Par, for instance, for the 18-handicapper is not 72—it's 90.

Most courses have four short holes (par-three), four long holes (par-five), and ten other holes of varying lengths over which the scratch player's par is four. Therefore, the sensible amateur must figure the numbers printed on the card so that they come within his own abilities. For example, a long par-four will be a par-five for him—and if he gets a four he has, in effect, gotten a personal birdie. The same applies, of course, to those difficult par-three holes. They become par-fours for the average golfer. Now, using a little arithmetic on this imaginary game, you should reach the following conclusion. If you take four at all the short holes, fives at all the long holes, and fives again on all the par-fours, your total will be 86. That's playing 14-

handicap golf, and 14-handicap golf is a good deal better than average.

Just to realize your limitations is not enough, though. You must play within them on the course. However, too many amateurs play golf as figments of their own imaginations. They attempt shots that even the best professionals wouldn't dream of trying—shots that have no chance at all of succeeding. For instance: taking a two-wood from the rough, with the ball nestled down in four inches of lush grass; bouncing a sand wedge from ground baked as hard as fieldstone; or using a four-iron from a steep-lipped bunker.

Even when he doesn't go quite this far, the average player doesn't use his head as well as he might. Although less absurd, the following examples are still rather ridiculously dangerous. Let's say you hit a perfect four-wood from the rough but you're still left with another wedge to the green. It is best, even if you couldn't make it with one shot, to hit a certain six- or seven-iron from the rough and then hit to the green with perhaps the same club.

Then again, how many times have we seen players try to carry the ball beyond some distant water hazard, knowing (but ignoring the fact) that they could only make it with their absolute best shot. Unfortunately, best shots occur for the average player at the rate of never more than one in ten. The point here is, why ignore the law of averages? After all, the high-handicapper who goes for a 200-yard carry and lands in a bunker around the green, or in a stream or pond, is highly unlikely to score less than six. Yet he can almost always make five on such a hole with a couple of medium irons and a pitch. Overall, if the average player were never to try shots that would lead him into trouble unless the odds were 70–30 *in his favor* (not Arnold Palmer's odds), he would very soon be better than average.

To be more specific now in attacking a golf course, let's examine the strategy of each kind of golf hole.

Strategy and Par-Threes

We suppose that just about everybody who becomes pleasantly addicted to the game of golf becomes a Walter Mitty in two-toned gold shoes at one time or another and dreams of overwhelming the pros head to head. In his fantasy, Walter imagines himself booming a tee shot 25 yards past Nicklaus . . . flipping a high, biting wedge shot that spins back well inside Player's pitch to the green . . . stroking a

50-foot putt that runs smartly over two ridges, breaks sharply just as planned toward the hole, and plunks into the cup to close out the match with Sanders on the eighteenth green. Then he returns to reality and knows very well it was all a pipe dream. No matter how competent the amateur golfer is, he simply is not skillful enough to outdrive a Nicklaus or outpitch a Player or outputt a Sanders except with an occasional "miracle shot." And the duffer might as well forget it.

But wait. There is a place on the *average* golf course where even the player of mediocre ability could take on Arnold Palmer or any of the other touring pros and feel he has a chance to match or beat them. That's on a respectable par-three hole. Notice, we say, respectable. We object to the abnormally long par-three holes some course architects are designing these days and some that have been constructed in the past. More about that later.

The point is that all golfers, from the pro down through the weekend player of sufficient ability to get the face of a club on the ball and propel it in the direction of the green, can reach the putting surface of most par-three holes with the tee shot. Oh, the less-talented player of limited physical strength may need a three-wood on a hole that a pro reaches easily with a five-iron. How many times have you read about a golfer making a hole-in-one with an unlikely club, say a three-iron on a hole that normally calls for a seven-iron tee shot? It's not how it's done, but that it *is* done.

So, when he comes to a par-three hole of moderate proportions, the occasional player of modest ability gets a psychological lift. After scratching 6–7–6 on his scorecard for the last three holes, he steps onto the tee of the par-three hole, thinking: "Well, at least I ought to be able to get a 4 here . . . maybe even a par . . . make the score a little more respectable."

And he should—if he uses his head and doesn't waste the opportunity. Good judgment, as we said many times, is of the utmost importance in golf. Of course, good scoring begins with the proper execution of the shots, but a player can lower his score tremendously by using good judgment—and we mean constantly throughout the round. You have no doubt heard or read remarks of the pros, saying they "went to sleep" on a shot that resulted in a bad hole. They simply weren't thinking for the moment. Sometimes it resulted in a badly hit shot. Other times they used bad judgment in sizing up a hole or shot, or selecting the club, or evaluating weather or course conditions.

This is particularly important on the par-three holes. You have just

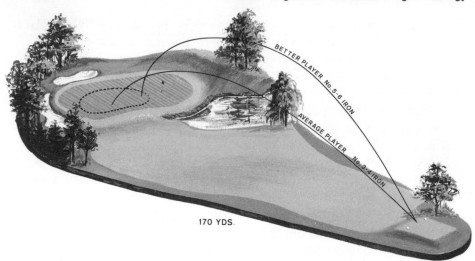

170 YDS.

The smart golfer on this 170-yard par-three hole will angle the shot to the safer left side rather than chance the right front water hazard. Good players may use a five- or six-iron while the average golfer will hit a three or four.

the one "full" shot on them. Make an error of judgment or execution and you have probably lost your chance for a par right then and there. On the longer holes, you still have another shot or two with which to rescue yourself from the first mistake. So, let's step onto the tee of an average par-three hole, one that calls for an iron shot to the green, and begin to exercise some of that good judgment.

Look for the trouble. It's a rare par-three hole that doesn't have some sort of hazard around the green—almost always sand traps, frequently heavy grass around the collar, severe slopes, occasionally ponds or streams. This should be weighed seriously in your mind as you select the club and plan your shot strategy on the hole.

Where is the worst trouble, and how bad is it? If you have severe trouble on one side of the green, you should consider how severe it is and try to protect yourself from getting into it. For instance, if there is a water hazard to the right of the green, you would be a little better off even to wind up in a sand trap on the left than in that water. So, naturally, the smart thing to do on such a hole would be to favor the left a little bit. This involves stance alignment more than anything else. Sure, the better player will be shooting for the pin practically all the time and, with his greater skill, will be more likely to hit the shot on target, but even he, if he uses good judgment, will be guarding against the severe trouble and trying to stay on the "safe" side. That is, the idea is simply to put your tee shot on the green; almost any place will do. The tee shot should be aimed to the "fat" part of the green; i.e., to a spot that involves the least risk of landing the ball in a nearby hazard.

Now that we have discussed the left and right sides, let's consider trouble in front of and behind the par-three green. Here we get into the matter of club selection. To make the point here, let's use as an example the fourth hole at Baltusrol Golf Club in New Jersey. This 183-yarder has trouble both front and báck. A three-foot stone wall girds the front of the green, threatening to ricochet a low shot back into the water, and directly behind the extremely large putting surface are three sand traps. Also the two-level green slopes toward the water hazard and narrows sharply to the right making the hole more difficult when the pin is placed in that location. Hitting against the prevailing wind into this double-tiered green can call for as little as a four-iron or as much as a three-wood. Most pros agree that on this course a golfer should hit for the traps in back, for more pars are made from there than from the pond side. That is, the thinking golfer, if he's in doubt about which club to use, will take the stick that may be "too much club" rather than one that might not be "enough club" and put the ball in the drink.

Speaking of putting a ball in the drink, it's a good confidence bolster, as we said earlier, to use a good ball on a water hole. Those players who promptly drag out a cut-up ball for a shot over the drink practically admit defeat before they swing. Use a good ball, perhaps

The 183-yard par-three at Baltusrol Golf Club.

even a new one, and swing away with confidence. Remember that those who *think* they'll pull off a good shot have a much better chance of doing it. Thus, a new or good ball can help build this confidence.

On most short and average par-three holes you should generally

The average golfer should realize that many holes are too rugged for him to hope for par. If a par-three hole calls for your absolute best shot to get home, then it's wise to play short and try for a good chip. The worst you'll make is bogey.

TARGET
AREA

160-180 YDS

200 YDS PAR 3

shoot for the green. Don't lay up to avoid trouble unless you can't reach it because of severe weather or because the hole is abnormally long for you. On these long backbreakers, it's generally wise to miss short, than to miss on either side where the hazards most often lurk.

Most average golfers don't really penalize themselves as much as they might think by playing short on *long* par-threes. Such golfers are usually better-than-average chippers, simply because they are forced to make more of these shots. Frequently they will chip close enough to par the hole by holing the first putt. Sometimes even the pros play safe on par-threes. The sixteenth at Cypress Point in California is a good example (see page 176 for layout of the hole). The way the wind usually blows into your face off the ocean, it's often foolhardy for even the top pros to attempt to play for the green across more than 200 yards of churning water. Unless the weather is unusually calm, it's more often than not a lay-up par-three. We know that many spectators, perhaps a little sadistic, seem to relish watching the pros gamble and lose at that hole as the balls drop into the whitecaps or

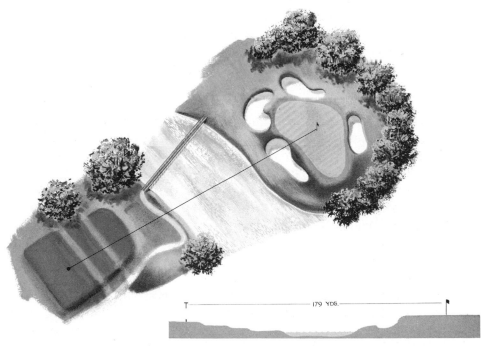

Some par-three holes, like the seventeenth at Medinah Country Club in Illinois, have problems front, back, and to the sides.

onto the beach below, or bury in that impossible iceplant on the hillside.

As for selecting the right club for more reasonable par-threes, we don't think the average player can be precise enough to club himself right to the pin unless, and this is unlikely, he has stepped off the yardage and knows exactly how the positions of the pin and tee markers affect the yardage. You can assume the yardage pretty much, though, from the locations of the tee markers and pins generally just by looking at them. The yardage the club lists for the hole is usually figured from the middle of the tee to the middle of the green, so you can then make allowances for the locations of the flag and tee blocks. You, as an individual, should know what club to hit for that particular yardage. If you are undecided about what club to use, select the longer club. Most average players, as stated earlier, tend to underclub on par-threes.

There are two or three other factors that enter in club selection. One, certainly, is weather, particularly the wind. Naturally, you will want to take "more club" if you are hitting into the wind and "less club" with the wind behind you, remembering, too, that the shot into the wind will stop more quickly than one with the wind, which tends to take off any backspin you may have imparted in making the shot. Since you can see the green easily from the tee of most par-threes, be certain to look there in calculating the wind velocity and direction. See how the flag on the pin and trees in the area are blowing. As your shot loses its velocity near the green, the wind will have its most pronounced effect, and that area sometimes will be more or less exposed to the weather than the spot on the tee where you are standing.

Consider, too, the relationship in elevation of the tee and green. The distance will be greater to an elevated green and less from an elevated tee. Naturally, the ball will go a little farther when you are shooting downhill because the ball will stay in the air a little longer. On the other hand, the ball, dropping at a greater angle, will tend to stop more quickly when hit from a tee higher than the green. Since these two differences tend to balance each other, the elevation will not make too much difference in club selection.

One final point of strategy. You should have some idea of the condition of the green—soft or hard. If you are hitting to well-constructed greens or in or just after wet weather, you can count on the shot holding the putting surface fairly close to where it lands. But, if you know or suspect that the surface is hard, you will be smart to

Weather conditions certainly influence the tee shot. Don't be deceived by a calm tee area. Look out to the green and carefully observe which way the flag is blowing. This should reveal the real wind direction and velocity. Since the wind here is from right to left, hit to the right side, letting the wind push the ball in as it descends.

WIND

TARGET
AREA

CALM AREA

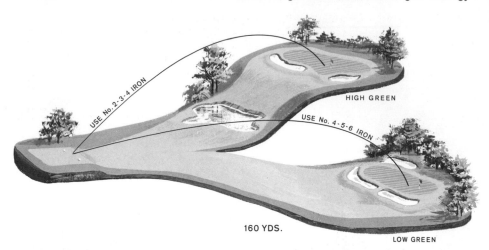

Shooting 160 yards to an elevated green or from an elevated tee to a low green requires thoughtful club selection. In general, to a high green use more club, and from an elevated tee count on extra carry.

select a club that will allow the ball to roll quite a bit and not go over the green or far beyond the pin. With the hole properly sized up, you are ready to make the shot, and, as they say, it's one thing to know how to do something and another thing entirely in being able to do it.

Most par-three holes require an iron shot; and in playing the iron, the average golfer could often make the shot a good deal easier for himself simply by playing the ball off a wooden tee. What the average golfer usually does instead is to toss the ball on the bare ground, give himself a good lie, and then play the shot as though he were hitting the ball off the fairway. Quite often, in addition, he will tee the ball up on a tuft of grass with the clubhead, thus nullifying almost any chance he had for attaining backspin. What you should do is place the ball on a wooden tee which has been pushed into the ground as far as it will go. In effect, this places the ball level with the ground, yet leaves the ball on a firmer surface than the ground itself, giving you a better lie than you could possibly get in the fairway. This trick won't guarantee the success of the shot, but it will help. And no good golfer plays a shot without getting all the help the *Rules of Golf* allow.

We have discussed the strategy of iron play in Chapter 2, but we would like to stress here that most bad shots off the tee on par-three holes are missed because the golfer presses the shot and destroys the rhythm and arc of his swing. He is too fast with the backswing or tries to swing too hard into the ball.

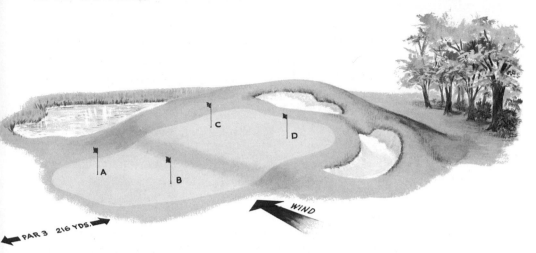

This par-three test can present different problems depending on wind, pin placement, and whether you are leading or behind. In any event, check out all possibilities, decide on a plan, forget what may have happened on previous holes, face up to the challenge with confidence. What would you do?

Take it easy. The face of the iron, contacting the ball firmly and with normal impact, will get you the distance for which the club is built. Just be sure you have enough club to get there, and then you won't feel the compulsion to overpower the shot.

Strategy and Par-Fives

Most playing professionals and scratch amateurs look on all par-fives as potential birdie holes and consider a par on many of these holes as a stroke lost, or at least a chance wasted to offset past or future bogeys in the round. But players of medium ability, usually shorter hitters, don't have to think often about getting home in two at a par-five hole. They usually can't do it and should concentrate on controlling that second shot. If they are facing a green guarded by a water hazard or even tough bunkering, they should lay up short in most cases. Otherwise, it will cost them strokes and perhaps a golf ball or two.

The average player should think mostly of position on that second shot, getting the ball in the best area short of the green to open up the easiest third shot to the pin. He can get his birdie that way, or at least make the par in relatively easy fashion.

Chop the normal par-five hole into three equal parts, and you have shots averaging about 175 yards that most duffers can handle and often less distance than each of the two shots on the normal par-four. On this basis, a par-five should be easier for the poorer player than the par-four. Yet, for some reason, the over-all length of the par-five hole seems to intimidate many duffers. They rarely manage pars on these holes, taking sixes, sevens, even eights instead.

More often than not, they get themselves in trouble with the tee shot. They figure they have to get off to a big start with an extra-long (for them) drive, so they overswing and wind up smothering the shot or whacking the ball off to the right or left into trouble. Then they compound the error by gambling out of the rough or trees or try to make up for lost distance on the topped drive by attempting to hit the ball with a wood out of the rough or uneven lie short of the cut fairway. Before they know it, they have taken four or five swings and still aren't on the green. By now they are upset and have little chance of being able to concentrate on the chip that could save at least one stroke or the putt that could do the same.

The way for the duffer to master the par-five hole is quite clear. He shouldn't try to get any more distance off the tee on the par-five hole than he does on the par-four but should, instead, try very hard to hit an adequate tee shot *into the fairway*. If he succeeds in that, he has

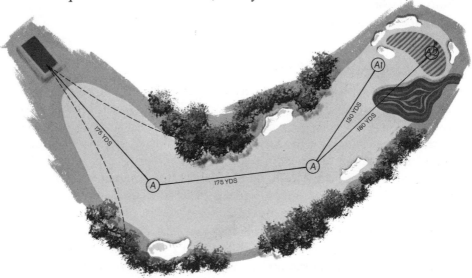

This 530-yard, par-five dogleg tempts the golfer to press for more distance and trouble (dotted lines). With the hole broken into three equal parts, the third shot is a matter of discretion: the discreet move (A1) gives you an easy chip for your par; a greater gamble (A2) lies in carrying the water and chancing a stroke penalty.

definitely saved one stroke and possibly two or three if the off-line or topped shot winds up in severe trouble that costs penalty strokes.

The same effort to avoid overswinging should be made with the fairway wood on the second shot. This is the shot that gives so many of the below-average players much trouble. Many of them tend to swing too hard and lift up as they swing. The result is the famous grasscutter that bounds along the ground maybe 50 or 75 yards. We've noticed that many women golfers of just average ability do better with their fairway wood shots than many men, mainly because they don't—really can't—swing as hard. With the easier swing, they seem to stay down with the shot and give the ball a nice little trip through the air straight down the fairway.

Even if the green is still not within reach after two decent shots in the fairway, and a lay-up third shot is necessary, the duffer still has the opportunity to get on the green with his fourth and either salvage a par with one putt or two putts for a bogey that certainly is better than jotting a seven, or eight, or even worse on the scorecard. For him, discretion is the better part of valor most of the time in a challenging situation, such as a 180-yard carry over a water hazard to the green. He can waste two or three good shots in a hurry by taking a gamble with his lack of top ability stacking the odds against him.

On most par-fives, there's usually plenty of room to drive. Take the famous eighteenth hole at Baltusrol. This is a fine and challenging 542-yard par-five dogleg left to an elevated green. If you aim to the right a little, there is plenty of fairway to hit. But if you're a gambler, the left-side short-cut is trouble. There's a stream there and heavy rough. Let's assume your drive is 200 yards out in the fairway. Your second shot poses a real thought-provoking choice. Should you aim to carry the stream that cuts across the fairway 200 yards away, or should you play short (175 yards) and have a third shot of about 170 yards? This is where knowledge of yourself and your game comes into play. If you've been hitting the ball well and you're confident, go for it. But if there's any doubt, play it smart—play it short.

Let's assume then that you've played it short of that stream. Since the elevated green slopes from left to right and then flattens out, with traps left, right, and front, pick out the worst spot you can be in. The answer is that left trap. If you're bunkered there, it's almost impossible to prevent the ball from skidding downhill across the green, and into another trap. Therefore, the best shot (regardless of where the pin is) is going right for the heart of the green. At least if you catch a trap

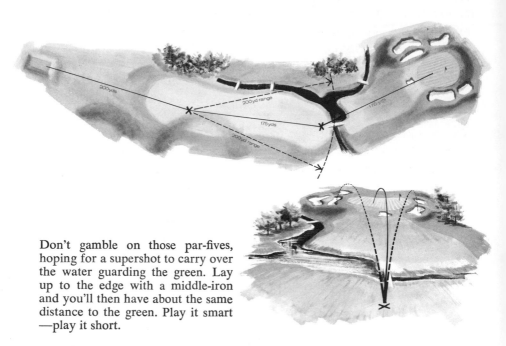

Don't gamble on those par-fives, hoping for a supershot to carry over the water guarding the green. Lay up to the edge with a middle-iron and you'll then have about the same distance to the green. Play it smart —play it short.

front or right, you'll have a blast shot against the slope of the green. Once again, it's all a matter of thinking of the possibilities, playing in character and playing the percentages.

While going toward the green, take a little time to study the approaches and greens on adjacent, advanced holes. That is, make special mental note of the flagstick placement, the size and slope of the putting surface, and the position of the hazards around the green. Plan where you'd like your second shot and where your third should be hit so as to leave yourself with the easiest possible putt. This advanced knowledge is especially helpful on par-fives where you'll be far from the green when you plan your second shot.

No matter how carefully the duffer plays, he will still get into the rough on occasions on the par-fives (and the par-fours, too, of course). This is when he should use his head to save strokes. In most cases, the ball will be nestled down in the deep grass. The player may still have 300 yards to negotiate, but he should resist the temptation to flail away with a wood in such a tough lie, sacrifice distance by using an iron with sufficient loft to dig the ball out of the grass and get it back into the fairway. Such a shot will almost always be farther along toward the green than the one that is muffed with a wood and moves merely from one bad lie in the rough to another not many yards away.

By and large, what advice we have given to the average and below-average male golfer applies to many of our ladies of the links except, of course, the growing group of very capable girls and women players who can give many of the finer men a good tussle on the golf courses.

Strategy and Par-Fours

The long par-four is something nearer a par-five for the average player—so play for that five. But, when you come to a short par-four—a scoring home for you—play it the safe way if it is tightly framed by trees. Nothing is more demoralizing and self-defeating than to take six on a hole where you hoped for a three and were "convinced" of a four. Leave that big stick in the bag and drive with a four-wood or a three-iron. After all, a four-wood plus a six-iron add up to no more shots than a driver and a nine-iron. The safe way is to make sure you're going to get at least your par. Remember, when you finish, it's only the total on your scorecard that counts and not where you played the ball from, what club you took to do it, or how you swung.

When playing par-four holes, it is *very* important to plan your approach, or second, shot before hitting your drive. Too many golfers simply tee the ball up and hit aimlessly down the fairway. But by checking the flag position, you can aim your tee shot to one side or the other, depending on which will make the approach shot easier. For example, if the flag is positioned in the left corner of the green behind the trap, you would want to hit your tee shot down the right side of the fairway. This gives you a better angle for your second shot approach and more green to shoot for. In addition, look for level ground to use as a landing area when planning your drive, one that will give you a good stance for your second shot. True, you might have to sacrifice a few yards to avoid bumpy terrain, but even with a longer second shot you will be more accurate and will reach the green more frequently from the level lie. Thus by thinking about position every time you tee off, you might well save three or four strokes a round on par-fours. It will also be of value even when you miss a tee shot and roll it out there, because by being on the proper side of the fairway, you'll have a better chance to recover and maybe save par.

Cutting the corner on dogleg holes can, in some instances, save a few yards, but usually not enough to risk the gamble involved. Heavy rough, bunkers, or trees generally guard the corners of most doglegs, and you're taking an unwise risk to try to carry across all of these trouble spots. If the hole bends around the right, for instance, the general tendency for the average player is to attempt to fade the ball over the right side. However, on the average doglegs, it's far wiser to play away from the bend, to the opposite side of the fairway. From this position the green usually opens up for a clear shot, while the approach from the dogleg side of the fairway is often blocked by additional trouble near the green. That is, in our example, it's better to be on the left side with your drive so that you have the opening of the green to work with, instead of arcing a shot over a trap. And if you want to place your drive on the left side of the fairway, generally it's best to tee off from the right side of the tee. The same goes for the second shot on a long hole. Play it to the opening or the open side of the fairway. Be honest with yourself and realize that you can't be on the green with every shot, but make your mistakes the kind that can be recovered from.

On most par-four holes of more than 400 yards, and on nearly all par-five holes, you will want to take out your driver and go for maximum distance. But on many par-four holes in the 325–375

Use the tee position to your best advantage when driving at your target area.

range, you can assume that the design of the hole is such that there is some danger awaiting your drive. You can look for some sort of water, sand hazard, or narrowing fairway out there in the normal range of a big drive. When they make a hole easy as to distance, they usually make it tougher with hazards. This is why you see so many pros using long irons or fairway woods off the tee on short par-four holes. In fact, most golfers are more accurate with their shorter woods, and while they lose distance, they can obtain a better position

When the fairway is narrow, why not drop down to a four-wood off the tee? The chances of keeping the ball in play will be much greater, and it will only mean that you might have to hit a six-iron instead of a nine-iron for the second shot. Too many golfers go for broke with the driver on every hole, and it costs them strokes in the end.

on the fairway. Thus on your second shot you'll be hitting, say, a six-iron instead of an eight- or nine-iron, but you'll have obtained a better position while sacrificing just a little distance. The percentages of this strategy are all with you.

In addition, the use of lower woods is a good idea if you're having problems with your drives. It's far better to lose a little distance than to be in trouble with a driver. Solve your driver troubles out on the practice tee, not during play.

The second shot on par-four holes should always be aimed to the area with the least amount of trouble. Most greens have more trouble on one side than the other. By hitting away from trouble, you'll be in a safe position to get it up and down for a possible par or sure bogey. Hitting the ball straight for the pin generally brings you closer to the hazards, and anything less than a perfect shot will put it in the sand or water, practically eliminating a par and making a bogey anything but sure.

One of the trickiest situations when playing any hole, especially par-fours, is when you're playing to a blind green that is down behind a hill. Part of the problem, of course, is mental. You go up to the brow of the hill and decide what club to take, but by the time you get back to the ball, you've forgotten the exact distance and again toy with club selection. Even if you have grabbed the right club, you probably won't hit it right. You'll either give it too much or let up on the shot. The way to gain confidence in hitting this shot is to have a method which will help you determine the distance from the ball to the flag: Walk to the brow of the hill and note the pin placement. Say it is 100 yards

Method of hitting to a blind green.

from the brow of the hill to the pin. Judge what club it would take to go from this point to the hole, taking into consideration you need less club when you are hitting down to a green. In this case, you would perhaps select a nine-iron. As you walk back to the ball, be pacing off the distance and walk back along the line between the pin and your ball. Let's assume it's another 30 yards. That's approximately three clubs more. So, in this case, you would take your six-iron. Now, forget everything except the line. Hit the shot you intend, and let the club do the job.

As you can see, attacking a golf course for the lowest possible score demands more than strength, timing, and a repeating golf swing. You must: (1) Know your own game; (2) Know your limitations; (3) Play within them; and (4) Think! And you must never forget that the name of the game is "Keep the ball in play."

Strategy Designed for You

The information on playing the various par holes is generally good regardless of handicap. Golfers of all shapes, sizes, and handicaps take lessons on the practice tee to improve their swings, and to learn the mechanics of various shots. Very few, in comparison, will ever go out on the course with their professional and take a *playing lesson*—perhaps because they don't realize how valuable it is.

Golfers who take time for a playing lesson invariably find that their score for nine holes is several strokes better than their average. Some of this improvement, no doubt, can be attributed to the friendly encouragement of the pro, but what really makes the difference is that they are buying the pro's playing "know-how." Actually, there's much more to playing "scoring" golf than merely swinging well. Many golfers will tell you that learning how to play a course is just a matter of "experience." But what they don't tell you is that the playing lesson is the short cut to that experience. It's like "on-the-job" training in golf.

There's something to be gained from a playing lesson for any golfer —regardless of handicap. Let's take the Class "A" player, who has a handicap, say, between scratch and seven. This player usually can hit the ball hard and fairly consistently. His biggest problem is not so much how to hit the ball, but making his golf skill pay off on the course. It comes down to course management. Where should he hit the ball and with what club? He can learn more from a few playing lessons than if he hit balls on the practice tee every day as often as does Trevino. Often the "A" player has the ability to maneuver the ball, but rarely explores to the fullest his actual potential—such things as consciously drawing or fading the ball, or keeping it high or low. The "A" player can also make the course play easier by hitting the ball over corners or fairway traps. Sometimes, by sheer conservatism, an "A" player blows three to four shots a round.

The "B" player's problem (say 8–14 handicap) is usually in the area of overconfidence in his power to hit a golf ball. For example, how many times have you seen a "B" player watch an "A" player crack a two-iron onto a long par-three, then hit a two-iron himself and leave it fully 15 yards short of the green? In a playing lesson, the pro would tell him to take a four-wood.

The "C" player (15 handicap and above) is the one who is usually besieged by golf theory and is constantly experimenting on the golf course with any number of swing nostrums. He doesn't know which of his "swings" to use and, in the end, he forgets the primary purpose of the game, namely, to "hit the ball."

The most valuable lesson to be learned from a round with your pro is that, while you are playing a course, you must make the best use of whatever degree of golfing skill you possess. If there's one thing it doesn't pay to kid yourself about, it's your golf game. Here you will see how representatives from these three levels of skill—the class "A," "B," and "C" players—should utilize their golfing ability in playing actual golf hole situations.

A PAR-FIVE HOLE

On the illustrated par-five dogleg to the right (opposite), the player has driven to this position some 190 yards from the flag by the direct route. Now he must decide how much water, if any, he should try to carry on his second. The "C" player's choice is limited by the distance he can hit the ball, and the fact that he doesn't strike it solid every time. The pro would tell him to pick a club that would get him to the spot marked C. With his next shot, he can then get on or near the green. The "B" player can be a little more ambitious—but not too ambitious. He should hit to the point marked B, well left of the tempting short route to the pin. The pro would advise a club that is certain to carry the "B" player's ball over the water—even if he mis-hits it a little. He will then have no more than a short-iron to the green. The "A" player has the hardest choice. He has the ability to go straight for it, to the point marked A, but hitting to a spot between A and B,

When faced with a problem like this, bite off as much as you can chew depending whether you are a Class "A," "B," or "C" player.

leaving only a short approach, is also good. The pro would advise a decision based on your lie and how you are striking the ball that particular day.

A PAR-FOUR HOLE

On the par-four, 400-yard dogleg right (page 154), pro directed "A" player to shoot over trap (out about 190 yards) to make second shot shorter (line A). "B" player, pro observed, could not carry trap for certain, but the brook was no problem. He should try to drive onto top of plateau, left (line B). He'll have flat, elevated lie for second, which would make up any distance lost by driving left, and leave open shot to green. Pro told "C" player to play short of the brook, as his average

Plot your attack on this par-four according to your ability.

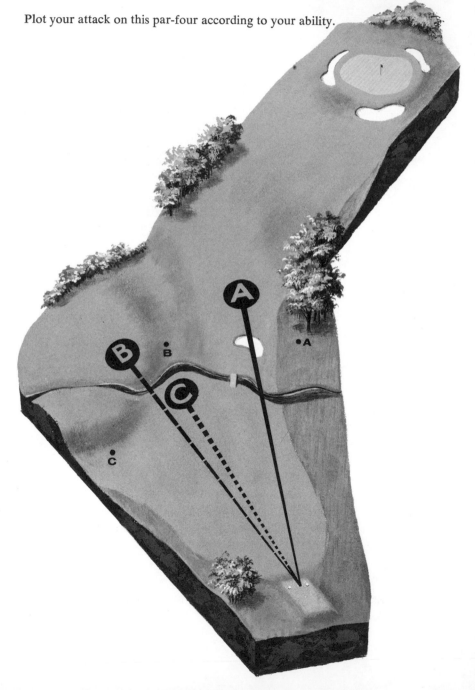

drive might drop in. He should play for a personal par of five on this hole. Unfortunately, players missed their targets, but, with pro's advice, each came out of the hole in good shape. The following tells how the pro helped them on their shots.

Class "A" Player. "A" player landed in right rough, with trees blocking his second shot. He had a four-iron in his hand to chip it safely back in the fairway, when the pro pointed out he was lying well, and should attempt to cut the ball around the trees onto the green. Even if the shot did not fade enough, he would be nearer the green than if he played it safe. Had the lie been poor, then chipping out would have been wise. To cut ball, draw left foot back slightly from the line, "weaken" the grip, and restrict hip turn, so you feel you're hitting with shoulders and arms only.

Class "B" Player. "B" player missed the plateau and wound up on a lie with the ball below his feet (point *B*). He realized that hitting from this lie, the ball would tend to fade. He, therefore, took up his stance slightly to the left of target to allow for this. The pro advised him to play short of the traps protecting the green, from where a good chip could get him his par (it's difficult to catch it flush from this type lie). Stand closer to the ball, the pro said, with knees well flexed. Above all, stay down on the shot. Otherwise, you'll hit it thin or top it.

Class "C" Player. "C" player pulled his ball short and left of his target area, leaving him behind a large mound. He grabbed his four-wood, thinking he must gain as much distance as possible. The pro stopped him, pointing out that even if he hit the shot perfectly, it was doubtful he could clear the mound with that club. And if he hit the mound, his ball might wind up in the brook. The pro advised him to take a more lofted club, which would put him in position for a short iron to the green. He should, however, aim to the left side of the fairway, to open up the green.

A PAR-THREE HOLE

The three-par (page 156) is 175 yards long, trapped front and left, with a deep grass bunker to the right. The green slopes from left to right and from back to front. The pro told the "A" player to have confidence in his ability, and go straight for the flag, but to aim a little left to allow for the left-to-right break (line A). He advised the "B" player to aim for the center of the green (line B), to avoid going over the trap or risk going into the grass bunker, right. The "C" player was advised by the pro to take a similar line (line C), but a little more left to allow for his tendency to slice. With no trouble at the back of the green, the pro advised the "C" player to take enough club to avoid the trouble short of and to the sides of the green. Both the "B" and "C" players could expect their balls to break right because of the left-to-right break on the green, so they should be in good position. Let's follow the action.

Our three "class" players hit to a target on a par-three.

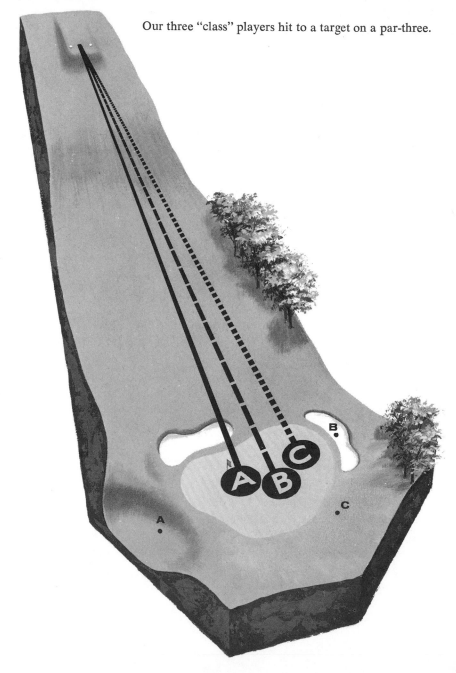

Class "A" Player. The "A" player pushed his iron right, landing in the grass bunker. He was faced with a shot that demanded that he get the ball up more quickly than on a normal pitch shot. The pro advised him to take his most lofted club—his sand wedge—and to play the shot slightly to the right of the pin to allow for the right-to-left slope from the back of the green. With a good lie, the pro said, play it from an open stance, position the ball off the left heel, and open the clubface a fraction. Hit well down on the ball, and it will "jump up quick."

Class "B" Player. The "B" player pulled his ball left and buried it deep in the left trap. He was all set to play a normal trap shot with his sand wedge—open face, open stance, and slightly outside-in swing. However, the pro warned him that this technique could not get the ball out of a buried lie, because the flange would "bounce" off the sand, causing a skulled shot. Take a square stance, and close the clubface, so that the leading edge digs well under the ball. The shot won't bite, so aim for a spot halfway to the pin, and slightly left, to allow for the break.

Class "C" Player. The "C" player hit his shot so well he carried right over the green. He faced a downhill chip to the pin, which would break from left to right. To control the ball better on the downhill slope, "C" decided on a pitching wedge. However, the pro pointed out the slope wasn't severe enough to demand a pitching wedge, and anyway it was far too delicate a shot for him to attempt. Take a five-iron, the pro said, and run the ball. This is much safer as it's much easier to fluff a wedge shot than a five-iron chip. As the fringe was too long, he shouldn't use a putter.

How a Champion Puts Strategy to Work

To study golf strategy at work, we sent Oscar Fraley, *Golf* magazine's contributing editor, to the Doral Country Club in Miami, to record, in addition to his stroke-by-stroke play in a competition, Arnold Palmer's comments on the way he played each hole. The Doral is one of the toughest golf courses in the United States, and the No. 2 course—on which the event was held—has been dubbed by the PGA touring professionals as the "Blue Monster." The day was sunny, but there was a 25-mile-an-hour wind. Here is the stroke-by-stroke play with Palmer's comments in italics. (The 18 holes are illustrated on pp. 159–161.)

No. 1, 533 yards, par five: Gently rolling terrain, with traps on the right at 225 yards; four traps surround the green plus a large trap 50 yards in front of green on the right; line of small trees bordering center of left rough.

Palmer, with a cross tailwind from left to right, hooked too severely and finished in the left rough 10 feet behind a bare-limbed tree on hard sand. Without hesitation he selected a four-iron, played a hook to the right of the tree, the ball curving into the opening to the green 25 feet short of the flag. His first putt was barely three inches short, and he dropped the putter at his feet and turned away before going up to tap it in.

I tried to keep away from that trouble on the right and also to get into position for a clear shot to the green. There was no doubt in my mind that the four-iron was my shot, and it came off perfectly, if just a little short. I thought I had that putt for an eagle but, even so, you can't knock a birdie.

No. 2, 366 yards, par four: Heavily trapped at 225 yards on the right, with a mound on the left at the same distance. Slight dogleg to right forces direct route to green over three traps.

Driving long and straight down the middle in a quartering right-to-left wind, Palmer was 70 yards short of the green. His wedge-shot second was dead to the pin but rolled 20 feet past to the back fringe. Sizing up the putt carefully, he rolled it in for a birdie three.

The drive and the wedge were ordinary shots, but that putt really made me feel good. You sink one like that, and it really makes you feel good.

No. 3, 402 yards, par four: A dogleg to the right in which most of the fairway is bordered on the right by a lake extending right up to the green.

Hitting into the wind, Palmer's drive was down the right side, flirting with the lake and stopping behind a widely spaced line of palm trees along the shore. His second shot, through this giant picket fence, again was strong and ended up 25 feet past the pin. Palmer's up-putt was a foot short, and he ran it down for a par.

I was going to hit a six-iron on that second shot, but I was afraid that the ball might fly. So I took a five-iron and tried to choke it down. I guess I didn't choke it down quite enough.

No. 1: 533 yds., par 5.
He missed eagle putt.

No. 2: 366 yds., par 4.
His 20-foot birdie putt dropped.

No. 3: 402 yds., par 4.
Two putts for a par.

No. 4: 225 yds., par 3.
He three-putted for five.

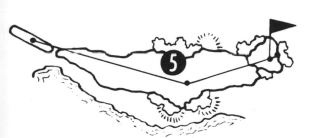

No. 5: 374 yds., par 4.
A par here with two putts.

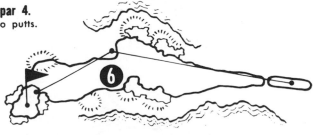

No. 6: 437 yds., par 4.
Birdie putt was six-inches short.

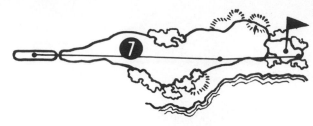

No. 7: 427 yds., par 4.
Another birdie putt miss.

No. 8: 528 yds., par 5.
Palmer canned long eagle putt.

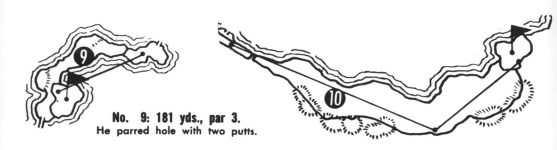

No. 9: 181 yds., par 3.
He parred hole with two putts.

No. 10: 496 yds., par 5.
Three putts but still a par.

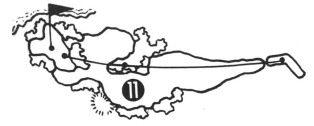

No. 11: 361 yds., par 4.
He got the par using two putts.

No. 12: 608 yds., par 5.
Three putts from fifty feet for a six.

No. 13: 246 yds., par 3.
Another bogey, and two more putts.

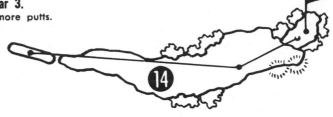

No. 14: 419 yds., par 4.
His birdie putt stopped on lip.

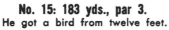

No. 15: 183 yds., par 3.
He got a bird from twelve feet.

No. 16: 379 yds., par 4.
Only one putt for the par.

No. 17: 426 yds., par 4.
Missed bird from four feet.

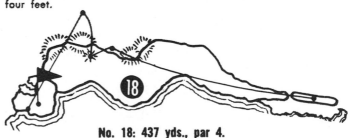

No. 18: 437 yds., par 4.
A closing bogey with two putts.

No. 4, 225 yards, par three: Carry over water to a narrow green with postage-stamp apron in front and traps in rear. Safe route to left avoids lake but requires extra stroke to reach the green.

With a following wind, Palmer's tee shot fell short, just missing the water and ending up on a narrow rocky beach 40 yards short of the pin. His chip shot skidded 40 feet past the flag. The first putt was four feet short and to the left, and he missed the second three inches to the left for a double bogey five.

The key to my trouble here was my failure to judge the wind properly and thereby selecting the wrong club for my tee shot. I wanted to hit a four-iron, but after a great deal of indecision, because the wind was blowing so hard at that moment, I dropped back to a five-iron. The wind tailed off just a bit as I hit it, and I fell short on the beach. There, off the stones, it was impossible to hit a well-judged chip even with the wedge. As if that wasn't bad enough, I played the up-putt too soft because the green ran downhill toward the water and looked slick and fast. And how do you explain missing a four-foot putt?

No. 5, 374 yards, par four: A dogleg to the left, with extensive traps on both sides of the fairway in the 225-to-275-yard range and with traps both in front of and behind the green.

Palmer blasted a low wind-cheater straight down the center of the fairway. His second was dead on the pin but rolled 20 feet past. The first putt was a bare two inches short of the hole, and he shook his head but remained expressionless.

Hitting straight into the wind, I kept my drive low and straight, without trying to hook or fade. The second shot usually would have been a wedge but, because of that high wind, I punched a seven-iron and got just a little too much of it.

No. 6, 437 yards, par four: Dogleg to the left, well-trapped on both sides of the fairway at the 225-to-275-yard "pro range." Three traps around the green, but with an open approach.

The left-to-right cross-wind carried Palmer's drive to the right side of the fairway. His second was on the green, 25 feet short of the cup. The first putt was a scant six inches short of the hole, and he tapped it in stoically for a par four.

Johnny Pott, playing with me, hit a four-iron past the pin from just behind me. I figured the five-iron I hit would get me hole-high, but I eased off on it a little too much and left the ball short.

No. 7, 427 yards, par four: A series of traps on the right and one on the left at driving distance. Four traps surround the green.

Palmer unloaded on this one, and, with a following wind, passed the right side traps and ended up 50 yards in front of his rivals, Johnny Pott and Gary Player. They had to wait momentarily for the threesome ahead, which still was putting on the green. The gallery was restrained by a rope stretched across the fairway behind the drives of Pott and Player. Palmer walked ahead to where his drive rested on the far right side of the fairway and, while waiting his turn, stared off to the side where a three-year-old boy, holding his mother by one hand, was throwing stones into the lake. Palmer stood watching, a relaxed smile on his face. Then he pulled himself back to the business at hand, hitching up his trousers in that unconsciously characteristic gesture of placing a thumb knuckle on each hip. His second shot was 20 feet past the pin. He putted back six inches past, barely missing the cup for the fifth time in seven holes. He took a deep breath and expelled the air by puffing out his cheeks in mild exasperation as he tapped in his par four.

It was a good drive. But I hit the wedge shot too firmly in the following wind. What can you say about missing a putt like that?

No. 8, 528 yards, par five: This was the thrill hole, the tiger he tamed with an eagle. At driving distance a yawning pit of sand looms in front of a lake that encroaches from the left. Shoot to the right and another and broader lake stands between you and the doglegged path to the green nestling high on a seemingly unreachable plateau behind the water.

He "unloaded" on a drive that climbed low with the trajectory of a jet takeoff to escape the full fury of the wind and thus retained its power on descent. It bounded and clawed its way down the right side of the fairway, along the edge of the grasping rough, and finished a full 40 yards ahead of the others. It still was a long way to the green, some 235 wind-bucking yards and most of those across the lake. Then he derricked a three-wood from his bag with a flick of the wrist and addressed the ball with a stern concentration you could almost feel. It wasn't a particularly good lie. Yet not a bad one, either. He swung and there was a moment of craning silence followed by a rising roar from the crowd as the ball bulleted homeward. There sat the ball, 25 feet short of the pin, the manicured grass was sloping slightly upward as it meandered toward the shrunken smallness of the cup. Arnie crouched momentarily behind the ball, stepped up swiftly and stroked it smoothly toward the hole. There was a swelling crescendo of acclaim as it dropped.

It was a "go for broke" spot all made to order. I had hit a good drive, and I had a decent enough lie. Pulling it off meant the difference in being in good shape or not being in good shape. It never even entered my mind that I might miss the shot. Even so, it gave me a big lift when I saw that ball stop on the green.

No. 9, 181 yards, par three: The entire hole is surrounded by water with a crescent-shaped fairway to the right. A full carry over water from tee to green, with a trap at the left side.

Palmer's tee shot was pin high and 20 feet to the right. Stroked evenly and with great concentration, his putt stopped a mere six inches to the right of the hole, and he shook his head slowly as he tapped it in.

Hitting into a quartering wind, I played a four-iron and it was the right club if a bit to the right. I thought I had that putt, but it just didn't break in quite enough.

No. 10, 496 yards, par five: A sharp dogleg to the left, bordered on that side by a lake clear to the green. Large mounds at intervals on the right.

Against a strong right-to-left wind, Palmer kept his tee shot low and to the right side. His second, from an uphill lie, was hole-high and 30 feet to the right of the cup. Hunkering down to study it briefly, Palmer stroked the ball two-and-a-half feet past. Coming back, he missed it to the right.

I hit a four-iron second shot to the green, and it was the right club, although the wind didn't bring it in as I thought it would. As for missing that short putt, most of the time you blow them because you were careless.

No. 11, 361 yards, par four: Slight dogleg to the right, with a full acre of sand on the right 245 yards from the tee, the green heavily trapped in front.

Palmer's drive hit that large tract of sand as he drilled his drive straight into the wind. With a level lie 125 short of the green, he punched a shot to the narrow green 20 feet short of the pin. The up-putt slid a foot past, and he knocked it in for his par.

The only question in my mind was whether to hit an eight-iron. But the wind was strong, so I decided to punch in a seven-iron. However, even that was short.

No. 12, 608 yards, par five: Well trapped on both sides at 225 yards and with a large sand waste area at 445 yards. The green has traps on three sides.

With the wind from right-to-left, Palmer drove a trap on the right side. He had a level lie, but there was a three-foot bank about six feet in front of him. His second was to the left side of the fairway 180 yards from the green. The third shot was hole high but 50 feet to the left of the flag. Palmer's first putt was eight feet past. As he stepped up to his second putt, a plane roared overhead, and he walked away and watched it into the distance. Then he missed it an inch to the right to take a bogey six.

I hit a five-iron out of the trap on my second to get in position for a shot to the green. Then I hit a three-iron and, with the pin in the neck of the green, it was a touchy shot. That first putt was a bad one; the kind you don't alibi even if you wanted to.

No. 13, 246 yards, par three: Four traps hug the green, with a large grass waste area in front of the apron.

With a following wind, Arnie's drive landed on the green but rolled to the back fringe some 40 feet from the cup. Chipping back, he left it eight feet short. His first putt slid past two feet on the left side, and he shook his head as he holed that one for a bogey four.

I hit a four-iron off the tee and, with the wind that was blowing, it was too much club. Then, because I had been putting rather erratically, I decided to chip back with a six-iron. I almost went with the putter but then figured I'd better try something different and was sorry I had when I left it so short.

No. 14, 419 yards, par four: A dogleg to the left with traps on both sides at 225 yards and four traps on both sides of the green.

Still with a following wind, Palmer lofted a high tee shot down the middle which finished 60 yards short of the green. His pitch was dead to the pin but 30 feet short. When he left his birdie putt on the lip, Palmer grimaced as he flipped his club to the caddie.

That tee shot felt good, just the way I wanted it. But the wind didn't take my wedge shot in as close as I thought it would. And when you keep missing those putts like that, you begin to wonder whether you're ever going to get a birdie again.

No. 15, 183 yards, par three: A broad, shallow green, well trapped in front, with a narrow entrance and a trap in the rear.

Palmer's tee shot, a hook into a left-to-right cross-wind, was hole high and 12 feet to the left of the flag. As he walked to the green, he winked at a friend in the gallery. Sizing up his putt carefully, he rolled it in for a birdie two and, leaning down, slowly took it out of the cup with mocking care.

I hit a six-iron just the way I intended and felt as I walked up there that I was going to make this one or bust. Up until then, I'd been wondering whether I was ever going to drop one.

No. 16, 379 yards, par four: A 90-degree dogleg to the left with extensive sand wastes starting at 225 yards, a large face trap in front of the green, a narrow entrance and two traps behind.

The tee shot had to be hit into a cross-wind from left-to-right, and Palmer gave the shot two big doses of body English as the wind caught the shot and carried it to the right side. With a downhill lie, 120 yards from the green and hitting dead into the wind, he knocked it to the back apron, to the right and 60 feet from the cup. His chip was three feet short and he knocked it home carefully for his par.

You certainly couldn't call that drive well planned, but on days like this you just have to keep plowing. On my second shot I hit an eight-iron too strong but then pitched it back pretty fair on the down-sloping green with that same club.

No. 17, 426 yards, par four: Traps on the right and a bunker and trap on the left at 225 yards. The green has one trap on the right and three around the left side.

Against a left-to-right cross-wind, Palmer hooked his tee shot down the middle 150 yards from the green. He grinned widely at the cheer when his approach shot curled in four feet short and to the left of the pin. But he frowned when his birdie putt slipped four inches past, and he had to settle for a par.

Normally I would have hit an eight-iron on that second shot. But I punched a six-iron to keep it down out of the wind. With this kind of shot you have to figure both wind and distance. I try to figure the distance first and play the kind of shot which will be least affected by the wind, although the lie, of course, dictates a lot what the shot will be.

No. 18, 437 yards, par four: A dogleg to the left; the fairway has a lake on the left which extends all the way to the green. The right side of the green has a large trap.

Palmer attempted to hook his drive but the hook didn't take and, as the wind carried it down the right rough, he exclaimed, "Look out there, ball." The drive ended in a hard-packed sand roadway where he had an uphill lie 200 yards from the green, with a small tree 30 yards in front of it. His second shot struck the tree and caromed off it to the right and into the adjoining fairway 100 yards from the green. His third shot, dead into the wind, went 40 feet past, and he knocked it in for a bogey five and an even par-72 round.

On my second shot, my alternative was to lay it up and then pitch to the green, but I wasn't about to do that. In this game, it's all or nothing. So I took a one-iron and, well, hit the tree. Then I hit a four-iron to the green.

His Card

Par out	544	344	453—36
Palmer out	434	544	433—34
Par in	545	343	444—36—72
Palmer in	546	442	445—38—72

I wouldn't say it was a brilliant round by any means. But from the time I started, it was one of those days when I couldn't get myself pulled together. So I had a poor round.

A poor round for Arnold Palmer—even par.

7. Good Strategy and Percentage Golf

It's the golf professionals' business to watch and to analyze. In other words, they profit by each other's mistakes. Making spectacular shots is their business. And yet, if you, too, will analyze the games of the various professionals under tournament conditions, you'll find that they are hitting the shots they know they can hit. Only in the clutch, when he has to gamble or toss in his cards, does a pro throw all caution to the winds.

On the whole, however, they play the percentages. And as we said so many times in this book, you should, too. Because it's an accepted fact that you'll make more pars and birdies out of the fairway than you will out of a trap. Make certain that gamble is going to pay off before you take it.

Let's play a hypothetical hole of 400 yards that has a ditch crossing the fairway at the 250-yard mark. Normally you'd expect to clear it with your drive—if you hit a perfect tee shot. If you did, you'd have only a nine-iron to the green. Yet if you hit short of the ditch by design, you still have only an eight- or seven-iron shot to the green. In this case, why take the risk of missing your drive just a fraction and hitting the ditch? What you are doing is gambling a stroke against a mere 20 or 30 yards. Now if getting over the ditch means a cinch birdie, that's something else again. Here you are equalizing your chances—picking up a stroke against losing a stroke. The case also would be altered if you left yourself a long-iron second shot by not clearing the ditch. Now, let's say, you are driving the ball well, but you aren't hitting your long irons too well. In this case, you might as well shoot the works because the odds favor a bogey in any event.

Gambling on your drive also can be predicated on where you expect your second shot to end up. Consider the thirteenth hole at the

Masters, a par-five hole with a ditch in front of the green where a gamble can really pay off. Here a good drive means you have a three-wood, let's say, for your second shot and a fine chance of holding the green. But if you drive short on this hole, you have to lay up short of the ditch and you have a downhill lie. This one you can easily wedge right into the ditch. The probability of that dangerous downhill wedge shot means that you have to tee it high and let it fly off the tee.

Augusta No. 13

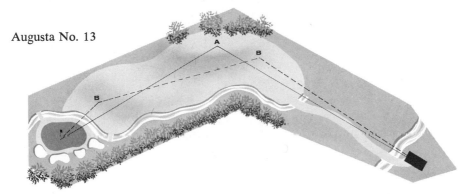

The fifth hole at Augusta National, where the Masters is played, is another gambling hole. This one is a dogleg left with a bunker on the left side. Now you can play it to the right side safely, but you leave yourself a full two- or three-iron to the green, always a risky shot. But if you gamble successfully with your drive, flirting with the left side, you wind up with only a five- or six-iron shot to the green. Here again the percentages are with you.

The average player merely hauls off and clobbers the ball, in most cases, figuring that the only thing he can do is get as much yardage off the tee as possible so that he's closer to home. But there is a right and a wrong way to play every hole, and a little study of the trouble side should convince you that the shortest distance between two points isn't necessarily a straight line . . . not in the par and birdie department.

Position Is Everything

We would like to discuss the holes that have stood out in the mind of *Golf* magazine's instruction editors as some of the toughest in the United States. The reason is that it will help you see how you should plan your attack with a minimum of gamble for a maximum of success. Forgive us if the yardages in all instances aren't exact because we're playing them from notes given to us by our experts.

The first is a 425-yard layout at New Orleans that has trees to the right and a bunker guarding the left front of the green. Play a fade here and you're really in trouble because you're either under the trees or you have a long second shot over the bunker. Ideally, you should play the right side, with a slight hook to make certain you don't run down to the right, thus leaving you an opening to the green. It sounds simple, but it's the type of hole that seems to act like a magnet to draw your ball far to the right and into trouble.

For our second hole, we would take the 510-yard second at Pebble Beach. The short way home is up the left side because there's a ditch in front of the green, and from the right side you're hitting to the skinny part of the green. Here you have to hit a good drive up the left-hand side, which puts you in position to clear the ditch on your second. From the right side, there's nothing to do but lay up and then pitch to that skinny target. The drive, as you can see, is the key shot.

Pebble Beach No. 2

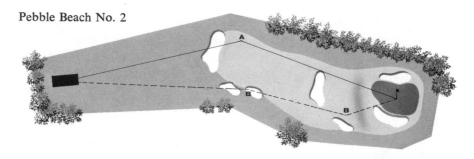

As our toughest third hole, we'd pick Firestone Country Club at Akron, Ohio, where the American Golf Classic and the World Series of Golf are held. This one is a 450-yard back-breaking four-par where your drive must be to the left or center to have a four-iron second or longer to the green. Hit the right side and there's no way you can shoot at the green on this dogleg monster. Again, it's the placement of the tee shot which is the key because if you wander up the right side you've had it—a bogey that is.

Our fourth hole is at Westchester Country Club in Harrison, New York, another lulu. It's about 420 yards with a blind tee shot up over a hill, a big dip in front of the green, which is small, and trouble to the left. Here you have to hook your tee shot to make certain you hold the

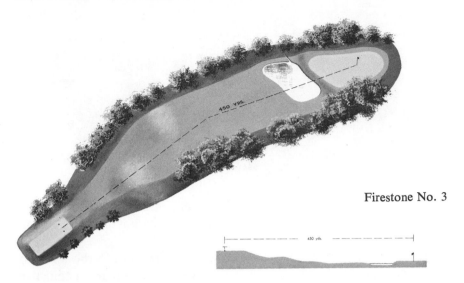

Firestone No. 3

left side, opening up the green. Put it on the right side and, while you have a shot at the green, you also can be shooting straight at that trouble on the left side. Here you are striving for the position that will make your second shot less of a gamble. (This hole is *now* the thirteenth at Westchester, but when our experts played there during the Thunderbird it was the fourth.)

You'd have to search a long way to beat the fifth hole at Colonial, in Fort Worth. It's 459 yards, a dogleg right, with a river on the right and a ditch on the left. The prevailing wind makes this a real long hole. Blueprinting this one, we'd sacrifice distance for accuracy, taking a three-wood to just cut around the corner. Even so, you still have a four-wood or a long three-iron for your second. But it's murder

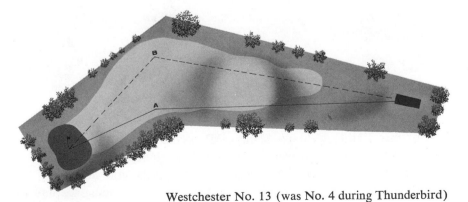

Westchester No. 13 (was No. 4 during Thunderbird)

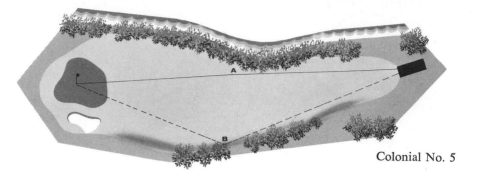

Colonial No. 5

on the left side, with tall grass and overhanging branches, and from there you still have to hook the ball to get in any kind of decent position.

The par-four, 390-yard sixth hole which stands out in the minds of our experts is the one at Atlanta's East Lake Course. It's a four-iron shot to a green surrounded by water, and if you hit the left side you can spin back down into the drink. There's also a big bunker in the back of a long green for the poor unfortunate who uses too much stick. No matter where the pin is, you have to cut the ball into the right side of the green, and it's really a finesse shot.

The seventh at Augusta is only about 365 yards, which makes it sound as if it should be a very easy hole to par. But while it's short it still is a very difficult hole, straight but uphill with trees on both sides and a severely trapped, elevated green. On top of this, the green is usually hard, and the pin is placed in front. There are always more bogeys than birdies on this baby. The second shot, usually with a wedge, should be played to land on the front edge of the green.

Augusta No. 7

For our eighth, we'd go back to Pebble Beach, about 450 yards uphill to a blind green, well bunkered. The right side of the fairway slopes to the ocean, and there's a ravine 150 yards wide in front of the green. Complicating matters is the wind. Here it's a must to play up the left side. Next you have to decide what to play into that wind. Most pros use a four-iron, but when wind is stiff, they go to a three-wood.

Pebble Beach No. 8

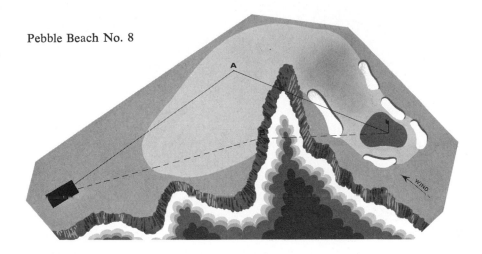

Stay right there at Pebble Beach for the ninth hole, which also is about 450 yards but can play like 500. It's an easy driving hole, within reason, but your second shot is to a green below that has water behind and to the right and a king-sized bunker to the left. Most pros never hit less than a drive and a two-iron here and generally you have to play two wood shots. In this case, it's just haul off and say a prayer.

For the tenth, we'd select the 496-yard par-five tenth at Miami's Doral Country Club. This dandy is a dogleg to the left with water inside the dogleg. You can flirt with the left side here and set up a birdie with a three-wood or three-iron to the green, shooting over the water. But if you have the wind in your face, take the safe way by firing up the middle or even to the right. Then you can safely play short of the green and hopefully put your wedge to work. The danger route is an almost certain birdie, or a well-watered bogey if you can cut it too fine.

The eleventh at Augusta, about 445 yards, is another demon (see page 174). Here you have a lot of driving room, straight downhill, and playing the left side you have only a four-iron to the green. But there's a water hazard to the left, and the green curves into it. The way to play this is safely to the right, lay it up and chip on. Not as flamboyant but an awful lot safer.

Augusta No. 11

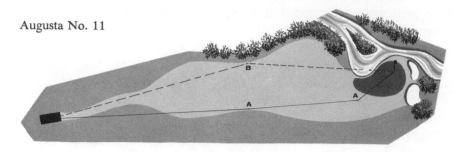

One of the most scenic and treacherous holes in the country is the short twelfth at Augusta. It's only about 155 yards, but there's a lake in front of a long, narrow green with a swale behind the green. Adding to the difficulty is the manner in which the wind swirls and shifts where this role is situated. Here you've got to hit a good six- or seven-iron with bite on it. The concentration is in hitting down and through the ball and, once again, saying a little prayer.

The thirteenth at Dunes Golf and Beach Club in South Carolina sticks out in the minds of our experts as one of the truly great holes. It is 560 yards alone and is a horseshoe-shaped affair that looks around Singleton Lake, one of the largest water hazards in the United States. The tee shot, which must be taken in a general direction away from the green, has to be straight and long, coming to rest approximately 220 to 240 yards out and near the lake's edge. Such positioning is necessary if the second shot is to be from an ideal setup. If you slice your drive, the ball will go into the water or the stand of bushes and trees that grow on the lake's edge. A hooked drive takes you too far away for a correct second shot. This second shot, by the way, is not easy since it requires a fairway wood (generally a three- or four-wood) to make it across the water. Then depending on how "brave" you were on the second, you can use anything from a three-iron to a seven- or eight-iron. This approach shot to the rolling thirteenth green is also demanding. This is *not* a gambling hole, and it should be played as safely as possible. Actually the ability of the player determines how the hole is played.

For the fourteenth hole, most pros still liked the old 440-yard layout at the now closed Tam O'Shanter. It's a straightaway hole, but there are trees lining both sides of the fairway with a fairway bunker at the 225-yard mark. The green is well bunkered with four traps coming out on the left front and only one on the right side. You can carry the bunker in the fairway, but you have to favor the right side for a second shot that can be anything from a three- to a five-iron. But, from the right side, you only have that one bunker with which to contend, and any time you have a chance to minimize the trouble between you and the green, that's the way to go.

We seem to keep returning to certain courses, and heaven knows that there are great holes on practically every course the touring pros play, but we had to go with the ones which stand out in our experts' minds. Ask about a fifteenth hole, and we must go back to Augusta, a 530-yard five-par. This is one hole that many pros like to attack. There's a lot of driving room, but there's water in front of the green with the fairway sloping down steeply to it and mounds require a fairly careful shot. There's also water in the back with a damaging downslope, and a trap to the right. You can play it safe with a five-iron short of the creek in front of the green, but then you have that ever dangerous downhill lie for your wedge shot—an easy one to drop into the water. In this case, many pros think it's time to gamble, so they go to the three-iron or more for a shot at the green. It's a calculated risk because of the dangerous lie you might get on your layup shot.

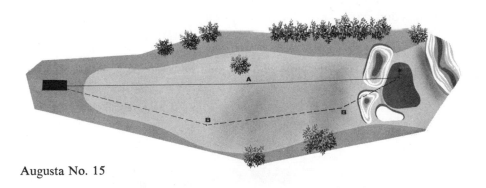

Augusta No. 15

Let's go back to Cypress Point again for the sixteenth, a par-three of about 225 yards (see page 176). The large green makes an inviting target, but you have to shoot over a ravine where the ocean comes in. You can make it with a three- or four-wood, but you're flirting with disaster. Much better to play a three- or four-iron to the left, laying up so that you only have a 40- to 80-yard wedge shot into the flag. Discretion here is much the better part of valor.

For the seventeenth hole, it's a return to Firestone and, while only 390 yards, a real great four-par. It's an uphill hole with four bunkers

Cypress Point No. 16

on each side at the driving distance. Go ahead, unlimber your driver, and if you hit it absolutely on a string, you'll get up to or past those bunkers and have a possible birdie pitch to the green. But the odds are that you'll wallop it right into one of those traps and, by the time you get to the green, you're laying three. It would be wiser, therefore, to play a three-wood just short of the traps. Then it's a four- to a six-iron to the green, which slopes both ways. Don't just settle for the green. You hit to the side on which the pin is placed, and you don't have that tricky camel hump to negotiate.

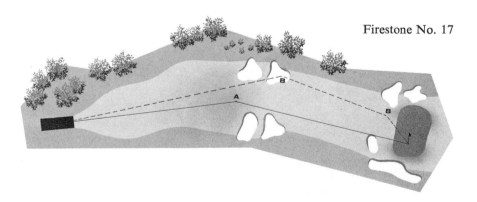

Firestone No. 17

For our eighteenth, we'll go back again to Doral, which has a closing hole of about 440 yards that is a real dilly. There's water all the way down the left side and a quick little dogleg into the green that is elevated slightly and runs from right to left. Here's the lure: go down the left side, and you're saving distance and have anywhere from a nine-iron to a five-iron across the water to the green. Go down the right side, and you're safe. You'll have to hit a wood for your second, and playing it right all the way you won't catch the water. But you won't make any birdies either, in all probability.

Doral No. 18

But let us repeat that there's a time to gamble and a time not to gamble. Go back to that seventeenth hole at Firestone, and you'll see how silly it is to try to pull off a perfect shot when there's no necessity for it. There are many, many times when it's smarter to lay up short of a well-bunkered green than it is to go for the whole ball of wax and fall flat on your face.

Position is one of the most important phases of golf, even if you have to sacrifice distance in the process. Watch how many pros use a three- or even a four-wood off the tee to get that pin-point position. That's why we suggest you quit trying to pull off the perfect shot and play the safe one you know you can handle. Don't gamble unless the percentage is in your favor. It's better to be short of a trap than in it and, if you'll blueprint your round to avoid the hazards instead of challenging them, we're sure you'll see a tremendous difference in your game.

Charting Your Course

Sure, Jack Nicklaus is a great golfer. This man is not only a superb striker of the golf ball, he also knows, as previously stated, how to play the course—any course for that matter. Actually, one of Jack's trademarks is the pad of paper he always totes around with him during practice rounds. He records how he is going to play each shot from the tee through the green. Jack's great distance could have been a disadvantage to him, if he hadn't learned early in his career how to think out his rounds of golf—and we might add this is reminiscent of another all-time great strategist, Ben Hogan.

Today almost all your Tour players use some type of charting system to speed up the learning process about the course and to avoid depending too much on memory. On your own home course, it's not necessary to carry a chart of play, but we strongly suggest that you make a pro-type charting at least once on your regular golf course. You'll probably learn some significant facts that you haven't realized, and the training method will certainly help you when playing on a strange course.

Start your charting right at the first hole. Check the scorecard for distance and carefully survey the terrain of the hole with particular emphasis on where you wish to place the tee shot. Then formulate your *tentative* strategy. This plan, of course, is subject to change as play progresses. Sometimes your first judgment is confirmed, or your strategy may have to be revised as you get a closer and better look at the hole while walking to it. Further revisions may even be necessary after you have reached the green or you have finished the hole.

The easiest part of charting a golf course—but most important—is determining the yardage to a green from a location near which you will normally be playing your second shot. Say that the hole is 380 yards, and you figure you have driven 220 yards (your average drive from a tee). Thus your estimate of the second shot would be 160 yards. To confirm your estimate, pick out a tree, bush, or some other fixed object that is nearly alongside your drive, and pace off the dis-

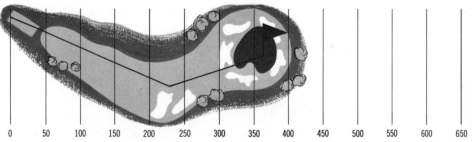

0   50   100   150   200   250   300   350   400   450   500   550   600   650

A typical chart for a par-four hole

tance to the center of the green. Say that it comes to 157 yards. Make note of this fact on your scorecard, or in a small notebook that you can carry just for this purpose. Then in subsequent rounds all you have to do is to step off the yardage from your drive to your 157-yard-to-go mark and add to or subtract from that yardage as indicated by the position of your tee shot to exactly where you are at.

Chart all bunkers, water hazards, trees, bushes, deep rough, and particularly out-of-bound lines either in writing or mentally. The basic idea here is to calculate the margin for error for any shots you must take. In your notebook record all the basic data about the green, too. In other words, when you have completed your chart of the first hole, you have *all* the necessary information to determine your strategy regardless of where the ball is at.

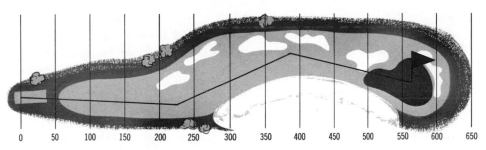

| 0 | 50 | 100 | 150 | 200 | 250 | 300 | 350 | 400 | 450 | 500 | 550 | 600 | 650 |

A typical chart for a par-five hole

You should use the same method of charting for the remaining 17 holes. On par-fives that you don't feel that you can reach in two, measure from a point where your second shot is most likely to be. On par-three holes, measure from some particular fixed location on the tee, so you can make your calculations based on the placement of the tee markers. The scorecard gives the basic yardages on these holes, but it must be checked.

Speaking of scorecards, do you throw them away in disgust after a particularly bad round? Don't do it! Those double and triple bogeys staring up at you with scorn may eventually help you to lower scores.

Every average golfer has certain holes that "bug" him. The procedure some players have used with success is simply to think hard about these nightmarish holes, and play them over and over in their mind—not just while standing on the tee waiting to drive, but at home, on their lunch hour, or in any spare time.

Some golfers go even a step further. They draw a chart showing name of course, hole number, par, and the scores they have made. Naturally they disregard the holes they parred or bogeyed with any regularity. The chart is important because it keeps them constantly aware of the dismal scores and reminds them to picture each hole more vividly and study it oftener. Determination to improve is increased because marking a par or a bogey on the chart where higher figures once prevailed is quite a thrill.

In some instances when a hole seems to have put a complete whammy on them, they draw a large-scale rough sketch of it, marking in all hazards and estimated distances. This visual study permits them to improve their selection of the proper club to ˙use from various locations on the fairway.

Remember that the golfer who learns all he can about the course he is playing is more able to plan his game around any likely situation and is the one who will consistently score well. More and more amateurs are following the lead of the touring professionals, who pace off each hole so there isn't any guesswork on distances, no question on the length, width, and type of greens and their openings, pin placements, trouble spots on the fairways, trap locations, and where the "go" and "no go" line is on those long holes which require a big fairway hit. This is the pre-game strategy that makes it unnecessary to ponder over club selection and eliminates the hesitancy that can affect the execution of the shot.

Golf Strategy and Your Caddie

The dictionary says that a caddie is "one who assists a golfer especially by carrying his clubs." With a good caddie, it's the "assists" that are important, and carrying the clubs is only incidental to his main purpose: helping his golfer any way he can. The player and his caddie make up "the side," and it is the only trace of teamwork in an otherwise individual sport.

Ideally, of course, the caddie should *help,* but it is up to the golfer to use him wisely. In the first place, it's true that except for a few notable exceptions, most touring pros don't make extensive use of their caddies except as psychological buffers from the pressures of the play and the galleries. They may perhaps exchange a few words to relieve tension, but they don't tend to ask for advice. Their example is a misleading one for the beginner, however. Professionals know the game so well that they have formed habits of self-reliance in situations requiring critical decisions. The tyro, on the other hand, cannot have the same self-knowledge at his disposal. He doesn't necessarily know the course or his own game.

A good caddie can be invaluable even to a pro. Arnold Palmer has attributed much of his success in the Masters to his "teammate" Iron-man; and Jack Nicklaus, when he plays at the Firestone Country Club, has a boy who goes out and charts the course with a tape measure before play begins. Gary Player likes to use his caddies to help him line up putts, and Doug Sanders has his caddie travel with him, serving as a chauffeur and valet when he isn't on the course. Some tournaments may have been won by caddies. Gene Sarazen thinks that his British Open victory in 1932 was due in a large part to the efforts of his seventy-year-old caddie, Dan Daniels, who gave Sarazen all he had and died a few months later.

Try to evaluate your caddie. If you think he is capable and knowl-edgeable, ask his advice, but ask it before you voice your own deci-sion, so he will be objective. In quizzing him about distances to the green, ask him how many yards it is, not what club he thinks you need. Only you know how far you can hit with each club; only you know whether you are going to hit the shot full or punch it. Above all, remember that you may ask advice only of your caddie or your playing partner and his caddie, and you are permitted by the *Rules of Golf* to have only one caddie.

The player may send his caddie ahead to a hill to mark the line to the green, but he may not have him drop the bag there and go on ahead. Similarly on the putting green, the caddie may point to the desired line and even remain pointing at it while the player putts, but he may not touch the line with a club or other marker to indicate how much break should be played. Anything that the player is forbidden to do, such as repairing spike marks on the green, his caddie is pro-hibited from doing also. If the golfer's shot hits his caddie, he loses the hole in match play and is penalized two strokes in medal play. If this situation occurs in best-ball, only the offending player is affected. He is disqualified for the hole, but his partner is not penalized.

Golf Strategy in Various Sections of the United States

Part of the secret of winning, as we have seen, is knowing all you can about the course you're playing, because every stroke, whether it travels 300 yards or 3 inches, has to be recorded. You may feel you can always pull a "type" shot out of the bag to avoid trouble, but it is better for the heart and wallet to know what you are doing and why. For example, from the close lies of the lush bent-grass fairways up North, the ball will sometimes fly out and travel farther than off Bermuda, a strain usually found in warm climates. Fortunately, the Northern greens are normally soft, and the ball would hit on, take a little hop, and come back, or else would spin back from the spot where it landed. If Bermuda grass in the fairway is still in the dormant stage, the ball will set up on top, and hitting controlled shots is a bit easier. But Bermuda greens are sometimes overseeded with rye, and under this top growth the greens will be very firm. The ball can be expected to hit on and take a long hop before checking. Instead of pitching directly at the pin, carry the ball about ten yards short. If the pin is in back and the green is large, hit what might be called a precaution shot, a low wedge into the front of the green with a reasonable amount of backspin that lets the ball skid to a stop near the hole. The elements, such as the heavy, damp air of seaside links, the dry, thin air of high elevations, as well as the wind and the rain, must also be considered, because each affects club selection.

For the vacationer with one eye on golf courses in various sections of the United States, we would like to point out the various conditions you will face as compared with your own home area. So let us repeat that, as has been pointed out several times in this book, you should change your thinking, or strategy, according to the conditions, but in no manner or means should you attempt to change your game.

Northeast   Generally, in the Northeast and New England, you will find that the principal difference, as compared to most other sections, is that you are always looking at a variety of lies. Even on seaside courses, you will be called upon to hit downhill, uphill, or sidehill lies. (See Chapter 4 for details on the strategy of making these shots.)

You will find, too, in the Northeast, that the turf for the most part is bent grass with very soft soil, the most favorable kind of turf to hit out of. Bent greens in this area are usually very true, but they can be slick and undulating. There is a tendency for a golfer from other sections to hit the ball a bit "fat." To counteract this, simply be more conscious of keeping your head still.

The rough usually is very thick and dense, much as it is in England. And, because of the many trees, you very rarely have the chance to hit a full shot to the green. Just be satisfied in getting any stray shots back on the fairway. Get it out for certain, or you'll find the shots mounting incredibly.

Southeast In the Carolinas, Georgia, and Florida, you will find that the soil here is a bit harder, being comprised of sand and clay and with Bermuda grass and rye grass the standard types.

In the Northeast, both the turf and the soil are soft, and you have no difficulty driving the clubhead through. Even with a tight lie, you can "go after" the ball without fear of a mis-hit. This is because you don't have to worry about hitting it absolutely flush. But in the Southeast the great percentage of tight lies, with a concrete-like soil, demand great concentration on hitting the ball squarely. Thus instead of a descending swing, you must concentrate on staying with the shot. The key here is to concentrate on keeping your head fixed, so that your arc doesn't move and cause you to drive the clubhead into unyielding soil or bounce up and belly into the ball.

As to the greens, which will be either Bermuda or rye or a combination of both, you can almost always expect them to be slower than they are in the North. While they may appear fast, you will find that you are leaving most of your putts short unless you become a bit more aggressive with your putter. On the greens you also will have a minimum of break with which to contend. This is because the coarse blades of grass prevent the ball from sliding off too much.

The rough in the South is not as deadly as it is in the North because, for the most part, you will find tall pines or palm trees where the foliage starts growing out at a good height. Under such conditions, you will find it possible much of the time to make fairly successful recoveries from this type of rough.

In Florida, on the whole, you will find a rough much less demanding, and at times your lie can be even better than if you were on the fairway. This is because the grass is so thick and wiry that the ball tends to sit right up on top. We've seen instances where it sat up so well that you could take a driver if you so desired. There are courses in Florida, however, where there is a great deal of sand in the rough. Under such conditions, once again be certain that you keep your head still, plant your feet firmly, and it also is a good idea to use one more club—say a five-iron instead of a six- —than you would if you were playing a normal shot.

Midwest The bent-grass fairways are in general very lush, and are similar to those in the Northeast. Here again, in certain sections, you will find a great many uphill and downhill lies, and it is well to refresh yourself on how to play these types of shots. (As pointed out in the section on playing in the Northeast.)

We are inclined to think of the Midwest as flat country. But most of the better golf courses have been planned around streams and lakes. For example, you couldn't find a much more uphill and down-dale course than Wakonda in Des Moines, Iowa, where the U.S. Amateur Golf Championship was held several years ago.

The rough on most Midwestern courses has been planned also to try the patience. You can get tall trees, but the underbrush is thick and tenacious and, when in doubt, you'd best be certain to concentrate on getting the ball safely back into play.

One of the major Midwestern dangers is the abundance of clover in the fairways. Complete details on the strategy of shots in clover were given in Chapter 4.

Southwest   In this section, taking in Louisiana, Texas, Arizona, and New Mexico, the courses primarily are very flat, and the turf is usually very hard. The visitor playing courses in this area will discover that, because of the flatness of the terrain, the distances have a habit of becoming distorted. What appears to be a mere 160 yards may in reality be 180 yards. It's the same principle involved where a mountain on the horizon appears to be five miles away and it may actually be 20 miles off. Thus, unless you have a good caddie to club you, chances are you probably will find you are hitting everything anywhere from 10 to 20 yards short. Until you have become accustomed to this factor, take one club more than you think you will need, say a five-iron instead of a six-iron. There is possibly one exception that should be kept in mind: The rarefied air of Arizona sometimes gives you extra length off the tee, and you could enjoy drives of 15 to 30 yards over your best at home.

You also will discover that many courses in the Southwest have very scrubby fairways. By "scrubby" we mean that it is quite possible to slam a ball down the middle of the fairway and still wind up on bare ground. The answer here is to hit the ball as close as possible to the bottom of the swing.

You have heard the term "Texas wedge," and there's a good reason why the putter is called this in this section. It's because the ground is flat and hard and the greens are hard and fast. Pop your ordinary wedge shot up there and, no matter how much "stop" you might be able to give the ball, in most cases you're likely to run right on over the green. Run the ball up there with the putter, and your chances are going to be enhanced considerably. As we said, and will repeat again, don't change your game. Change your strategy.

The rough varies considerably in the Southwest but, on the whole, it is nowhere near as thick or severe as in the Northeast or the Midwest. You get a few tree problems here and there, but, on the broad plan, you are better off in the rough than on a burned-out fairway. The grass doesn't grow very long or thick, and you can pull off a shot out of it without too much difficulty.

The greens, as we pointed out, are hard and can be extremely fast but are usually very flat. You will find mostly Bermuda in the summer and in the winter rye or bent overseeded. They are extremely difficult greens to putt, primarily because you need a feathery touch or you're likely to wind up in the next county.

Northern California   Here you will find some of the finest courses in the country and, because of the wind, playing conditions very similar to those you find in England. However, because of the general dampness throughout the Northwest, you will discover that the greens hold the ball well.

Wind is the major factor, for example, on the Monterey Peninsula. Here there are several world-famous courses, and your best bet is to play the safe shot that you know you can pull off. Start gambling, and it's an odd-on proposition that there will be times you'll wish you'd never seen a golf club.

The greens are a type of bent, and you will play on a lot of poa-annua, a grass with which everybody in the golf business is familiar in all sections of the world. It isn't too difficult to putt on, particularly soon after it is cut. But it grows rapidly in very warm weather and can quickly become rough and uneven. Unless you carry your own lawn mower, all you can do is grin and bear it.

Southern California   This is one section in which you will find more types and varieties of golf courses than in any other section. In the Los Angeles area, for instance, you will find a number of extremely flat courses. Then, on the other hand, others are very rolling.

In the Palm Springs area, an area of desert and mountains, the courses are lush, man-made beauties. They can be considered flat, and yet the next minute you'll think you're making like a mountain goat.

Here, we would venture, the over-all premium is on accuracy because the fairways are not extremely wide, and the well-irrigated rough can be tenacious.

Much of the hazard in this area is caused by undulating greens which contain a great deal of break. In most cases, the hot, dry weather makes the greens difficult to hold, and they will putt differently from day to day, depending on whether or not they have been freshly cut.

Summing up vacation golf, where you are going into an area with which you are not familiar, we would have to hold that you will play better if you think more about how to defend yourself against strange courses rather than in trying to attack them. Analyze your own game thoroughly, and apply its strength to the weakness of the courses. If the greens are hard and fast, use your head and play a pitch and run to the opening. And if the terrain is baked out, don't overlook that "Texas Wedge." On the other hand, lush, holding greens are built to order for the shot that's hit to stop at the flag. The entire answer as you pack your golf bag and start for alien parts, however, is right there in your head. We'll say it once more: THINK!

8. Match-Play Strategy

While virtually every tournament on the professional tour is conducted at stroke (formerly called medal play) play, for the over-all public, golf basically and fundamentally is a match-play game. That is, almost 90 percent of the golf played at clubs throughout the United States by the nation's amateurs is in the form of match play.

In match play, strategy can often serve you as well as your ability to bring off shots. In every match there must come a crucial point in the struggle—usually on the green. If you can correctly judge this moment, you can turn this judgment to your advantage. One stratagem which the late Walter Hagen, the all-time master of match play, often employed in this respect was to concede all short putts to his opponent early in a match, providing they were only for halves. Then, when Hagen's opponent was faced with a short putt for a crucial half later in the match, the Haig would stand by while the player coped with the almost unbearable pressure of sinking his first short putt of the round. He usually missed.

How to Win Matches

Confidence is what wins matches—that and bold playing. To give yourself confidence, it's essential to have a plan of action. Hitting and hoping is not enough. And how can you be bold unless you have a clear, realistic picture of what you are trying to do? Believe us, fuzzy thinking ends in excuses—and lost matches.

Actually, the difference between stroke and match play involves strategy, the thinking which is so important to successful golf. You certainly don't change your game technically or mechanically.

In match play, you don't have to worry about a bad hole. Naturally you don't ever want to have a bad hole, but, in match play, you can take a risky shot that you would hesitate to take in stroke play. You can really afford to take a gamble to win a hole that you wouldn't take in stroke play.

Of course, even in match play, the smart gamble is relative. It depends on its importance and the position of your opponent. In fact, the position of your opponent has a great deal to do with what you do in match play. Let's take an example:

Your opponent has put his tee shot in trouble, pitched out into the fairway and lies two. You are one. In such a case, you certainly wouldn't take a big gamble because, from all outward appearances, normal play will win the hole. You know your opponent will take the gamble when it's his turn to shoot, but you still should play the more conservative shot since you already have the advantage. This should be pretty much the pattern of your strategy throughout the match.

Once you get the advantage, you shouldn't give it away by taking unnecessary gambles. You might have to take a necessary gamble to get the advantage if you don't already have it. Figure it this way: When you get one hole up in a match, your opponent must win two holes, not one, to get the advantage himself. It's always important to get the advantage on your opponent and get as many holes up as possible. Once he is down, he is likely to free-wheel it more. It's his job to catch you and he knows, too, that, even if his gambles fail, he will only lose one hole at a time and not the entire match.

It's most important that you work out a plan of attack. Think out the course beforehand and decide such things as where you will just keep the ball in play. Having made up your mind, don't change it, unless it means losing a hole.

Another thing we find the average golfer never thinks about is the matter of "key holes." Every course has certain holes that are extremely difficult. You should figure out how you can best play them. If you can get by them at or near par, you are going to pick up a lot of match-play holes. When playing a strange course, find out all you can about the key holes. Check with the local professional, the local caddies, or local players.

Many people get suckered into handicap matches that are unfair from the start. One fellow merely says, "My handicap is twelve," and the other, without thinking, starts giving away strokes—without proof. If you're going to play a handicap game, ask your opponent for proof of his handicap.

With your plan of attack all squared away and a fair match set, now let's consider the match itself. Here are our twenty golden rules for success:

1. Know your own game. Never figure you will do better than your average. You will have some good holes and some bad holes. Your opponent will, too. This sort of thinking will keep you from blowing up when things go wrong or being too elated when they are right.

2. Study the course conditions—as you learned in Chapter 5 they will radically affect your play. For instance, on a dry course, play run-up shots, play to hit on the apron and bounce onto the green. On a wet day, play a pitching game. On a windy day, you again want to play low, bouncing shots. Remember, as previously stated in Chapter 3, that the speed of the greens can change during the day. In the early morning, the dew will make them slow. In the afternoon, when the sun has dried them out, they will be faster; but in the afternoon, watch out for a lot of spike marks around the hole.

3. Play the shot you know you can make—not a fancy shot out of a book.

4. Study your opponent's style during the first few holes. It can often give you a lot of confidence! A player with several faults will surely come ungrooved before the end.

5. Play your game shot by shot, and don't worry about your bad shots. Remember that a bad shot in match play can, at worst, mean one lost hole. Never give up on a hole and waste strokes. In singles many a hole is won with a bogey. Actually, it's usually wise to play only pars. Remember: Play the course, not your opponent.

6. Always try to take the offensive, if possible. Sure, we can say play your own game, but few things in a match can produce more pressure than trying to hit a green after your opponent has already reached it. There he is, just two putts away from his par and possibly only one putt away from a birdie. And there you are, faced with the distinct possibility that you will lose the hole if you don't hit the green. The burden of the match is, therefore, constantly on your shoulders. The trick, then, is to switch it to your opponent's shoulders, to take the offensive. To do this, it is sometimes expedient to use a three-wood off the tee in place of your driver. By doing so, chances are you'll be shorter but also more accurate off the tee than he. And since you are shorter, you will be hitting first to the greens. He, then, will be the one who will have to match your second shots.

7. The strategy of putting in match play frequently differs from

that of medal play. In medal play the thought uppermost in your mind is to hole every putt you can. In match play, however, it is often obvious that two putts will win the hole, particularly when you are putting after your opponent. In this event you have to "lay up," as the pros say; that is, you leave your first putt in such a proximity to the hole that your second putt remains well-nigh incapable of being missed. It may even be conceded. To insure this it behooves you to "miss" your putt, as it were, on the lower side of the hole always. A three-footer uphill is immeasurably easier to hole than a two-footer downhill—always.

8. If you miss a few putts early in the match, don't let it upset your train of thought. Don't panic and try to make up everything at once. Remember that an 18-hole match is long enough for you and your opponent to blow hot and cold several times.

9. Remember that the first hole is just as important as the last one. Actually, it is a good idea to start fast since this immediately puts the pressure on your opponent.

10. Always play with what you have. For instance, if a fade is what you have, make allowance for it. Don't try to straighten your game out in the course of a match. You can only do that in practice, and it is difficult enough then.

11. Play position with every shot. Always plan one shot ahead to make your next shot easier.

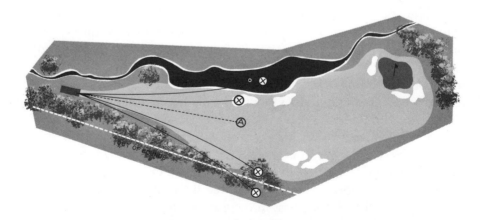

Opponent in trouble. If your opponent (X) flies his tee shot out of bounds or into some hazard, then it's wise for you (A) to sacrifice distance and play your ball with planned accuracy right down the middle.

12. Try to hole everything from 30 yards in. Not that you will hole all of them, but because this positive attitude will bring you closer to the hole than a wishy-washy effort. Once in a while, one will drop and really shake your opponent.

13. Play away from trouble. We know this sounds obvious, but so many players will dispatch a beautiful drive straight into a fairway bunker, when with a little care they could have been in good shape.

14. Always play at your own pace. If you usually play slowly, don't allow your opponent to speed up the game and throw you off your normal pace. If you normally play fast and your opponent is playing slowly, keep yourself in motion by walking forward and studying your next shot some more.

15. Don't let up when you are ahead. This is fatal. Keep playing each hole according to plan.

16. Be sure to play in turn. Out of ignorance too many golfers re-tee a ball immediately after hitting out of bounds. Strictly speaking, then, they are hitting out of turn. They should stand aside until their opponent plays his first shot. In addition to being rude, such a practice is also very stupid. By standing aside before hitting your second tee shot, you open up the possibility of your opponent also hitting out-of-bounds. Thus you stand even with him before exposing the nature of your second tee shot.

17. Don't gamble unnecessarily when you are down. When down, too many people try to play better golf shots than they are capable of playing—out of desperation. What they should do is to hold their position at all costs and wait for their opponent to make mistakes. The exception to this is when on the last few holes of a match.

18. Always be prepared. Nothing is more frustrating than to find yourself a mile from the clubhouse without an umbrella in the middle of a thunderstorm. Should this happen during an informal match, you can just call the whole thing off and run for cover. Should it happen during a tournament, however, you have to continue playing. If you are not protected against the elements, you leave yourself with a distinct disadvantage. Use your head before you tee off: Be prepared for any eventuality. Make sure, for one thing, that your umbrella is attached to your bag even though there may not be a cloud in the sky.

19. As we all too well know, most matches are won or lost on the first tee. It is up to you to make the wisest match you can. There are innumerable ways of taking "a fair advantage" as the smart boys say.

If, for example, you are faced with the choice of giving an opponent either strokes or "ups," give the strokes. Let's say that you give your opponent four strokes—two on each side. It is almost a sure thing that one of these four strokes will fall on one of the last four holes. Quite possibly, you may have closed out the match before he ever gets to use the last stroke. Had you given him "ups," however, the match would still be alive.

20. Get your proper rest. Sleep as late as you possibly can before an afternoon match. It can be an awfully long day if you wake up at seven in the morning and have to pull yourself through a tight golf match 11 hours later. Sleeping through the morning has become a standard practice among touring pros who are often faced with starting times as late as two-thirty or three o'clock in the afternoon. Frequently, to make sure that they can sleep late, they will very often stay out late the night before. Early to bed and early to rise is a great practice for Boy Scouts. But you are planning on winning a golf match, not on taking a hike in the woods.

Four-Ball Match Play

Two-on-two (four-ball) match play is a great deal different, for you have a partner to help you and, instead of being cautious, as in one-on-one, you just turn it on and hit the ball as hard as you can off the tee. Then you aim your second shot for the pin, no matter how precarious its location, and you ram the putts to make sure the ball gets to the hole. You have to try to birdie every hole because when four of the best players are trying, someone is bound to birdie most of the time. That is, holes are seldom won with pars.

Successful four-ball play begins with the choice of your partner. It is most important to have a partner who is compatible. In other words, if you are a bold player and a big hitter, it would generally be best for you to team with a rather conservative player who consistently keeps his ball in play. Or vice versa. But your selection should be largely psychological; select a partner whose attitude will generally complement yours. In addition, make certain that you fully understand one another. Know his game, his strengths and weaknesses. Know which types of shots and holes he plays well and poorly.

To cover every situation in four-ball play would require a book in itself. True, most of the information previously given for one-on-one play remains good. But, we will zero in on those points that many players overlook. In essence, all the hints we could give you add up to two golden rules:

1. Give your partner confidence.
2. Give your opponents fits!

All other considerations flow from these two.

Both you and your partner should concentrate on your *own* games as much as possible. Don't try to do it all yourself. Remember that it takes two to win best-ball matches. That is, always have respect for your partner; assume he's doing the best he can.

On par-three's the better iron player should shoot first. Having the accurate iron player already on the green can give the weaker iron shooter confidence. In fact, it is wise always to let the straightest driver tee off first on every hole, unless the other prefers first spot. If you have the honor, this puts the pressure on your opponents.

Before teeing off on any key hole, the side's strategy should be discussed and decided. Of course, the state of the match will sometimes reverse your original plans for any key hole. In fact, it is a good idea to elect a captain at the start of the match for your side—usually the player with more experience. It is this player's job to make the tactical decisions.

One of the things amateurs forget is that if your side is away, either of you can shoot next. Don't confine your use of this option to the putting green. It can work in your favor on any approach shot, or even on seconds on par-fives.

Remember, the idea is to give your partner confidence. So, when your side is away, the player with the best chance of making the shot should play first. A successful shot on his part will encourage his

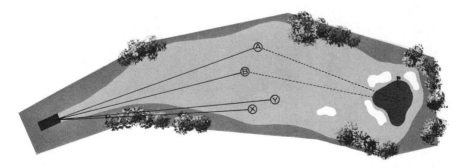

Four-ball play: Players "A" and "B" can put pressure on players "X" and "Y" by easing up a little to get the first shot at the green. With player "B" clear to the flag, player "A" should aim for the flat part of the green.

partner to make a success of the more difficult shot. And two successful shots can really put the pressure on your opponents.

While we're on this subject of options, there may be times when you
prefer not to surrender the option. By this we mean have the player
who is nearer the hole play first—regardless of the difficulty of the
shot. The thinking here is to get two shots near the hole before your
opponents have the chance to match your shots. Where options and
the matter of giving confidence to your partner conflict, each case will
have to be decided on its merits. But always think about the situation
before making a decision. A clear plan can give each partner a better
picture of what he has got to do and increases his chances of making a
successful shot.

Most veteran match teams usually have a rather odd rule: *No
matter where the first team player to putt may end up, he never putts
out; mark the ball!* Suppose your partner has a long putt and you have
a ten-footer for a bird. Your partner then leaves himself a three-

Putting strategy. With player "B" away, his partner (A) should putt first since
he is closer to the flag. If player "A" drops the birdie putt, player "B" can
pick up without giving player "X" the line. If player "A" misses but gets his
par, player "B" can boldly go for the birdie.

footer. If he misses, your attitude toward your putt now changes from positive to negative. You are no longer thinking in terms of making your ten-footer but in terms of not three-putting yourself. If, on the other hand, your partner had marked his ball, you would still feel he would make it in case you miss. Besides, if you do miss, what are the chances against you both missing your second putts: We should say they were very slim.

It is considered wise play to be bold when your partner is safe and to play it ultracautious when he is in trouble. Let's say your partner is on the green in regulation and is only 20 or 30 feet away from the cup. By all odds, he should get it down in two for your team's par. At the same time, however, you have a chance to get closer for a possible birdie putt but you must play a ticklish shot across a trap. Let it fly for the possible birdie.

On the other hand if your partner is trapped, play your shot safely to the fat part of the green. It's surprising, when pressing for birdies, how often both partners will wind up with a bogey.

Remember that confidence will not come from ignorance, but will be fostered by planned knowledge. Playing bold does not mean playing with the blinders on, but rather knowing what you must do and then doing it!

Gamesmanship

In country clubs from coast to coast, millions of players daily are knocking heads in a divot Donnybrook where the total number of strokes taken has little to do with the financial outcome. Ordinarily, it is hole-by-hole Nassau competition which the average player is battling, and that gamesmanship—sporting, and to put it very mildly, unsporting—usually winds up as the "name of the game." On the Tour there are little or no shenanigans. So high is the honor factor that players call penalty shots on themselves even when no one possibly could detect an infringement of the rules.

How many ordinary players could say the same? Yet without questioning the honesty, integrity, and arithmetical ability of your average golfer, from long observation of "friendly" golf, we would have to hold that gamesmanship bordering from the sneaky to the downright dishonest is with us an immorally high percentage of the time.

There is a bold line between strategy in match play, and the ruthless tactics of the brassie bandits who would take advantage of their aging

Aunt Priscilla to win a press. You'll undoubtedly recognize a great number of these sharpshooters.

They come in many different categories. To start with, there are the "destroyers." These are the fellows who, if you happen to be playing particularly well in one department, innocently press home their inquiries as to how you do it. Say, for example, you are putting well. Immediately they will press the inquiry as to whether you apply most of the pressure with your right or your left hand. Once you have started thinking about it, your putting stroke has gone the way of all flesh.

In this category, too, falls the gent, as separated from gentleman, who informs his partner in a stage whisper you are certain to hear that "Poor old Harry just can't seem to keep from looking up on every shot today." And let me tell you, Harry, that's what you'll be doing from there on in.

Then we have the "advisors" who are particularly cute around the greens. They'll stroke a putt too hard with the grain and go past the hole. This provokes a lamentation: "Boy, are they fast today. You really have to baby them." Facing a putt from the other direction, or against the grain, you have been subconsciously conned and hit it so fearfully that you wind up shorter than a circus midget.

This works in the opposite direction, too. In cases where the "advisor" is short while putting against the grain, he'll scream to the heavens that "I really walloped that one and look what happened." What happens is that you step up from the other side, with the grain going straight down your line, and you've been so brainwashed you're lucky to keep it on the green.

With this breed, like in making a police confession, anything you say may be used against you. Idly drop a hint that you only recently have overcome the shanks, a scourge worse than the bubonic plague, and we'll lay you two to one this will be his subject for the afternoon until, you're right, you'll be doing it again.

Whisperers, sneezers, coughers, cigarette lighter snappers, change jinglers, and club droppers are top-ranking members of this gamesmanship cult. It is absolutely amazing how innocently they can spurt into action just as you reach the top of your backswing or are beginning to stroke your putt.

In this day of the golf cart, these concentration shatterers have added such refinements as picking a vital moment in your play to let the brake snap off or scrape the metal of the cart with their spikes. Accidental, purely, you know, old boy.

Another mid-iron menace is the windy day opponent with the loose-legged trousers who somehow always seems to be somewhere in your line, or barely visible out of the corner of your eye, while his trousers flap in the breeze like the sails on "Old Ironsides."

Then there is the elephant who constantly, albeit "unconsciously," trundles over the line of your putt until it looks only slightly rougher than a freshly plowed field. One of his best tricks, if he putts out first, is to casually plant one of his brogans close to the rim of the cup but pointing off obliquely to the right or left of your line. Reaching down to retrieve his ball, his entire weight is on that foot. When you putt, no matter how truly, the ball is certain to follow that groove, much akin to the gutter in a bowling alley, and skid off and away from the hole at the last moment.

Everybody knows the character who pursues his ball eagerly into the rough, flounders around ambitiously in the cabbage, picks up a ball and holds it to his eye with the intensity of a diamond cutter, identifies it triumphantly by waving it high in the air, and then carefully replaces it—well teed up on a tuft of grass. This type could hit a full driver out of a quicksand bog.

This fellow is a full-fledged member of the improvers of the lie, no relation to the improvers of the breed, although irate members of the opposition could find some sort of an equine equivalent.

These are the ones who, when facing a tight lie on a wet fairway, carefully place the clubhead behind the ball and during a lengthy address press down so hard behind the ball you'd think the shaft would snap. By the time they get around to taking their swing, the ball is teed up so high they could hit it flawlessly with an Italian salami. This type also has a masterful technique in the rough.

It reminds us of a story about Bob Hope's caddie, and, knowing that Hope is the soul of honesty on a golf course, we will tell it only for a chuckle. Anyhow, somebody saw Hope's caddie sitting on the 50-yard line at the Rose Bowl with his wife and two children.

"Hey," he asked, "where'd you get the seats?"

"From Bob Hope," the caddie glowed.

"Man, they're the best seats in the house."

"They'd better be," retorted the caddie. "I've been caddying for him 10 years, and he hasn't had a bad lie yet."

Maybe there have been times when you've had one of those days where you never ever had a bad lie. Well, I can tell you that it's a distinct possibility that your caddie is betting on you against your opponent's caddie. It was a situation which almost became a scandal at sacrosanct Augusta National a few years back when Ed Dudley was the head professional there.

Dudley finally assembled the caddies and gave them a stern lecture against improving situations during the course of play. The very next day, Dudley faded a tee shot far into the woods and, when he arrived at the spot, the ball was sitting up in a nicely cleared area and branches had been broken from the trees to leave a clear opening to the green. The caddie was waiting angelically. Dudley took in the situation at a glance and became furious.

"Didn't I tell you yesterday," he barked, "that absolutely nothing was to be done to improve a player's lie?"

The caddie rolled his eyes pitifully, shrugged plaintively, and said softly:

"I know, Mr. Dudley, but ain't it pretty?"

There is a great deal of petty larceny on the greens, and it's no idle expression when you hear someone say, "If George marks his ball two more times it will be in the cup."

One of the best dodges used is in replacing a ball, marked with a coin, which has been lifted from a slight depression. Just the barest fraction of an inch one side or the other in replacing the ball makes certain that the ball doesn't have to be tapped out of a spike mark or some other infinitesimal declivity which might alter its course when the ball is stroked.

In this category are the "forgetful" souls who originally faced a downhill, sidehill putt of three or four feet. Fortunate are they, indeed, if they are in someone else's line and are asked to mark. Naturally, they meticulously mark a putter head's length to the side— to the side away from the break. Then, "forgetting" that their line has been changed to a straight-in putt, they replace the ball at the coin's new position and casually putt out.

There are, of course, match-play stratagems which are perfectly legal and do not bend let alone break the rules of sportsmanship. One which well may be considered a borderline case is to play rapidly when you are hooked up against an opponent you know likes to play slowly. Or, on the other hand, to play with studied deliberation when you are going against a man who prefers to play speedily and is upset by delays.

Disregarding your opponent's shots from tee to green is, of course, almost virtually impossible. Yet you can conquer this to some extent by not even watching when he hits but going about the business of mentally planning your own shot. Do everything in your power to concentrate merely on shooting the best score you can.

John Ball, undoubtedly one of England's most phenomenal match players in that he captured the British Amateur eight times, proved this point with a pointed remark during one match in which his opponent drove into a bunker on a par-five hole.

"He's in the bunker," commented a friend. "You didn't see that, did you?"

"No," Ball replied. "Why should I? It's my business to get a five here."

You can, of course, use a certain amount of strategy to legally "keep the heat" on your rival. If you are equal drivers, it isn't a bad or unsporting idea to ease off a little so that he will be in front of you and you will get the first shot to the green. If you're on the putting surface first, there is always a little extra pressure on him at this point to match your shot.

There is, of course, a time to play your opponent instead of the course, and that's when you can play it safe and make him gamble. Also, if you're a couple up, this is the time you can afford to shoot the works. It keeps the pressure on him and forces him to gamble.

Another time you have the pressure tight on him is when he hits the ball out of bounds. Ordinarily, you might think this is the time to really lace it out there and break his back. Not so.

At this point you have two shots to play with, so distance isn't a factor of any consequence whatsoever. What you must concentrate on here is to hit the safest, straightest shot right down the middle that is humanly possible. Play it safe and play it for position, and you've got him in your hip pocket.

An example would be again the sixteenth hole at Cypress Point, where you have to go over the water to reach the green with your tee shot, but you can play it far out to the left and have a relatively easy approach shot to the green. If he dunks his tee shot in the water, he's now hitting three from the tee. Your percentage is to play out safely to the left and reach the green with your second shot. That still leaves you one putt before you're even in strokes with his second tee shot.

But, on those out-of-bounds decisions, make certain that he is out-of-bounds. Or at least in deep, dark trouble. A case in point was a match in which Walter Hagen was playing Leo Diegel. Hagen far outdrove Diegel but was in the rough. Diegel fiddled over his shot and then decided to walk up to see what kind of a shot Hagen faced. But as he began to walk toward Hagen, Sir Walter whipped out a brassie and took his stance on the edge of the rough. Diegel, thinking Hagen had a clear shot, retreated to his ball, took a brassie and not being able to get home anyhow buried it badly in a bunker short of the green. Hagen then replaced his brassie in his bag, walked over to where his ball was dead behind a tree trunk, knocked it casually out into the fairway and put his third within a few feet of the pin. The rattled Diegel exploded out poorly and needed two putts to get down. Hagen holed his putt and won the match.

It is illegal for another player to ask you what club you hit for a certain shot, particularly in playing a three-par, but it isn't illegal for him to stand close by and watch with hawk eyes while you select your club. There are several ways of dealing with this without completely mutilating the soles of your clubs so that the numbers don't show.

You can take less club and hit it harder or you can take more club and hit the ball softer. In selecting your club, snap it out of the bag and, after you hit your shot, bury the club back in the bag quickly with a scrambling, concealing motion. On the other hand, you may guess properly or even see what club your opponent is hitting if he has the honors. But, in this case, remember to see how far down the shaft he is taking his grip and how far back he takes the club so that you will know whether he is playing the club half, three-quarters, or full.

There is nothing against "going to school" on a rival's putt if you have the same line and he has a 20-footer while you face a 10-footer. But watch first how he contacts the ball, whether he stroked it firmly or pushed or pulled the putt. You still will have time to catch the last 10 feet of the roll to ascertain exactly how the green breaks, and that last 10 feet is all you are interested in.

Another factor you should consider is that of keeping your comments to yourself. If you goof a shot and it still comes off, don't let anybody know you blew it, but let them think you simply have a wide variety of shots. Your opponents may get a mental lift if you start complaining about your game and, even worse, you may convince yourself. But, above all, always hit the shot you can pull off. Ben Hogan once said, "Don't ever try a shot you haven't practiced recently."

Much of four-ball match play is psychological. This is why it's so important to build up your partner's confidence constantly. At one point in the famed CBS Match Play Classic between the team of Tommy Bolt and Bo Wininger and that of Gardner Dickinson and

Sam Snead, the latter put his shot into a bunker and began to fuss to his partner about his line to the green.

"Well, Sam," Dickinson grinned at him, "I can't think of anybody in the world I'd rather see playing that shot than you."

Sam looked back at his partner and gave him a big smile. "Yeah, I'm pretty good at that shot, at that." And he knocked it stony to the pin.

"One reason we do so well together," Sam told us after the match, "is that Gardner never fusses at me." Two guys who get along have a tremendous start toward beating two guys who are constantly beefing at each other.

How to Bet

Betting is a paradoxical factor in golf. It is the element that makes golf unique (because it is the participants who are doing the betting), but at the same time, it is the catalyst that makes golf like other sports because it establishes the competition with another player. Remember that we are always referring to casual, weekend golf and not tournament play.

On a less philosophical level, the high incidence of betting in golf is surely attributable to the game's admirable handicapping system. It is necessary for a good bet that the opponents be roughly equal in ability so that there is some doubt as to the outcome of the contest; golf's handicapping techniques effect such an equality, even between two players of disparate skills.

Ellsworth Vines, who was a champion tennis player before he became a pro golfer, recalled that when he was at his peak in tennis, there were only a handful of players in the whole world who could give him an exciting match, but with golf's handicap method, he could have a close, interesting game with any kind of player.

If you are going to bet at golf, you had better be like a poker player and know the house rules before you start. Most wagers are won or lost on the first tee when the game is made up, so know what you are playing, and above all, know your opponents. And never gamble heavily—even if you can afford it. The worst thing that friends or members of a club can do is to make big bets with each other. There's no way you can keep playing and beating the same individual every day and still keep getting a game—in fact, you probably won't even stay friends. We believe in making the game fair so that the money evens up in the long run. If you give a man five strokes and beat him, next time you should give him six. If you beat him again, then you should give him seven. Then if he beats you, give him seven again, and if he beats you again, then you'll drop back to six shots. This merely creates an even golf game, and the only one making any real profit out of it is the pro shop—which is as it should be. If you want to make a living playing golf, get out on the Tour. Don't try to take it away from your friends.

Now we didn't really intend to lecture anyone on the dangers of getting up a golf game, because, perhaps more than anyone, we know how much fun it is to get a good, competitive game going on the course. So let us pass along a few tips on how to become a better player in head-to-head match-play situations.

First of all, it is a wise rule not to gamble much on a strange course. You've got to know the course on which you're playing, because if you don't then sooner or later it's going to reach out and grab you— and it'll probably cost you the match when it does.

A lot of people are known for actually winning the match on the first tee. What this means is that they maneuver their opponents for so many strokes that they can't possibly lose. What you have to realize is that everybody is going to ask for as much as he can get on the first tee, and it's the fault of the man who accepts the bet if he loses later. We've found, however, that most amateur players tend to overestimate their own games rather than underestimate them. Don't fall into that trap, because you'll lose for sure. Don't base your handicap around what you shot on your best day. We've found that if you ask a player what he shoots, and he's had one 78 in his life and never broken 80 before, he'll say he shoots around 78–79–80–81. He just wants you to know that he can score 78. Actually he should play at around 84 or 85. You've got to be realistic with yourself—unless you want to give your money away.

Now for a little bit about analyzing your opponents. Handicaps are set up to even any match. So if you put four 16 handicappers together in one foursome, they should all finish about even, if all four play to their full capabilities. But you can usually tell which one will win. The man who gets a lot of pars and then has one or two bad holes is going to be a stronger player than the straight bogeyman. The first fellow will win more holes and, therefore, the match. So if you're playing in a foursome like this, consider your chances. If you're the man who gets a lot of pars, then you're in good shape. But if you're not, you may need some help to keep from being a consistent loser. You've got to judge your opponents on how they play—not simply what they score or on their handicaps. And if you feel that your opponent is better than you, always request that you begin the match one-up—not one stroke but *one hole*. You can always waste that one stroke by taking a double bogey on the stroke hole, but if you're one up when you start, no one can take that away from you.

As far as games that you can play around the country club go, there are several and here's a brief guide as taken from the *Encyclopedia of Golf* to the types of bets you may encounter:

NASSAU

The most common kind of bet. At match play, three points are scored: one for the first nine, one for the second, and one for the 18. If a golfer is playing a "one-dollar Nassau," he has three individual one-dollar bets.

BISQUE

A handicap stroke that may be taken on any hole at the player's option. Strictly speaking, a stroke that is given to an opponent must be taken at the hole indicated on the score card as being that particular handicap number. Thus, if a player is given "five strokes," he must use those strokes on the holes marked one to five on the card. The handicap numbers are usually circled to differentiate them from the hole numbers. A bisque on the other hand, may be taken anywhere.

SKINS

A skin is awarded to the winner of each hole provided that he is not tied by another player. If two tie, all tie. A deadlier version of this game (and not one for those who play a steady, unspectacular game) is called cumulative skins. In this little hair-raiser, holes not won by anyone because of ties are accumulated and awarded to the first winner of a hole. Also called "scats" or "syndicates."

BINGLE-BANGLE-BUNGLE

A fast-paced item with lots of action. Three points on each hole: one for the player who reaches the green first, one for the player nearest to the cup after all are on the green, and one for the player who first holes out. Charlie Coe sometimes plays this one with his friends to even out the game, since obviously a consistently good player loses his advantage over the short hitter and the lucky putter.

BIRDS

Points scored for birdies on any hole; double for eagles.

LOW BALL AND TOTAL

A four-ball team bet in which the best ball of each team wins one point, and the low total of the partners wins another. This game is a method of getting a good bet out of the situation in which there is one very good player playing with a poor one against two average players.

PRESS OR EXTRA

A new bet on the remaining holes. If someone wants to take a "dollar extra" on the seventeenth tee, he wants to play the last two holes for the dollar.

The best advice on betting, which was stated and is well worth repeating, is *never* to wager more than you can comfortably afford to lose, or else you may be putting yourself under unnecessary pressure that will probably hurt your game. Don't rush into an extra bet when you are losing unless you have been playing unusually badly and have suddenly discovered the cure, or you have been hitting the ball well, but have been unlucky.

Peripatetic golfers who do not play regularly at one course, and who get into games with strangers, should be wary of what looks like a sucker bet. There may be a hidden kicker. In the musical *Guys and Dolls,* Sky Masterson tells a story that is a good lesson for anyone who is betting with people he doesn't know. Sky remembers that when he was preparing to leave home and start out on his own, his father treated him to some advice in lieu of a bankroll. "One of these days in your travels," he said, "a guy is going to come to you and show you a nice brand-new deck of cards on which the seal is not yet broken, and this guy is going to offer to bet you that he can make the jack of spades jump out of the deck and squirt cider in your ear. But son, do not bet this man, for as sure as you stand there you are going to wind up with an earful of cider."

So if a guy comes up and offers to bet you that he can drive a golf ball two miles, do not bet this man, because remember that this bet has been won by guys driving balls off mountains and down frozen rivers. And a lot of guys have been left with earfuls of cider.

9. Practice Strategy—And How It Can Help Your Game

There probably isn't a golfer alive who hasn't at one time or another wondered just what was the secret of success of the Hogans, Palmers, and Caspers. Well, there is a secret all right, but it probably isn't what you think. The answer lies in practice and plenty of it. There isn't a man on the pro tour who hasn't spent hours upon hours in lonely practice—and every one of them still goes to the practice tee before his round and sometimes afterward. However, just practicing isn't enough in itself; the golfer must know what and how to practice. You can go to the driving range every night for a month, but if you aren't working on something specific, all you'll have to show for it will be blisters—and the same old slice.

Practice is not merely a routine of hitting ball after ball. It has a definite purpose and needs careful thought and planning. We all have seen golfers stride over to the practice tee with a couple of woods and maybe hit a couple of hundred balls either teed up or nudged onto the top of the most luscious tuft of grass. It may help their driving, and they may be able to hit an adequate three- or four-wood off the fairway from a good lie, but golf is more subtle than that. Let's say they find a poor lie off their drive so they hit their second into a trap. They then take three or four to get out. Why? Because they don't have the know-how. They have never practiced the stroke-saving shots.

Bunker play, as we have said previously, costs the longer handicap player more strokes than any other facet of his game, yet a lesson on trap shots and a few practice sessions devoted to this alone would

probably have him master of the shot in a matter of weeks. Trap shots
are but one of the trouble shots that golfers neglect. Seldom do you
see players drop a bag of balls in the rough, yet how often do they
drive into it? Do they practice from uphill, downhill, and sidehill
stances? No, yet all these shots call for different techniques. No one
can be a complete golfer until he has mastered all golf's many contingencies, but the incongruity of it all is that it is the longer handicap
player who is more likely to encounter all the trouble spots.

Don't practice when you're feeling tired; it'll do you more harm
than good. By all means go out and practice after your round, but
take a breather first. Quit when you feel you are really in the groove
and hitting the ball well. Even if you go fresh to the practice tee, an
hour's practice, or so, is ample. After that you will get arm weary and
undo the good you have done your game.

The longer handicap player, having a greater margin for improvement, can show greater dividends from practice, but, conversely, the
low handicap golfer's swing is much more finely grooved, and the
slightest discrepancy is more likely to manifest itself. So, you see,
practice is for everyone, even if it is merely to maintain your present
standard.

Practice at Home

This is a do-it-yourself age, and it applies to your golf game as much
as to anything else. Because whether you are getting ready for a new
season or merely trying to improve yourself, there is no better place to
do it yourself than in your own backyard.

The beauty of backyard practice is that you can work on various
phases of your game without interruptions, and you can work on your
swing or your chipping whenever you have a few minutes to spare.
You will discover quickly that one of the greatest advantages is that
these sessions will develop a new "feel" for your clubs.

First of all, building your own net in which you can hit full drives
isn't very complicated and doesn't require much room. All you need is
a large square of canvas, which you can nail to two poles planted in
the ground. If you feel permanent installation would be unsightly, all
you have to do is set two pieces of pipe into the ground just below the
level of the turf, and the poles can be lifted out and the canvas rolled
around them for easy storage. We would suggest that before the
canvas is attached to the poles that you wrap the poles with burlap

and fasten it down. You can also do this with a cross-piece at the bottom to keep balls from dribbling under the canvas. This burlap will take the bounce out of any ball that might inadvertently hit the supporting poles. Now you can bang away with regulation golf balls to your heart's content.

"Feel" is the total answer in golf and, while interminable practice is the only answer to obtaining it, you don't have to go near a golf course in the process. You can do it with a padded wall in your garage, one of those fiber doormats, and the rug in your living room.

However, you needn't even go to this minor trouble if you don't feel like it. Because you can groove your swing in your own yard by hitting readily available plastic balls that will only go a few feet through the air no matter how hard you hit them. Remember, whether you use the net or the plastic balls, you aren't striving for distance. What you are striving to do is forget the ball and perfect your swing.

Accurate pitching when you are on the golf course can save you a fantastic number of strokes if and when you get to the point where you can consistently get the ball close enough to one-putt. It is in your backyard that you can really sharpen your chipping and pitching game amazingly. What you are trying to develop here most of all is "feel" and the ability to hit the ball to a certain spot where it will make its run to the hole. We must take into consideration that in most yards you will not get a true bounce or the type of run you would get in landing a ball on a putting green. However, you can develop the "feel" and the knack of lofting a ball to a precise spot.

What we suggest here is to pitch or chip a ball to an ordinary peach basket or bushel basket, or even to a small piece of canvas about two feet square. Soon you will find that you are landing the ball exactly where you want it with an ever increasing consistency. What you are developing is a burglar's touch around the greens, and you'll see it reflected in your scoring week by week.

Now it stands to reason that the lady of the house may not want her backyard pitted with hundreds of divot marks. To escape any possible vocal retribution you can, if you so desire, hit your shots off one of those bristly cocoa mats. Let's face the fact immediately that this isn't practicing under ideal conditions. When you take a divot, as you should on most pitch shots, it should appear just ahead of your ball. This means that you have contacted the ball before you take the divot. Naturally, you aren't going to be able to take a divot on a cocoa mat. But if it's a question of a cocoa mat or no practice at all, by all means use the mat. You won't take a divot, of course, but you can learn to contact the ball before you dig down into the mat. It might even be better, the experts notwithstanding, because you will learn in the process to contact the ball exactly and precisely—which means keeping your eye on the ball all the way through the stroke.

So, you may say, this way I'll learn to contact the ball squarely and smoothly and develop "feel," but how will I know what club with which to chip when I am faced with a shot to the green? There is one solid tip we can give you in this department. Picture every chip shot as one in which you are going to toss the ball underhand toward the stick. And keep in mind that the lower you can keep the shot the less hard you will have to strike the ball, and, therefore, the more accurate your shot will be. If you will keep this theory in mind on every chip shot, you will find that—once your backyard "feel" and touch is developed—the easier your shots will become.

One of the biggest banes of the average player is the trap shot, and yet this is one bugaboo you can conquer easily in your own backyard. If you are serious about your game, and yet haven't too much time to practice, those occasional few minutes you can pilfer around the house can make you an expert in getting out of the sand. It is, after all, a matter of rhythm and timing as you swing the club through the ball.

Do you want your own sand trap? Simply get one of those plastic children's wading pools, which are less than knee deep, and fill it with three or four inches of sand. If you have the room in your backyard you can then swing away to your heart's content, as long as you don't face the picture window in the living room. But, until you get the confidence and control that is so easy to acquire, start out once again with those plastic balls that won't go more than 30 or 40 feet, and, if they did, wouldn't dent a cream puff with a direct hit. The sand trap soon will lose all its terrors for you.

When it comes to putting, there are several schools of thought as to whether it does you any good to wield your blade on the living room rug. Let's face the fact that under the proper conditions you can grow and mow as perfect a patch of green in your backyard as they have at the world's finest country club. Yet we must feel that even on a flat rug putting practice has to be beneficial because you are developing a "feel" for your putter and training yourself to take a smooth even stroke at the ball. But one thing we would like to stress is *always* putt at a target smaller than the actual hole you will be shooting at when you line up your putts on the golf course. In other words, if you are putting at a tumbler on your living room rug, use a shot glass. If you are lucky enough to be able to groom your own little putting green in the backyard, have the hole cut appreciably smaller than the normal golf course cups.

Mental practice is important, too. You may not have the time or the facilities for physical practice at home, but you can improve simply by thinking constructively about your game. Analyze your abilities and determine which are your strong and weak points.

Practice at a Driving Range

Probably the most familiar complaint heard on golf courses is, "Can't understand it, I hit the ball a ton at the driving range last night, and today I can't do a thing."

If you learn proper practice procedures for driving ranges, you can easily transfer your range ability to the golf course. The first thing to remember is that the word "driving" in driving range does not belong there if you plan to improve your game. You should think of the range as a *practice range*. Too many golfers only care about playing "long ball" when they get on a driving range, and no matter how many poor shots they hit, they are satisfied if they can clear the 250-yard sign on at least one poke. The object of the game of golf is not to see how far you can hit the ball, so why practice only distance?

You should try to duplicate golf course conditions when you visit a practice range. Use your own clubs whenever possible. Too often driving-range clubs are purchased mainly for durability. Wear your golf shoes, and if you use a glove, take it along.

It is best to start your practice-range work with a nine-iron. You can gradually work up toward the woods. Too many driving-range customers practice nothing but drives, hitting balls as fast as they can be teed up. Take your time between shots, give your hands a chance to rest, and give yourself a chance to study the results and make corrections. If you hit ball after ball without a rest, you will find your grip becomes tighter and tighter, and you are only slugging the ball. You won't be controlling the club, the club will be controlling you.

There are two main reasons why a golfer who does well at a driving range may scrape the ball around on the course. The rubber mats used at ranges make a golfer look good. You can hit several inches behind the ball on a mat and the club will slide along the rubber into the ball, and you will still get a decent shot. But the same thing doesn't hold true on a golf course. If you hit too far behind the ball, the club digs into the ground, and a "fat" shot results. It is important that you hit the ball cleanly off the practice-range tee, so that you won't fall into a sliding habit. If at all possible, forget about the tee mats and find a grassy spot at one end of the range, where you won't bother anyone. At some ranges this is not possible, but if there are grassy tee areas, take advantage of them.

Lack of pressure is another reason for good range results. There are no out-of-bounds, water holes, or other hazards on a range, and if you miss a shot, you still have a bucketful of balls left. However, you can add a form of pressure at the range that will benefit your practice.

Rather than blast balls into the wide open spaces of the range, build an imaginary fairway, using distance markers or some other objects for boundaries. Consider any shot that lands outside of your make-believe fairway out-of-bounds. As you improve, narrow your fairway.

One major advantage that a driving range has over other practice areas is the yardage markers that virtually all of them have. These markers make fine target lines. You should always select a specific target when hitting practice shots, either woods or irons. And you can add more pressure by playing games at the range. If you're with a friend, bet soft drinks or some other token item on the number of shots that stay in the imaginary fairway. You can play the same game with irons, hitting to designated spots. See how many shots you can put within six feet of the 100-yard marker.

You can also play a mental round of golf at the range. Pretend you are playing your favorite course, and go through the shots hole by hole. Let's say the first hole of your course is a 350-yard four-par. Your drive carries 230 yards, leaving you an approach shot of 120 yards. Pick out a spot 20 yards in back of the 100-yard distance marker and use it as your flagstick. Imagine that the green stretches 10 yards in any direction from the pin. If you hit the "green" more than six feet from the pin, allow yourself two putts. If your approach shot is within six feet of the pin, consider you got down in one putt.

If your approach shot misses the 10-yard limit of the green, estimate the distance left, and pick out a spot in front of you equal to that distance. After completing your chip, the same putting rule applies.

You can play 18 holes at your favorite course from the driving range tee in this manner. You can make it a competitive game or you may wish to make up your own rules. Naturally you can't get birdies, as you must count two putts per hole, but you can test your tee-to-green precision. If you feel you have only hit half the greens in regulation figures and the others in one over regulation, you would be nine over par.

If you flub a shot, don't worry about it, just continue to play the hole through. Don't suddenly take a timeout and hit five or six practice shots. You wouldn't do it on the course, so don't do it during your practice exercise. It would defeat the whole purpose of conditioning your mind and swing to actual playing conditions.

This tee-to-green exercise will give you practice in a variety of shots. Normally, most people practice by hitting every shot full, but on the course usually half or three-quarter shots are called for more often than a full shot. Therefore, by playing your course visually, you become accustomed to hitting those half-wedge shots you normally need to execute. This gives your game the edge it would have if you played six straight days. Naturally, at all times you must be honest with yourself. A flubbed shot is a flubbed shot, and at least a stroke penalty must be paid. But don't forget, no matter how well you swing you'll occasionally miss a shot, but don't be alarmed. If your swing is sound, don't change it. Too many golfers change their swings whenever they miss a shot. This only breaks down the repetition and continuity of the swing. However, if you have completed several practice rounds visually and you chronically mis-hit the same shot, then try to correct the fault, or see your pro. He can usually analyze in a few minutes the trouble that might take you weeks to discover by trial and error.

The golf range is also an excellent place to practice trouble shots. Most ranges have sand traps, and since it is almost impossible to practice trap shots at the golf course, take advantage of the driving-range opportunity.

Since many shots must be hit from poor lies, try several shots from self-made poor lies. It is also advisable to practice shots where your backswing is restricted or ones where trees form an obstacle. Work on hitting approach shots over bunkers or make-believe water hazards. A hedgerow can serve as a bunker.

Not all your shots on a golf course will be clear approaches to greens. Use the practice range to develop a controlled hook and slice.

One important thing to remember about using the driving range— plan ahead of time what you want to work on. Work out a practice schedule, with particular emphasis on the shots that are giving you trouble. If possible, hit several shots with every club in the bag. But don't purchase too many driving-range balls. Keep in mind that even a high-handicap golfer probably hits no more than 50 full shots in an 18-hole round of golf, and to go greatly beyond that figure may in a single practice session create an undue strain on the average golfer. That is, an overly long practice can harm the average player more than it helps him. It is no good to go on hitting shot after shot with tired muscles. Remember that no matter how hard you practice, if such fundamentals as grip and stance are not correct, the practice will not help.

On the Practice Area

One of the more popular "if" stories is the nineteenth hole one about "The great round I could have had if I hadn't started double bogey,

bogey, double bogey. I would have buried you guys but for those first holes."

Surprisingly enough, the fear of a bad start is just as much a good player's problem as it is the weekend golfer's. And as far as "play for pay" characters go, that first hole can look to them like hitting down a railroad track. This is why the professionals make the practice session —before that first tee shot is hit—a kind of ritual. And we don't care how relaxed or blasé a tour player may appear before he tees off, he still is tickled pink to walk off the first green with good old par.

Let's just take a close look at what we've done before, and what the amateur golfer makes a bad habit of doing. For one reason or another, our amateur will charge helter-skelter to the club for an afternoon round. Sometimes if it's late afternoon he's trying to squeeze in as many holes as possible before dark.

First of all, his mind is still cluttered with the problems he wrestled all morning, and he isn't geared mentally to concentrate on golf until after playing a hole or two. Chances are, also, that he just came from an air-conditioned office or locker room after bolting his lunch. So he takes a few hurried swings with his driver and then tees it up and lets loose a hefty swing designed to blast the ball right down the middle. Under these conditions, it isn't difficult at all to pull a muscle right there on the first tee. Yet, even if he doesn't, the combination of taut muscles and lack of concentration causes him to blow his score on the first few holes. Consider other sports—football, basketball, baseball— and you'll have to admit that even the juvenile competitors warm up at least a half hour before playing. The muscles must be loose to perform at maximum efficiency.

The practice area at the golf club is really the ideal place to practice, because the conditions are—or ought to be—identical to the ones you'll find on the course. The turf is the same, the texture of the greens the same, the sand the same. But, the practice will pay off big dividends only when you have and follow a preconceived plan.

For instance, you may wish to start your practice with 10 minutes or so of putting, to get a sense of tempo and to unlimber your muscles gradually. Concentrate on making a smooth, even stroke, and repeat it consistently. A good idea is to put several balls down in a circle, with the cup at the center, and move around the cup as you practice. That way you'll be able to test different breaks in the green, and you'll regrip the club and set yourself up for each putt, thus making conditions more realistic. Start with short putts and work back.

Next hit balls for about 45 minutes from the tee area, starting with the shorter-range clubs and finishing with your driver. Aim at a target on each shot, and plan each as if you were on the course. Don't rush your shots just because you have a full bucket of balls at your side. We know some pros who place the bucket behind them, so they'll have to take the time to turn around.

Once you have mastered the fundamentals of the swing, experiment on the practice tee (much better here than on the course). Get the feel of hitting a few intentional hooks and slices. Eventually you'll be able to maneuver the ball around the course. Conclude your practicing with 15 or so minutes of chipping and putting, picking targets on a practice green.

But regardless of your practice plan, start off easy. Take some minor exercises, such as a few easy bends and twists, nothing earthshaking or violent, though, before you pick up a club. Get the hands, fingers, and wrists warmed up before hitting a ball. And start off by using the nine-iron or wedge. The biggest mistake a person could make would be to take the driver and begin booming the ball out of sight. Your body is not ready for the demands of a big hit, and you might never be able to recover from the strain. Such a beginning would not make any sense at all and your golf game would be hurt, not helped by it.

Actually, there's more to starting your practice sessions with the nine-iron or wedge than loosening up tired or unused muscles. Knowing how to use these clubs is necessary for low scores. In fact, the wedge is really the difference between the game as played today and during Bob Jones and Gene Sarazen's time. It is a versatile club, and practice sessions should include your hitting all types of shots with it. Duplicate playing conditions as much as possible. Learn how to hit the low shot into the wind or the high loft over a hazard, with a full swing, a three-quarter swing, and a half-swing, from an open, closed, or square stance, with the wrists fully cocked or almost stiff. The short irons can help with your timing, and can lead to your getting into the habit of anchoring the head and swinging through the ball.

When you start to practice, as previously stated, always have a target to aim at. It can be your ball bag or a handkerchief on the shorter shots, or the flagstick itself if you are practicing from a trap. On the longer shots you can choose a distant tree or any other suitable landmark. If you find you are pushing them out or hitting them left of target, lay a club along the line of flight and check your stance. Lay another at right angles to correct the position of the ball in relation to your feet. Incorrect alignment is one of the most common faults in golf. It is easy to fall into, but just as easy to spot and cure.

The practice tee is also the place to try out all that your pro has taught you and what you have learned from reading, adapting them to fit your particular game, swing, or build whenever possible. But don't overdo any experimentation. You cannot continually change your swing or approach to the game just for the sake of changing. Bad habits should be cured on the practice tee, not compounded. Unlearning faults can be a long, drawn-out ordeal, but do not get impatient or panic. Space your lessons, your practice schedule, and your playing time so that each complements the other, and improvement will be assured.

Remember, however, that often the practice area is a meeting place for friends, most of whom are altogether too eager to offer bits of advice, to tell you what you are doing wrong, and how to correct any and all faults. Be careful. This sort of thing can only increase your woes. It is always better to have one man teach you, one man who knows your game and who can help you when things go bad. Once you acquire this kind of tutelage, stay with it.

You can learn more about the game on the practice area than anywhere else, and the higher your goal, the more time you must spend there. There is no question about it. To develop a game that will withstand the pressure of tournament golf, analyze your strong and weak points and get acquainted with practice. It will make you play better; it will satisfy any curiosity you may have about the game, the way you play it, and the mechanics behind the correct approach. These personal evaluations plus dedicated practice sessions by the top professionals and leading amateurs are the reasons for the high degree of expertness now noted in the game.

Always concentrate on what you are doing and use the practice time wisely. Select a particular part of your game, some phase that needs working on, such as grip, footwork, rhythm, or any or all of the mistakes your analysis has shown you are continually making, and work on it. But always keep the important fundamentals in mind. Never violate any of the basic rules of good golf, and if your swing happens to be in the groove, practice keeping the groove.

Preround Warmup Exercises

No matter how often the average player is told that he should go to the practice tee and hit some balls before going off the first tee, we have found that very few actually take the time to do it. In fact, the average weekend golfer's warmup usually comprises several grim swipes at a matchbox or a dandelion, whereupon he feels more or less equal to the task of driving off the first tee. But usually the stiff muscles fail to respond. He stands in tense, motionless silence over the ball. At the moment of truth he lunges spastically in a desperate effort to drive the green, sending a bounder hopping weakly off the tee, a wild slice out-of-bounds, or a chunk of turf flying majestically past a drag bunt. The traumatic experience may shake a sanguine linksman's confidence for several holes. On a sensitive soul it may leave a psychic scar healed only in the convivial anonymity of the nineteenth hole.

The vast majority of golfers, notably the publinxers, need a method of loosening up, especially when facilities for pounding out practice shots are absent. The purpose of the warmup is mainly physical, but partly psychological. Even a low-handicap player feels extra apprehension on the first tee if he hasn't hit some practice shots.

A good limbering up exercise begins with swinging the club easily and slowly, working gradually up to the effort of a drive. Place your feet much closer together than you do for a regular full swing: say about eight inches clear between the inside of the heels. The closer together your feet are, the easier it is to shift the weight and to pivot. You don't have to brace yourself to maintain balance against the thrusting weight shift of an actual drive. Concentrate first on being limber and lazy. Imagine the clubhead as a weight on a rope; you can't rush it. Swing it back low and straight, letting it lag behind your hip shift and pivot. Exaggerate the lag of the arms behind the body. Remember, you can't rush that rope!

At the top of the swing get extra lazy. Plant the left heel and begin to unwind the body well ahead of the start of the downswing. During the downswing concentrate on a smooth rhythm rather than clubhead speed, and swing through to a full follow-through. Now at the end of the follow-through, quickly but smoothly transfer the weight to the right foot and lazily reverse the swing. Keep the swing going continuously, alternating full downswings with full backswings. Concentrate especially on planting the left heel before starting the downswing and on planting the right heel before starting each full backswing. Try to lengthen the time interval between the planting of each heel and the reversal of the swing. Remember, the club shaft is a rope; you can't rush it!

A few minutes of this warmup swinging should help you cultivate

A good way to loosen up is to swing an iron with the left hand only and then with the right hand. Then take either a weighted club or two or three irons and swing these.

the feel and timing of a good swing as well as loosen you up. Continue it as long as you need a thorough mental and physical shakedown.

Now it's no secret that, as far as circumstances and conditions of play are concerned, the weekender is at a disadvantage to begin with. On weekends the course is more crowded; there're more waiting on the tees; a slow foursome ahead or an impatient group behind may create an undue pressure situation. Here, then, is an exercise that helps channelize pent-up energy and induces a state of readiness: Hold the club straight out and rotate the clubhead. This will help to relieve tension, relax the wrists, and give the hands feeling of club control.

Speaking of pressure, how does a golfer arrive at the right degree of tenseness without its affecting his play? Is the answer in the position and pressure of the hands? Most of our experts say yes. Normally, more golfers react to competition by gripping the club too tightly, rather than too loosely, and in so doing actually encourage tension, upset rhythm, decrease clubhead speed, and cause bad shots. What is really needed is less firmness, more sensitivity. If you feel that "pressuring the grip" is part of your problem, try these tips to help judge the right amount of grip strength:

1. With your hands on the club in your natural way, can you waggle the club, feeling the clubhead in your fingers? Continue until you can.

2. Relax your shoulders and arms as you prepare to swing the club back. There should be no tension in the forearms or restriction in the shoulders. The left shoulder begins the backswing.

3. Don't begin to cock wrists immediately. You'll discover that if you are relaxed, the wrists will swing the club into position very nicely. Repeat this exercise and you will arrive at the correct amount of pressure necessary for a full, controlled swing.

4. For a comparison, begin the swing again with a very tight grip and note the feeling of restriction. To play good golf it is necessary to maintain consistent pressure of fingers on the club throughout the entire swing.

Before teeing off find an out-of-the-way spot where you can hit at least one practice shot, possibly a plastic practice ball. This is an important part of preparation for the first-tee ordeal. You need to hit something as a test of how well you have learned your warmup lessons. Take a few full practice swings and then bang into the practice ball. But stay loose and lazy. Keep that club lagging behind the body, though not as much as in your warmup swings. Drag the clubhead back in a low straight arc away from the ball. Plant that left heel before you start the downswing, and arc the clubhead through the ball in the direction of your target. Repeat your dress rehearsal on the tee. And remember, you can't rush that rope!

A quick exercise to get ready for iron-play is as follows: Take a two-iron, choke it to about nine-iron length, keep the weight on the left foot and use a short backswing. Then "run through the bag," so to speak, by moving up on the shaft with your grip and increasing your finish until the last three shots are hit full, with the hands ending high. It will certainly help you to be loose and have more control once you

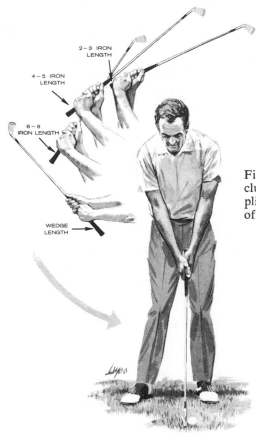

2 – 3 IRON
LENGTH

4 – 5 IRON
LENGTH

6 – 8
IRON LENGTH

WEDGE
LENGTH

Fifteen swings, all with the same club, say a two-iron, will accomplish nearly as much as a half hour of work with various clubs.

get out on the course. Try to concentrate on keeping the weight on the left side, the clubface square at all times, and stay with as short a backswing as possible. In this way, you can pour all your power into the hit itself. The result will be better control, more accuracy and better scores. Of course, if you can spend an hour or so on the practice tee before playing a round, then by all means do it. If not, then try the exercises just described and you'll find it won't take you four or five holes to "warm up."

Postround Practice

Many tour professionals maintain that one of the most profitable times to practice is immediately after a round. They stress correcting the things that they did incorrectly on the course, while they are fresh in their minds. You will find this practice worthwhile, too. Your muscles will be in gear, and you should have a clear idea of what you need to work on.

Is too much practice possible? The vast majority of tournament and club professionals believe that you *cannot* practice too much, up to your physical limits.

Physical Conditioning

Everybody feels strong on the first tee, but how many players poop out when they get to the fourteenth or fifteenth? And we're not talking only about amateurs. There are pros who have this problem, too. The importance of physical conditioning shows when you start the round off badly. Take a couple or three bogeys or double bogeys on the front nine, and then watch the man who's not in shape give up. He will shoot 80, 90, or worse. If he's in shape he has a chance to come back. At least he has the strength to come back. So many times conditioning means the difference between salvaging a round and having an absolutely horrible day. And another thing, it's easy to get tired mentally when you're tired physically.

The primary thing with any golfer is legs. When the old legs give out you sure can't function on the golf course, unless you want to walk on your hands. The legs are the big key to distance, because what hits the ball is the turn of the body, and what turns the body are the legs—the stronger the legs, the faster the body-turn. To work on your legs, jog as often as possible. Skip rope when you can't jog. As a rule, stay away from push-ups and lifting weights, because this tends to bind up the chest and back muscles—and this is not good for golf. The only muscles a golfer really needs to work on are in the legs, shoulders, forearms, wrists, and fingers. In fact, here are exercises which will help you to master the main essentials of the backswing, strengthen the hands and fingers, improve your timing, and add a new dimension to your game.

The whole art of swinging the club back from the ball to a position in which you are poised to deliver a solid and powerful blow is largely governed by a system of control running diagonally down the body from the left shoulder to the right foot. First, the shoulder, and with it that priceless knack which may seem elusive at first but which you must work to acquire—upper-left-arm leverage. Unless you keep that left shoulder UP you cannot hope to achieve upper-arm leverage, which comes as near to being a secret formula for success as anything in the golf technique. More than any other factor it made Hogan a phenomenal player of all the shots in the bag. Among the lesser men it can make a good player into a very, very good one.

This simple exercise should give you the feeling more readily than any other we know. You don't need a club for this exercise. Just take up the address position and with the left shoulder up grasp the extended left arm with the right hand at the point where the left hand joins the wrist. Now perform the backswing by turning the shoulders and chest over the stomach and carrying the hands to the top. Do this a number of times daily, and keep doing it until you develop the feeling of how the upper-left arm is operating.

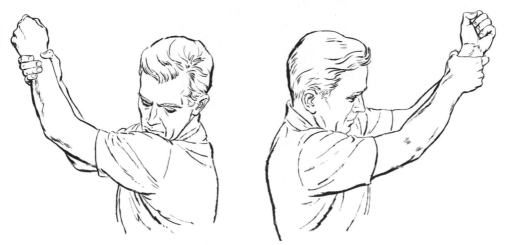

Upper-arm leverage comes as near to being a secret formula for success as anything in the golf technique. Perform the illustrated backswing and down-swing exercises until you develop the feeling of how the upper left arm is operating.

The second exercise, it could be more properly termed an expedient, is an aid to those who have trouble in keeping the weight on the inside of the right foot as the backswing develops, and the body-turn takes place under the control of the right knee and hip.

Many fine golfers have to fight against a sway creeping into the movement. To counter the tendency to sway and to maintain the weight on the inside of the right foot, practice with a golf ball wedged between the outside edge of the right foot and the ground. This not only acts as a buttress but helps to train the muscles as you require them to be set. In this way the right hip is prevented from riding too high and the right knee is held in the same position as at address. Go out onto the practice ground and try it yourself.

If you're a golfer, there are certain muscles that you don't want to build up, such as chest and back muscles. The important thing is to have strong forearms and wrists. A good exercise for this is to tie a weight on a rope attached to a stick and then roll it up and down with the arms extended. This one is great for the arm.

The best method of strengthening the forearm and wrists is by using a simple piece of apparatus which you can rig up in a few minutes. Take a broom handle and bore a hole halfway along its length. Run a piece of string through the hole, and fix a weight at the other end of the string. Holding the pole with both hands apart and parallel to the ground, turn it with the fingers clockwise toward the body, thus winding the string toward the pole and drawing the weight up to it. Release the weight slowly back to the ground by simply reversing the procedure. A two- to five-pound weight is about right.

To strengthen your fingers, use a wad of that "Silly Putty" that they sell in the dime stores. A lot of people have said that they use a rubber ball or a spring, but that makes it still a wrist exercise. With putty you can dig your fingers into it and really give them a workout. Squeeze and then ball it back up and squeeze again. The fingers are important in golf. They're what grip the club, and if you hit one on the tee with weak hands and fingers you're liable to lose the grip.

Developing strength in the arms, wrists, and fingers is really crucial. When anyone comes in contact with a golf ball, the club has some degree of kickback—or recoil. The stronger guy will be able to accelerate through the ball without having his swing slowed down. The weaker player may think he just hit a rock.

Before leaving the office, lie down on the floor, grab your knees and rock back and forth. This will help loosen you up before you get to the course.

Strength in the hands and fingers is crucial, and you can build up both of these by doing simple isometric exercises right at your desk.

In connection with strengthening your golfing muscles and grooving your swing, it has been the observation of many club pros that most people play with clubs that are too heavy for them. This is one of the many reasons why most average players are cursed with a slice. When they swing a club that is too heavy, they are not getting the clubhead through the ball.

One of the best methods of making your own clubs feel lighter when you swing them is to practice with a weighted club, which will build up your swinging muscles. For instance, Gene Sarazen always practiced with a driver that he had weighted to 28 ounces. Consider, by comparison, that the weight of the average driver is 13½ ounces. What this weighted club will do for you is make you swing more slowly—something 95 percent of the average players should be doing anyhow. In the process of slowing your swing, it will give you a more fluid motion and better timing and rhythm. Not only will you develop a slower and more rhythmic tempo with the weighted club but, when you go back to your lighter clubs, you will find that your tempo has been slowed automatically. In lieu of using a weighted club, you can buy a hood cover that has been weighted and will do much the same job.

Strategy of Preventing a Slump

Golf is great when all goes well, but, then, with a suddenness that can baffle even the most experienced player, strange things start to happen. You may *feel* as though you are doing everything exactly as you were before, but the results aren't the same. What is dangerous about this reversal is the golfer's reaction: his confidence shaken, he starts to tinker with his swing, and the deterioration is complete.

You must remember that all golfers, like baseball players, fall into slumps. When a ballplayer hits a slump, he may check with one of the team's coaches, then put in some extra practice to correct his faults. The same applies to the golfer who checks with his pro, discovers his mistakes and takes to the practice tee. Often, however, the golfer can iron out kinks on his own. A simple diagnostic method that many have found helpful is slow-motion analysis. Before a full-length mirror, take a 15-second swing with a driver. Carefully check every phase of the swing. If, at any point, there is an imbalance or snag in the pattern, stop at the suggested trouble point and concentrate on that phase of the swing. The flaw may be the result of a preceding action. You may even find yourself tracing the trouble back to something as basic as the stance. The object is to pinpoint the *cause* of the difficulty, then work to correct it. And if trouble still persists, you can be sure your pro knows what to do.

THE GRIP

We have seen great golfers with poor stances and swings that made them look like an old lady beating off a purse snatcher with an umbrella. But we have never seen a champion golfer who had a poor grip. The grip in golf plays such a critical role that we would venture to say that when a golfer gets into trouble, seven times out of ten it can be traced to the grip. Unfortunately, too many golfers don't bother to check their grip before each shot, and it's easy for small errors to creep into the grip unnoticed. The correct grip should have the palms facing each other, with the "V"s formed by the thumb and forefinger of each hand pointing to the chin. If you have slice trouble, place your left thumb farther over the shaft so that two knuckles of the left hand are exposed. Don't, however, turn your left hand in too much, or you'll have a hooker's grip. You can help correct a chronic hook by placing the right thumb more on the left side of the shaft, so that more of the back of the right hand is exposed. Again, be careful not to roll the right thumb too far over the grip, or you will slice. One of the chief causes of grip trouble is undue tension. The reason is usually that the golfer is trying too hard. As a result, he may unconsciously grip the club so tightly that it will be virtually impossible for him to execute a smooth swing. The grip should never be taken for granted and is the first thing you should check when you go into a slump.

THE ADDRESS

There is no reason for anyone to address the ball improperly. No physical work is involved in the address. It's all mental. The most important part of the address is the position of the ball on each shot. There are four basic areas of ball-to-feet placement. The driver is played off the left heel, the two-iron about two inches back of the heel, the five-iron in the middle of the stance, and the wedge should be positioned off the right heel. To make sure you are lining up your shots correctly, have a friend place one club to indicate the intended line of flight and another club leading from the left heel to the ball. If you are lining up the shot correctly, the clubs should form right angles at the ball for a wood or long-iron shot. Your feet should also be parallel to the line-of-flight club. The middle-iron address is slightly different from that of a long iron or wood shot. The hands are kept close to the body. When addressing a wood shot your feet should be spread the width of your shoulders, slightly more if you are tall or heavy. The arms are almost fully extended, which helps prevent an early wrist break on the backswing. And what better time, just before the swing itself, to remember to keep your head down!

THE SWING

The pattern of an effective golf stroke is determined in the first three feet of the backswing. The clubhead should be kept square to the line of flight. If it is not square, you will probably have to roll the club closed at the top of the backswing, and you may well be heading for trouble. In the so-called typical swing, note how the wrists are uncocked as the club starts back. At the top of the backswing the left foot is rolled in. But note that the heel is only an inch or so off the ground, so that the golfer will have a solid footing when he reaches the impact area. At impact, the arms should be fully extended to provide maximum power. The left arm should sustain the swing to avoid topping. And here is a tip for golfers who fall away from their shots: Place a golf ball under your right foot as you address the ball. The ball will force you to move into the shot, enabling you to get more distance and check slicing. And for still greater distance, delay uncocking the wrists as long as possible.

When in a slump, try slowing down your swing. Many "average" golfers merely compound their troubles by trying to hit harder. This makes just about as much sense as driving across a bridge that is about to be swept away by a flood. You would never think of overloading a bridge in that condition, so why impose further strain on a creaky swing? Next time you lose your timing, go out to the practice tee and set about it this way. Take a short iron and consciously draw the club back slower than you normally do. Swing back a little shorter than usual and meticulously time the hit, concentrating all your attention on making solid contact with the ball. Once you start hitting it on the nose, you can take a full short-iron swing, but still keep the tempo of the swing rather slower than usual. Then move up through your middle and long irons to your woods. Remember, swing slower than normal. You are trying to build up your timing, not hit the ball a ton. However, you will be surprised how far you can hit with this slow swing. Once your timing is re-established, then by all means increase the tempo until you have reached the speed of swing that is best for you.

PUTTING

Losing your putting touch is usually one of the first signs of a slump. Some days it's simple to figure the proper line and to keep the blade at right angles to the hole. On those too-rare occasions nothing can keep the ball from rolling into the center of the hole. Other days you find it impossible not only to find the correct path, but also the proper way to stroke the ball. Even the club itself, which you might have used for years, feels strange in your hands. Then it is time to re-evaluate your approach and actually begin all over again. The common faults are picking the clubhead up too quickly on the backswing and turning the wrists immediately on taking the club back. The first error requires too much of a downward hit, which pushes the ball with a skidding spin, more of a backspin than the needed overspin, and it will be completely at the mercy of the grain, often getting to the edge of the hole and turning away. The faulty wrist turns open the blade and makes the "square" return more difficult to achieve. Other errors that cause you to miss are excessive body sway and that ever-so-slight movement of the head. Assume a comfortable stance and keep your body locked into position until you hear the ball drop.

Strategy of Taking a Lesson

The old adage "practice makes perfect" holds good in golf only when a player knows what he is doing wrong and works along the proper corrective lines; then, of course, he is going to reap the benefit. On the other hand, there is a great deal of wasted energy expended on the practice tee by players who go out there with their heads full of well-meaning but misguided suggestions from fellow players whose knowledge of the theory of golf is just as flimsy as their own. They experiment by trying to correct one fault with another and never give themselves a chance to develop a smooth, well-grooved swing.

It is human nature to offer unsolicited advice, and nowhere is it more evident than on the golf course. A man hits a poor shot and all three fellow players have their own theories why. The misguided player gullibly swallows the proffered advice only to get himself deeper into the mire.

Though this advice is, on the whole, offered in good faith, more often than not it turns out to be backhanded gamesmanship. So if you value the standard you have attained and don't want to take a retrograde step, close your ears even to your best friend on the golf course and seek the advice of your teaching professional.

The average golfer, as we just stated, who has reached a reasonable degree of proficiency, seldom develops more than one fault if he suddenly loses form, and it is usually very basic—a slight change of grip, or stance out of alignment. If he would go straight to his pro and have a check-up, he could save himself a great deal of anguish and maybe weeks of bad play. Your pro is there to help you; it's his job. Many golfers have the quaint idea that they shouldn't bother a pro just as they shouldn't bother a doctor unless there is something seriously wrong. But the time that elapses may cause a long and arduous road back to recovery. Let's face it! Remember, as we stated earlier, that even the pros themselves take lessons.

If you're paying for lessons and they are having no effect on your scoreboard, maybe *you* are the reason. True, much has been written about the art of *teaching* golf. However, the importance of the art of *taking* a lesson has been generally overlooked. While it does not require any physical skill, you must use a modicum of common sense.

First and foremost, be honest with your golf professional and tell him exactly what you are trying to accomplish. Do you want a complete picture of the golf swing or do you just want to play along with the boys? Are you willing to practice or don't you have the time? Is this lesson to be one of a series or a one-shot deal? Having your objectives clear at the start and making them known to the instructor can save both of you a lot of grief.

Being honest with the pro doesn't stop there. Reveal any physical handicaps you may have—however minor—that could affect the way you swing. To cite an extreme case, a pro that we know once worked a solid hour with a pupil, trying to get him to transfer his weight to the left leg on the downswing. At the end of the hour, he confided to the pro that this would be difficult for him, since he had an artificial leg!

Another problem with many pupils is that they are not good listeners. Their one idea is to belt as many balls as they can in the allotted time. Remember, it's impossible to get your money's worth if you insist on hitting while the instructor is explaining something. Only by listening will you be able to absorb it.

There is, also, the golfer who comes onto the lesson tee with just a driver and says, "I slice everything." The pro takes a look at his swing—and the slices—and replies, "Well, if we could take your five-iron and get the swing going on the inside, then I think we can lick this." By now he's so mad he says, "If I can't hit the drive, I just won't play golf " There are none so deaf as those who will not hear!

Listening to your golf professional entails carrying out what he's telling you—even if it doesn't feel comfortable for a time. When you do anything new, it's bound to feel strange at first It means listening to him, not listening to well-meaning but mostly uninformed advice from your golf buddies.

Most times friends will say something like, "You're swaying." They may have spotted your fault, but they haven't told you what to do positively to get you swinging again. That's the job of teaching the golf swing, and it is your pro's business. Of course, if you prefer a medicine man to a qualified doctor . . .

A good listener also has patience. Don't expect miracles in five minutes or worry unduly just because you can't hit each shot perfectly. Don't be impatient when your pro tells you he liked the swing, even when you missed! What he means is that you are that much nearer to really swinging the club. So keep at it, and with hard work and patience, you'll be surprised how good you can become.

Like your play on the course, approach your lessons with a positive attitude. Think of them as a means of becoming a better player, not as an ordeal to be endured. Be sure to set realistic goals for yourself, trying to improve a *little* with each round. Learn in easy stages; don't move to more advanced stages until you have mastered the easier ones. In any case, be patient.

By patient we don't mean standing there like a lemon not under-standing a word the pro is saying! Every golf instructor has a golf language. He'll say, "Open your stance," for example, and take for granted that the pupil understands what he is saying. Often the pupil doesn't.

Never be afraid to ask your pro a question. After all, that's what he is there for. This applies to any point he is making, not just golf language. If he knows you don't understand, he can usually find an-other way of putting it which will be clear to you.

Many people are too anxious when they go for a lesson. They tighten up and can hardly hit a shot. Remember, fear and the golf swing don't mix. Confidence, on the other hand, is one of the best tonics for a golf swing we know.

Now, even if you have a reasonably good swing, don't imagine your lesson days are over. There is much more to golf than just learning to swing a club, though we'll admit that most golfers don't ever get that far. Do you have problems with that troublesome little pitch over a trap? Do you know how to play the ball to run? Can you get out of a trap? There are all sorts of shots where you must adapt the basic swing to different circumstances. Your pro is the person who can help you learn these finer points.

It is also a fact that even if pupils have all the shots, they don't know where to use them on a golf course. Or they just don't line themselves up to hit the ball in the right direction. As stated in Chapter 6, the best place to learn how to play a course is *on* the course during a supervised round. The trained eye of the professional will almost instantly spot flaws you might never discover yourself. Playing lessons with a teaching professional can benefit almost any golfer who lets this expert "think" for him and who tries to absorb as much of the reasoning and logic behind the professional's advice on the shots as possible.

It's really a shame that the golfers who could benefit most by seeing how a good golfer uses his head during a round, usually play with golfers who are not much better than they are. So they never learn to play a course. Most teaching pros claim that their pupils learned more during a supervised round than if they had stood on a practice tee for ten hours.

Taking golf lessons is like taking piano lessons: What good are they if you don't do any subsequent practicing? Too many persons expect a miracle from a meeting with their professional instructor, apparently thinking that the mere taking of one lesson should make them score better the next time they play. This is an impossibility unless they rehearse what they were taught and have made the lesson-session a part of their game. The biggest drawback to rushing out to play too soon after a lesson is that you end up devoting the entire round to thinking about what the pro has taught, and you miss the true benefits of the round of golf. Instead of showing improvement, your game retrogresses.

A good formula to follow is to practice about one hour for every half-hour lesson you take, broken up so that you devote no more than 30 minutes at any one time on the practice tee absorbing what was taught. Two half-hour sessions over two days following each lesson will set you up perfectly for more enjoyable golf. Only on the practice tee can you find the atmosphere to think about the points covered and the time to make them routine.

Strategy of Protecting Your "Image"

If you have read this book very carefully up to this point, and will promise to carry out all the information to the letter, then you don't have to read any further. But, if you're like most average golfers, you'll occasionally make one of your old mistakes. As a rule, your explanation of such mistakes may be blurted out without sufficient study of the situation. Not only do you dub your shot, but you dub the important public relations angle as well.

As golfers somewhere this side of flawlessness, the chart on page 232 can help you with the public relations of your game. It offers a choice of plausible instant alibis for almost any playing situation. Thus, after even the worst mistake, you can follow through immediately with a well-thought-out, well-executed explanation.

This chart is not only versatile but it is also portable. For best results, it should be carefully cut from the book and pasted in some discreetly accessible spot on your bag. It may not improve your game, but it should make it *seem* much better to some people. When that happens, you'll probably *feel* much better. And that's certainly one of the more important reasons for playing golf in the first place.

	WEATHER	YOUR CONDITION	CONDITION OF COURSE	INCIDENTALS
Too little yardage	"Quite a head-wind out there. It's like hitting into a brick wall."	"Uh-Uh! There goes my back again."	"You'd think they'd give this fairway a haircut once in a while."	"Well, never up, never in. Heh! Heh!"
Too much yardage	"In this kind of weather I don't know my own strength."	"I don't know why, but I just felt like really leaning into one, for a change."	"Well, that's the way the ball bounces—on a course like this one anyway."	"Put too little backspin on it, I guess."
Slice or hook	"Notice how the wind died down* the minute I swung?" *(or "started up")	"Guess the doc was right. This is one day I should have stood in bed."	"Say, did you see that ball move, just be-fore I connected with it?"	"Guess I might as well forget about that new grip." (Shake head impatiently)
Topping or other-wise dubbing the ball	Cool weather: "My hands are too stiff, I guess." Warm weather: "My hands are too sticky, I guess."	"Funny how a little thing like a lame elbow can just about ruin your game."	"If I'm going to keep playing this course, I'd better learn how to hit out of a hole."	"Well, I've really had it with this club."
Poor putt	Weather is nor-mally too cold or too hot. If perfect, then you prefer it other-wise: "Can't seem to get my 'touch' in this kind of weather."	"I knew this sore finger was going to give me trouble."	"Another one of those greens laid out by a practical joker."	"You fellows were so quiet there, you made me kind of nervous."

71 72 73 74 75 10 9 8 7 6 5 4 3 2 1